Fantastic Creatures in Mythology and Folklore

ALSO AVAILABLE FROM BLOOMSBURY:

A Cultural History of Animals in the Medieval Age, edited by Brigitte Resl
Riddles in Stone: Myths, Archaeology and the Ancient Britons,
by Richard Hayman

Fantastic Creatures in Mythology and Folklore

From Medieval Times to the Present Day

JULIETTE WOOD

BLOOMSBURY ACADEMIC
LONDON • NEW YORK • OXFORD • NEW DELHI • SYDNEY

BLOOMSBURY ACADEMIC
Bloomsbury Publishing Plc
50 Bedford Square, London, WC1B 3DP, UK
1385 Broadway, New York, NY 10018, USA

BLOOMSBURY, BLOOMSBURY ACADEMIC and the Diana logo are trademarks of
Bloomsbury Publishing Plc

First published in Great Britain 2018

A catalogue record for this book is available from the British Library.

A catalog record for this book is available from the Library of Congress.

ISBN: HB: 978-1-4411-4849-0
PB: 978-1-3500-5925-2
ePDF: 978-1-4411-3060-0
eBook: 978-1-4411-6676-0

Typeset by Deanta Global Publishing Services, Chennai, India

To find out more about our authors and books visit www.bloomsbury.com and sign up
for our newsletters.

For Saskia, Zac and Lela while they still believe in fantastic beasts.

Contents

List of illustrations

Acknowledgements

If only I could find a little hippogriff of my own, the experience of writing this book would be complete. However, in the real world, I would like to express my thanks to the many colleagues, students and friends who have listened patiently to my thoughts and theories on the fantastic creatures that have been included in this book. I am grateful to Cardiff University and to The Folklore Society for the opportunity to undertake research on so many aspects of this subject. My special thanks to Jacqueline Simpson for sharing her mermaid anecdote with me and offering excellent advice on dragons and to my husband and scientific adviser, Clive Wood, for his continued support.

I wish to express my thanks to many colleagues who have added their favourite beastly traditions to this book. I am especially grateful to Dr Patrick Carlin and Dr Walter Brooks for introducing me to 'Mi Unicornio azul'. Professor John Hines advised on Norse material and Dr Simon Brodbeck helped with the some difficult sources. I would also like to acknowledge the Librarians at the Special Collections and Archives of Cardiff University who have found lost books, answered questions and helped with the selection of illustrations, which are reproduced courtesy of Cardiff University Library.

Beatriz Lopez has been a patient and encouraging editor, and I would like to express my gratitude to her and to all in the Bloomsbury team.

Introduction

I sat upon a promontory, And heard a mermaid on a dolphin's back, Uttering such dulcet and harmonious breath, That the rude sea grew civil at her song

(MIDSUMMER NIGHT'S DREAM, ACT II, SC. I)

The pairing of a fabulous mermaid with a dolphin in this quotation from Shakespeare's *Midsummer Night's Dream* conjures up a beautiful world which blurs the fantastic and the real. Other writers view fantastic creatures from a different perspective. In St Jerome's history of early Christian hermits, an elderly holy man on a visit to an even older hermit receives directions from a centaur. Jerome questions whether 'this was an apparition sent by the devil ... or simply an animal spawned by the desert, which is a breeding ground for all sorts of monstrous beasts'.[1] Shakespeare and Jerome project contrasting views as to whether fantastic beasts are creatures born out of imagination, or real animals living in exotic and peripheral environments.

The fantastic beasts examined in this book have attracted a variety of myths, legends and traditions both old and new, and these terms require some clarification. In the 1960s, the folklorist William Bascom examined fundamental cross-cultural narrative categories of myth, folktale and legend. Although recent approaches to these traditional forms stress that rigid distinctions are not always possible,[2] the parameters Bascom suggested more than fifty years ago remain useful in dealing with different types of traditional discourse. Bascom begins with an overall definition of myths, legends and folktales as narratives in prose form. He noted that a term like myth can signify different things in different cultures, and that it had a variety of meanings from its use in everyday language to the more specialized usages in literary, religious and cultural studies. In everyday discourse, it can signify something that is untrue or a misunderstanding of science and the rational principles that underpin reality. As a literary construct, myth can be an aspect of the creative imagination or may express an 'archetypal' theme in contemporary literature. It can be a 'sacred narrative explaining how the world and man came to be in their present form',[3] or a narrative that embodies common values and ideals. To some extent, the definition depends on the theoretical framework. For some mythographers, myth is rooted in a fundamental aspect of the human psyche, or is the survival of some ancient belief structure. Nineteenth-century theories were likely to regard myth as a reflection of a more primitive world view, while recent approaches have emphasized mythic structure and function in specific cultural contexts, rather than a generalized and distant past. Psychologists like Freud and Jung were interested in myth as coded realizations of human impulses, while a more romantic perspective perceived myths and related traditions as a way to preserve ancient truths overlooked by modern society.[4]

As a generic category, folktales are fictional narratives that can be set in any time or place. This is not to say, however, that they do not serve a serious purpose. There are moral folktales to be sure, or at least folktales with a moral purpose. Legends are generally set in a real world, although one that may be remote in time and space.[5] What distinguishes a legend, according to Bascom, is that it is regarded as true (or at least there is a willing suspension of disbelief) by both narrator and audience. Given the popularity of contemporary fantasy writing and computer gaming, legends may even be set in a parallel world. By contrast, the events in myths are frequently 'cosmological' in the sense that they account for the origin of the world and the structures of human society. They may not reflect a literal reality, but they confirm the norms and values of a society and provide patterns of behaviour.[6] From this multitude of definitions and approaches, myths, legends and folktales emerge as oft-repeated narratives with changing cultural significance that can merge with other genres.

These varied concepts and definitions highlight different aspects of the fantastic nature of the creatures in this study. Many 'beasts' examined here, such as mermaids, griffins and dragons, are no doubt familiar. Some, like Pegasus and the kraken, have their origin in the traditional mythologies of different cultures or, like the hippogriff, are creations of literary imagination. Still others, like the unicorn, have become creatures of fantasy, as belief in their reality has waned. Different writers provide distinctive views of these creatures. For example, Lise Gotfredsen adopts a Jungian approach to 'the unicorn myth',[7] while Odell Shepard approaches unicorn lore from a literary perspective.[8] However, if one examines the entire spectrum of unicorn traditions, what emerges as a 'myth of the unicorn' is a creature that belonged to early natural history rather than classical myth. The unicorn became an important moral and chivalric trope during the medieval period and continues to function as a creature in contemporary fantasy writing. Animals like the dolphin, which have attracted classical writers and artists for centuries, have recently acquired an almost mystical quality as attitudes to our role in the natural environment have changed.

The present study has chosen to apply the term 'fantastic' to these creatures. A typical list would certainly include dragons, griffins and unicorns, hybrid creatures with human traits like centaurs and mermaids, and monstrous creatures like sea serpents or the basilisk.

In this study, they are organized according to certain dominant traits, whether they swim, fly, walk the earth or inhabit its hidden underground places, and whether they are winged, hoofed, aquatic or fiery. However, these creatures can slip easily from one environment to another. The hoofed Pegasus flies, and the winged phoenix is reborn in fire. Under certain circumstances, mermaids walk on land, and dragons, although linked to caves, wells and underground places, can fly and, in the guise of sea serpents, swim as well.

The earliest European sources for fantastic creatures were the writers of the Greco-Roman world. Classical writers like Aristotle and Pliny did not automatically assume that these creatures had no foundation in the real world. On the contrary, they were willing to entertain the idea that they could exist, most likely in far distant and exotic lands. During the medieval period, in the West at least, questions about their reality were less important than the moral principles they embodied, and medieval bestiaries, which were great repositories of this kind of lore, contain some overtly 'mythical' stories about animals we know are real, such as the tiger, the beaver and the boa constrictor.[9] During the nineteenth century, many of the creatures discussed in this book were 'eased out' of the world of real animals, while exotic species, among them the platypus and the kangaroo, became accepted and integrated into a newly developing scientific order.[10] Despite this, contemporary cryptozoologists continue to search, often in the same far distant and exotic lands as classical writers, for evidence that will transform a mythical beast into a real animal. [11]

The relationship between fantastic creatures and the cultures that create, or at least describe, them is as complex as it is fascinating. Dragons in Western culture, particularly in the classical and pre-modern periods, were fierce and dangerous entities that threatened an ordered cosmos or represented the dangers of sin. The Oriental dragon, by contrast, was an embodiment of natural forces rather than a challenge to them. The work of some palaeontological folklorists has linked dragons with those large, and perennially fascinating, extinct creatures, the dinosaurs. Contemporary fantasy writing, role-playing and computer games have kept elements of traditional dragon lore, but they have also introduced a more benevolent creature whose nature is, in effect, more human. Other creatures, such as the unicorn and the griffin, formerly the subject of much learned speculation, have passed completely into the realms of fancy where they now live and flourish. This study also includes creatures such as whales and dolphins that have become mythologized as attitudes to the environment have changed.[12] For many indigenous peoples from the western coast of North America to Polynesia and New Zealand, the whale is a mythical figure as well as a source for food, a cultural mediator rather than just an economic resource. It was associated with peril and sin, in early European descriptions, but by the seventeenth century, the whale had become a marine commodity to be harvested, and thus it remained until the mid-twentieth century when it was redefined as a symbol of our role as stewards, rather than exploiters, of the planet.

Ideas about the marvellous and the monstrous underpin much of European medieval discourse on fantastic creatures. The marvellous complemented the divine plan, while the monstrous challenged it, the former could be included, but the latter had to be tamed within divine order.[13] Western cosmology, for the most part, relegated such things to the periphery, the liminal world in which rationality confronts, and eventually conquers, chaos. The anthropologist Mary Douglas, in her classic study of cultural purity and cultural danger, characterized things that fell outside the ordered categories of culture as metaphorically dangerous,[14] and this is an apt characterization of the position occupied by fantastic creatures. While marvellous beasts might be seen as having a more positive overtone and monsters a more negative one, they embody degrees of ambiguity that test the parameters of what is real and acceptable, and at the same time, paradoxically, reinforce them.[15]

This sense of being at the periphery, of being 'other', is expressed in a variety of ways. Attitudes range from confirmation of a world that can include the idiosyncratic to one from which such deviance must be expunged. Creatures that embrace both the marvellous and the monstrous can function as symbolic boundaries that moderate threats or as mysteries that lurk just beyond the frontiers of civilization.[16] St Jerome characterized the desert as a breeding ground for the outlandish, and this notion has been an important factor in the categorization of the creatures considered in this book. Early travellers brought back tales of exotic creatures that were strange amalgams of characteristics: horses with horns, quadrupeds with human faces, beings whose upper bodies were human with fish-like, equine, avian or ophidian lower bodies, and hybrids made of equal parts of different animals. These combinations gave rise to unicorns, manticores, mermaids, centaurs and griffins. Once relegated to geographic and cultural peripheries, they now flourish in contemporary genres of film, fantasy novel and video game.

Studies of fantastic creatures often focus on their ultimate origin, which is revealed once the fantasy is weeded out from the biologically acceptable. However, traditions about these extraordinary creatures travelled with the ebb and flow of travellers, traders and changing civilizations. The interplay between concrete observations of real animals and speculative traditions about them is complex, and the notion of where the boundary between human and non-human lies varies considerably. Questions are often framed in terms of opposed, but complementary ideas of continuity and difference, and we continue to contemplate, imagine and speculate on mythical animals because we still feel that they have something to tell us about ourselves or about the current world.[17] To return to St Jerome's centaur, imagination and reality present two possible starting points for understanding the origin, function, meaning and development of fantastic creatures, but cultural, psychological, ecological and utilitarian considerations also play a part in their perception and interpretation. The creatures covered in this book can inhabit all these mythic categories as easily as they move from land to air and through water and, in this broad context, fantastic creatures provide ways for understanding how the world is structured and what it is to be human.

The rise of the ecology movement has altered the relationship between the human and non-human environment. This has affected traditions and myths, especially those associated with sea mammals like whales and dolphins, and has created a new mystique. Post-industrial Western society has become more ecologically conscious, and this contemporary process, which re-enchants the natural world, has moved away from the language of domination and separation. It now seeks to reconnect with nature and with the past, and the resurgence of fantasy writing, at least in part, reflects this new sense of a re-enchanted world. [18]

Sources

This book draws on a variety of sources: legends, folktales and myths; classical, medieval and Renaissance works; the writings of early modern scientists and naturalists; filmmakers; writers of fantasy; creators of role-playing games (RPGs); and even contemporary cryptozoologists. Many of the sources are interwoven with prevailing attitudes to mythical creatures and help clarify the ways in which they fit into a larger picture. Primary sources are listed in the appendix,[19] and specific relevant information is included in the text, but this section gives a brief overview of the sources used throughout.

Hesiod's *Theogony*, written in the seventh century BCE, contextualizes mythical creatures within the emergence of a coherent cosmos. On the one hand, these creatures are part of the ordering process of the world, but they are also monstrous anomalies that transgress the boundaries of accepted categories. Some of them originate from incestuous unions between divine siblings. As such, they fuse opposing qualities, which, in an ordered world, should remain distinct. Some female monsters are despatched by male heroes, which suggests a degree of gender opposition and conflict. Other creatures inhabit the liminal, and intrinsically ambiguous, spaces of both cosmic and earth-bound geography. The snake-haired Medusa and her offspring, Pegasus, embody the positive and negative ambiguities inherent in their geographical location and mythical natures. The demigod Perseus, himself the offspring of a human and a god, kills Medusa. However, this female monster gives birth to the winged horse, Pegasus who helps another demigod, Bellerophon, defeat the Chimaera, a fire-breathing hybrid. Medusa lives at the dark western edges of the world, but her offspring, Pegasus, sits among the stars.[20]

The ambiguity of that which is 'other' and 'liminal' finds expression in the varied, often overlapping, attitudes to fantastic creatures. The Roman writer Lucan catalogued the real and imaginary beasts met by Cato the Younger's soldiers in the African desert (*Pharsalia*, Bk ix, 19–28). The accounts of gory deaths brought about by a host of poisonous serpents, such as the two-headed *amphisbaena*, resemble a film scene created by a special effects expert. Undoubtedly, travellers' accounts exaggerated descriptions of poisonous reptiles as did Lucan in his desire to enhance the reputation of his hero, Cato, but the Roman author does share St Jerome's fearful distrust of the desert. The *Physiologus* (i.e. the Naturalist), a compilation of knowledge assembled by an unknown author in the third century CE, described forty-nine animals, both real and legendary.[21] It explained their habits allegorically in order to instruct Christians in proper moral behaviour, and it was an important source for the popular medieval genre, the *bestiary,* which, in turn, provided inspiration for architecture, church carvings, manuscript illustrations and literature.[22]

The world map in the Gerona *Beatus*, a tenth-century commentary on the Apocalypse, contains one of the earliest depictions of sea monsters. A watery band encircles the land in which a monstrous fish, with Jonah trapped inside, swims among other bizarre beings.[23] Narratives, especially those with traditional content, like the Icelandic sagas, also reflect this division between land and sea. Safe voyages and success in fishing depended on ambiguous forces that mediated between the two. Mermaids, sea monsters and 'real' species such as whales, which took on a quasi-supernatural role, embodied these contrary forces.[24] The ability to transcend categories and overcome these contradictions is a role often assigned to heroes or saints. St Brendan tames a huge whale, and by killing a sea monster, Perseus earns a bride and a kingdom.

For centuries, the inclusion of fantastic creatures was an integral part of map making. The fourteenth-century Hereford *mappa mundi*, the largest surviving medieval map, reflects both real and symbolic geography. Jerusalem is at the centre and East at the top enclosing the Garden of Eden. Monsters and marvels inhabit the margins, and the ocean surrounds the earth. Britain and Ireland, although somewhat compressed, are in the correct relationship to the rest of Europe, and the Faroe Islands appear for the first time. However, the Caspian Sea, which earlier explorers had reported as landlocked, flows into the ocean. The map positively teems with marvellous places, people, plants and animals. A mermaid holding her looking glass swims in the Mediterranean Sea; near her is a sword fish with its 'sword' sheathed in its belt like a proper knight. The edge of Africa is garlanded with strange hybrid tribes, but also contains the basilisk, unicorn, rhinoceros and the sphinx. Egypt is home to a phoenix, a salamander, the yale and a crocodile resting on an island in the Nile. Griffins fight the Arismaspeans in Scythia. Dragons inhabit the island of Ceylon (Sri Lanka) and the mountains near Paradise.

The world depicted on this *mappa mundi* was rich and multilayered in both meaning and physical dimensions. The material world is rendered in one dimension on a sheet of vellum, and is composed of four classical elements, fire, air, earth and water, but this does not mean that its creators thought of the world as flat. Different colours distinguished the land from the sea, serrated lines indicate the heights of mountains, a convention still found on modern maps, and textual explanations clarify many of the illustrations. Fish swim in the Mediterranean, and volcanoes spout fire, and some animals, like a Ceylonese dragon and the salamander, have wings as if to indicate flight.

On ancient maps, sea monsters embodied the dangers of the ocean. A flying dragon carrying off a hapless sailor, underscored the danger in the seas surrounding the mythical North Atlantic Island of Braçil.[25] The kraken was one of the most feared of medieval monsters, but the one attacking a ship on an early-seventeenth-century map is recognizable as a large cephalopod, anticipating the eventual identification of this monster as a giant squid. As geographical knowledge expanded, traditions about the exotic edges of the known world were relocated or reinterpreted. Maps reflect how the whale changed from a monster into a commodity. The *carta marina* of Olaus Magnus, published in 1539, maintains the early Renaissance view of sea monsters in which sea serpents swim alongside recognizable, if oddly shaped, mammals like the walrus. Scenes of whales being harvested in the Faroe Islands balance the infamous whale island that lured sailors who unknowingly lit a fire on its back.[26] The whale's monstrous reputation continued in the adventure literature of writers like Jules Verne and Herman Melville, until contemporary ecology transformed it into a symbol of man's exploitation of the environment.

The legendary locations of fantastic creatures can be as important as the beasts themselves. As one early traveller declared, 'The ends of the earth contain that which is both rare and fair.'[27] Monsters on early maps served as a warning, but, as exploration revealed more about the world beyond Europe, these mythical creatures began to represent man's conquest of the natural environment and were transformed into the ornamental mermaids and sea serpents of later maps. The periphery can also function as a refuge for wisdom and mystery. According to his biographer, Philostratus, the Greek philosopher Apollonius encountered numerous mythical animals, among them unicorns, dragons, griffins, a fiery worm and a phoenix, as he journeyed to the extremes of the Roman world. The author of the *Life of Apollonius of Tyana* used these traveller's tales as metaphors for the wisdom of its central character.[28]

For the most part, this book does not consider the strange humanoid races depicted on *mappa mundi* or described in travel literature. Such 'curiosities', as they were called, provided the subject for pamphlets and chapbooks, or were displayed at fairs and 'freak' shows. Some of these 'anomalies' were outright frauds, while others would now be considered birth defects. C. J. S. Thompson, a pioneer in the study of teratology and honorary curator of the Museum of the Royal College of Surgeons, offered rational explanations for many of these oddities.[29] However, fantastic creatures such as mermaids or dragons also appeared in pamphlets and fairgrounds, and the categories of monstrous, mythical and fantastic are not always easy to distinguish.

The changing world of the eighteenth-century European Enlightenment, the rise of the biological sciences and the advent of better communications dramatically altered perceptions of fantastic creatures. Classical and medieval sea monsters, which lurked beneath the waves, as a warning to sailors and a lure for exploratory curiosity, became ornamentation for buildings and maps as they were recognized and classified as animal species like walruses or whales. Scholars began to question their very existence, although occasionally, a seemingly legendary one, like the giant squid, has had to be readmitted into the biological system.[30] These anomalies keep the field of cryptozoology alive with its desire to make the mythic concrete, and its constant search for real species of animals that mainstream biology considered non-existent.

New phenomena, such as social media and the internet, have further blurred categories, in particular, the interface between written literature and tradition, and they have become an important driving force in the resurgence of interest in fantastic beasts. In 1974, Dave Arneson and Gary Gygax published the first version of *Dungeons & Dragons*, which combined the sword and sorcery action of Robert E. Howard's Conan series with the high-fantasy medievalism of J. R. R. Tolkien's Middle-earth. Fantasy RPGs have become a worldwide phenomenon in a comparatively short time, and their popularity has been significantly enhanced by the development of computer games that allow ever larger groups to participate in massively multiplayer online RPGs (MMORPG).[31]

New media forms reshape and expand the familiar. Fan sites, fan art and fan fiction have created contemporary mythologies around older traditional forms. They share features with fantasy works, books, films and graphic novels that incorporate fantastic creatures, and an ever-expanding fandom base, serviced by online discussion groups and other types of internet sites, supports this new subculture. The shared fantasy worlds of these games have given rise to new novels, comics, DVDs and ephemera such as calendars, figurines and other collectibles.

Fantasy gaming has been described as a form of interactive storytelling.[32] Since the early games were rooted in the alternative worlds of high fantasy in which a player negotiates mazes, acquires treasures and confronts monsters and magic, it is not surprising that its hero-characters pit themselves against fantastic creatures. Commentators have noted the similarities between RPGs and the quest narrative format of folktales, in which a goal achieved after a series of trials 'overcoming adversaries ... is virtually mandatory'.[33] Beasts make very good adversaries, and the first *Dungeons & Dragons* 'Monster Manual', a role-playing-game version of a bestiary, featured a unicorn, a griffin and a dragon on its cover.[34] Dragons, unicorns, griffins and manticores, all beasts that will be considered in this study, were among the earliest monsters in the game, and they still inform ever more imaginative monster permutations as gaming continues to develop. With their innate qualities of hybridity, ambiguity and the possibility of being real or unreal, fantastic creatures fit into the post-modern framework of play and intertextuality as easily as they fit into the world of maps as symbols for danger or conquest.

Fantastic creatures come in many varieties, inhabit many environments and have many names. They appear in such a wide variety of contexts and carry so many different meanings that a single book cannot hope to cover them all.[35] This study does not aim to present a comprehensive theory about fantastic creatures, rather it intends to focus on how differing views of these creatures embody complex concepts of 'otherness' and identity, and how they, in turn, reflect ways of understanding the world. A prominent theme in the approaches outlined in this introduction is a preference for contrasts and oppositions: safety versus danger, culture versus nature, self versus other, human versus non-human. However, these dichotomies are not fixed. They can be challenged, and often this dynamic process is key to the development of fantastic creatures at different periods and in different genres. If the medieval mermaid symbolized sin versus salvation, the dangers of material world versus cultural order, and the fluctuating world of water versus the stability of land, modern fantasy writing, literature and poetry often subverts these categories. The mermaid figure has become a way to challenge social structures that favour patriarchy, particular images of the female body and the mere fact of difference. The ability of fantastic creatures to undergo dynamic changes is one of the major themes of this book.

Questions about fantastic creatures are easier to pose than to answer. Is a mythical beast something that is exotic enough to differ sufficiently from ordinary reality that it deserves special comment or notice? Are they figments of our imagination or do they arise from the human psyche? Do they have elements of the anomalous or the monstrous, or are these creatures just distortions of an undiscovered species? This book hopes to provide at least partial answers to these questions.

1

When unicorns walked the earth: A brief history of the unicorn and its fellows

I always thought unicorns were fabulous monsters .... I never saw one alive before!
Well, now that we have seen each other ... if you'll believe in me, I'll believe in you.

Thus runs the conversation between Alice and a suave unicorn she meets on the other side of the mirror in Lewis Carroll's *Alice's Adventures Through the Looking Glass*. At first glance, the unicorn seems to have the clearest history of any of the fantastic creatures examined in this book. The first description, in the sixth century BCE, treats it as a real animal inhabiting a remote part of the natural world; a creature consistent with the strange otherness one could expect to encounter far from the safety of home. Later the unicorn developed into a complex symbol within the context of medieval religious allegory and the literature of courtly love. Its horn, in reality the tooth of an Arctic whale, was considered an antidote to poison and was fashioned into objects for the rich or pounded into powder for medicinal use. It was an important heraldic animal and remains popular in fantasy literature, and it has become one of the many symbols of what has been loosely called 'new age' mysticism. This silent mysterious beast is redolent with symbolic meanings, but, like so many other fantastic four-footed beasts like the *centaur*, the *manticore*, the *yale* and the *bonnacon*, the history of the unicorn is not as straightforward as it might appear. This curious animal enjoyed something of a heyday in European art and literature from the twelfth to fifteenth centuries. It is not really a creature of folklore, although it is regularly referred to as such. Travellers' tales about exotic animals contributed to descriptions of unicorns in classical accounts, but neither the Greeks nor the Romans incorporated this fantastic animal into their mythology. There is no parallel in unicorn lore to the rich vein of folktales and legends about mermaids or dragons. Essentially the unicorn is a product of classical and learned commentary, commerce and medical practice. Nevertheless, the interface between these different areas of discourse, as discussed in the Introduction, is very porous, and, it has helped to create a popular concept of this strange animal. The tale of the 'Brave Little Tailor', which the Brothers Grimm included in their iconic collection, illustrates this. It is an example of a well-known type of folktale about how cleverness can overcome superior forces. A tailor tricks a unicorn, whose horn becomes stuck in a tree, in the version printed by Brothers Grimm; although the ruse has precedents in earlier unicorn lore, the episode in the Grimm tale depends on a printed source.[1] Expeditions to find the unicorn, or at least the animal that inspired it, were still being undertaken as late as the nineteenth century, and the medical properties of unicorn horn continued to be taken seriously well beyond the era of Renaissance poison plots. The relation between the land-dwelling unicorn and the sea mammal that was the source of its most remarkable feature is a fascinating story in its own right, and the unicorn's entry into literature and fantasy has not diminished its capacity to engage our imagination.

Classical accounts

Greek and Roman naturalists whose writings span the period from the fourth century BCE to the sixth century CE, among them Ctesias, Megasthenes, Aristotle, Pliny, Solinus, Aelian and Cosmas, described the nature and appearance of the unicorn. They placed it in an exotic locale at the edge of the known world, but for the most part, accepted its reality. Descriptions emphasized different qualities of this remarkable creature, such as its size, strength, speed, ferocity, proud nature and solitary habits. Ctesias, a fourth-century BCE Greek physician at the Persian court, gives the first detailed account. He locates the unicorn in India and compares it to a wild ass with a white body, red head and dark blue eyes. It is too swift and fierce to be captured alive, but it will die to protect its young. The base of the distinguishing horn is white, the sharp upper part is crimson, and the central portion is black. The account adds that drinking vessels made from this horn prevented convulsions, epilepsy and poisoning, although this may be a later addition since classical medical tracts do not mention the pharmaceutical qualities of the horn.[2] Aristotle notes in his treatises *Historia animalium* (Bk 2, ch. 1) and *De Partibus Animalium* (Bk 3, ch. 2) that the unicorn is an exception to the rule that cloven-hoofed animals have horns, while hoofed animals generally do not. Aristotle's treatise presented a systematic description of the animal world, and for as long as it remained an authority on the subject, it was a significant factor in the acceptance of the unicorn's reality. Megasthenes, a Greek traveller who visited India about 300 BCE, mentions an animal with a loud bellow and spiral markings on its horn, which he calls a *cartazon*. Later authors such as Aelian (*Hist Animalia*, Bk 16, ch. 20–1), Strabo (*Geography*, Bk 15, ch. 1, sect. 56) and Pliny the Elder drew on this account. Pliny called the animal *Monoceros*. According to him, it had a horse-like body, stag's head, boar's tail, elephant-sized feet and long black horn. It made a fearsome sound and could not be taken alive (*Naturalis Historia*, Bk 8, ch. 31). Pliny's writings, like those of Aristotle, continued to influence perceptions of the natural world, and Solinus's *Polyhistoria*, (ch. 58), written in the third century CE, endowed the animal with the attributes noted in previous sources, plus a much longer horn.[3]

Aelian (Claudius Aelianus) in his treatise *On the Nature of Animals* attributed his detailed description to the authority of the Brahmins and located the animal among the impassable mountains and wild beasts of India. (Figure 1.1) He too calls it the cartazon with a spirally marked black horn and an aggressive temperament. During the mating season however, it grazed peacefully besides the female.[4] The first known picture of the cartazon appears in a copy of the work of an Alexandrian Greek, Cosmas Indicopleustes (the India Traveller), and it provided an influential addition to the natural history of the animal.

FIGURE 1.1 *A wild unicorn roams the forests of India in Sebastian Munster's Cosmographiae uniuersalis (1550), a description of the known world.*

In his sixth-century *Topographia Christiana* (Bk XI, ch. 7), Cosmas described a visit to 'Ethiopia' (perhaps the Armenian plateau). He did not see any live unicorns, only depictions of them in the emperor's palace. Cosmas's little creature resembles earlier Iranian bronze figurines,[5] and copies of the original drawing show an antelope-like quadruped with an upright horn and a collar around its neck to indicate that it belonged to the king. In an eleventh-century copy of his work, preserved in the Laurentian Library in Florence (MS. Laur. Pkt. 9.28, ch. 268r), an archer pursues a similar animal. This became a popular marginal illustration in manuscripts throughout the medieval period.[6]

Biblical unicorns

These classical descriptions were eventually absorbed through the prism of Jewish and Christian exegesis of biblical references into an animal that came to be identified with the unicorn. In the third century BCE, the cosmopolitan city of Alexandria was the setting for a translation of the Old Testament from Hebrew into Greek known as the Septuagint. Jewish translators seemed unsure of the meaning of the Hebrew word, *re'em*, but knew from context that it was a metaphor for something powerful. Originally, it may have been an ox-like animal, possibly an auroch (*Bos Primigenius*), the ancestor of modern cattle, so the translators chose the Greek word *monokeros* as the most appropriate equivalent.[7]

As Jewish laws and traditions were collected into a series of writings known as the Talmud, some Jewish scholars began to equate the re'em with the unicorn. Images of the unicorn, influenced by classical natural history as well as the biblical Psalms and exegesis, found their way into Jewish art and literature. A unicorn and a ram, the fighting beasts from Daniel's vision, illustrates a fifteenth-century printed copy of Isaac ben Solomon abi Sahula's thirteenth-century *Fable of the Ancients* (Meshal ha-Kadmoni), while a unicorn defeating a lion decorates an eighteenth-century silver Torah crown.[8] Talmudic literature also addressed the question of how the unicorn survived the Flood, as it was not actually a passenger in Noah's Ark. The enormous animal had to swim besides the Ark, and in some versions, the weight of birds that perched on its back caused it to drown beneath the rising waters.

The Torah, the first five books in the Jewish Bible, mentions the *tachash* that covered the tabernacle. Suggestions about the nature of this covering range from dyed leather to animal fur, but at least one source identifies the hide as that of a unicorn.[9] The fact that this was a unique appearance suggested to one Jewish naturalist, writing in the 1930s, a rationalization that brings an interesting perspective to the interface between science, tradition and commentary in respect to sacred texts like the Torah. The explanation acknowledges the identification between the unicorn's horn and the narwhal's tusk, a small whale (*Monodon Monoceros*) native to the Arctic. It compares the narwhal's distinctively mottled skin to the description of the tabernacle covering and suggests that a pod of northern-dwelling narwhals might have swum into the Mediterranean at the right time to provide an exemplar for some features of the *tachesh* traditions.[10] This somewhat tortuous argument illustrates how so-called rational solutions can be as imaginatively speculative as the travellers' tales themselves.

The creature that emerges from biblical commentary has something of the cosmic grandeur of the single-horned bulls that were common in Near Eastern and Indus art. These unicorn bulls may actually represent two-horned animals seen in profile, and they frequently appear on seals and temple walls opposing a royal figure or culture hero.[11] The re'em unicorn in the Book of Job, the Psalms and Daniel's vision certainly retained the fierceness of the single-horned bulls of Mesopotamia and the Indus valley in both Jewish and Christian tradition. Biblical commentators related the unicorn's power and fierceness to the power of God. References, such as the one in the Book of Job (Job 39.9–10), which depicts the animal as fierce, and the one in Ps. 22.21, which seeks salvation from the horn of the unicorn, were important factors in the integration of the unicorn into a Christian world view. St Jerome's Latin translation of the Old and New Testaments, known as the Vulgate (fourth century CE) used the Latin *unicornis* (and occasionally, *rhinoceros*) to translate biblical references to this mysterious animal. Later translations adopted whatever term equated with the one-horned beast in the relevant language. The Authorized Version of the King James Bible (1611) mentions the 'unicorn', while several contemporary translations revert to 'wild-ox'. Early Christian commentators transformed the unicorn into a symbol of Christ and included it in the scheme of creation as one of the animals in the Garden of Eden. (Figure 1.2) Tertullian (c. 160–220 CE), a Christian writer working from the Septuagint translation, distinguishes the unicorn from the rhinoceros. Elsewhere, Christ was compared to the unicorn, whose single horn 'pierces' mankind with faith. In the fourth century, three influential Christian writers, Eustace of Antioch (known as Basileus), St Ambrose of Milan and St Basil, bishop of Caesarea, linked the unicorn's power with Christ. Eustace refers to the role of a virgin in capturing the unicorn, but gives no details, while Ambrose stresses the unicorn's power over the lion, here a symbol of the devil.[12]

The *Physiologus*, a didactic poem written in Greek in the third century CE, combined Christian exegesis with classical natural history and commentaries on their moral or symbolic significance accompanied descriptions of real animals and birds, and a few fantastic ones. This widely translated and adapted work influenced the medieval bestiary tradition. It is the first Western

FIGURE 1.2 *A unicorn, traditionally a representation of purity and salvation, is just visible in the representation of the Garden of Eden from the first illustrated edition of John Milton's* Paradise Lost *1682.*

source to include the story about the virgin, the unicorn and the hunters. The seventh-century pope, Gregory the Great, a man well read in both classical and Christian scholarship, combined the creature mentioned by classical writers of natural history with the biblical rhinoceros in the Vulgate translation of the Book of Job ('Numquid volet rhinoceros servire te?' – 'Shall the rhinoceros be willing to serve thee'? Job 39.9). He interpreted the unicorn's capture by a virgin as an allegory of the Incarnation, the event by which Christ became human.[13] Isidore of Seville's *Etymologies*, compiled in the seventh century, identified the unicorn as a four-footed beast with a single horn. This horn could kill elephants by piercing their bellies, but a maiden could overcome its strength and fierceness (*Etymologies*, Bk 12, 2.12–13). The image of the virgin and the unicorn soon began to appear in art. A ninth-century copy of the *Physiologus*, the earliest that survives, depicts a classically draped female holding the unicorn's muzzle, and other copies show the lady leading the unicorn to the king.[14] Similar images appear in the margins of various manuscripts. An eleventh-century psalter, or mass book, depicts a lady blessing a unicorn under a roundel depicting the Blessed Virgin and child, a clear evocation of the Christian interpretation first described by Gregory.[15] The unicorns in these pictures have backward curving horns, and one even resembles a miniature rhinoceros.[16]

The unicorn and the lady

The bestiary tradition, which was central to the transmission and visual realization of medieval animal lore, included the unicorn with an account of its physical characteristics and Christian meaning. In a twelfth-century bestiary, translated by T. H. White, who incorporated a unicorn hunt into *The Once and Future King* (1958), the unicorn section epitomizes characteristics of the animal from earlier sources. It is small, fast and goat-like. It has a long, sharp horn, and the animal is captured after it rests its head in a virgin's lap. The text does not mention hunters or the animal's death, but these details appear in illustrations.[17]

In bestiaries, the unicorn appears as a delicate goat-like creature being embraced by a lady, generally with one or more hunters lurking among stylized trees. The image is deliberately ambiguous, embodying both innocence and carnality, religious as well as secular meaning. The lady, the unicorn, the hunters and the forest setting epitomized a subtle, multilevelled metaphor for the intricate rules of courtly love as well as the meaning of Christ's Incarnation. Sometimes the woman held a mirror, simultaneously a symbol of pride and the spotless reflection of chastity. The hunters who appear in the act of killing the beast with spears, swords or arrows, were often identified as sinners seeking salvation. Texts like the *Physiologus* and the bestiaries presented an increasingly elaborate exegesis of this complex image of the divine becoming human. Christ was the 'spiritual unicorn' whose single horn symbolized the unity between God the Father and the Son. A foliate border surrounding a Nativity scene in a Dutch Book of Hours includes a unicorn crouching before a crowned woman, and an inscription 'Egredietur Uirga de Radice Yesse'.[18] The unicorn's small size reflected the 'lowliness' of the divine being made flesh through the Incarnation. Although neither angels nor demons can capture it, the unicorn willingly enters the Blessed Virgin's womb in order to save humankind, a sentiment expressed in a line in a Middle English poem to Mary – this 'unicorne that was so wyld ... thou hast tamed and istyld'.[19] The Farnese Hours, a prayer book created for this powerful Renaissance family in 1456, depicts events from the life of the Blessed Virgin. Alessandro Farnese is illustrated wearing a helmet decorated with a lady and unicorn motif, and elsewhere, female figures tether unicorns with blue ribbons, the Virgin's colour.[20]

The mystic unicorn hunt, further influenced by the writings of St Bernard of Clairvaux, gained popularity during the thirteenth century, especially in Germany and northern Europe. The Annunciation narrative was reformulated. The angel Gabriel became a hunter who sounds his horn, and four dogs, representing the virtues of Mercy, Truth, Peace and Justice, accompany him. The Blessed Virgin sits in a *hortus conclusus* (enclosed garden) containing a symbolic fountain of pure water surrounded by flowers, such as lilies and carnations that have specific associations with her. A unicorn rests in the Virgin's lap with its horn pointed directly at her heart or womb. Other symbols from the Old Testament texts, such as manna, Aaron's altar and Gideon's fleece, which were associated with God's promise of salvation, also appear in the garden. This is undoubtedly the most elaborate use of the image as an embodiment of the Christian doctrines about the life of Christ.[21] Guillaume le Clerc's *Bestiaire Divin*, a rhymed thirteenth-century bestiary, emphasized the role of Christ as the 'l'unicorne esperitel' (spiritual unicorn) in an allegorical hunt redolent with Christian symbolism.[22] The mystic hunt appears depicted in prayer books, altar cloths and altar panels. An embroidered roundel on a thirteenth-century altar cloth, which inserts a little unicorn into an Annunciation scene, illustrates the way in which text and art informed one another,[23] but it is worth noting that the various strands of unicorn symbolism did not develop in isolation. A fifteenth-century Florentine engraving, for example, depicts a woman with the name Marietta inscribed on her cloak in the act of putting a collar on a unicorn attached to what looks like a pomegranate tree. This example combines religious allegory, which plays on the woman's name, with the more secular images of pomegranate tree and collar, symbolic of love, fidelity and eternal life.[24]

Bestiary descriptions influenced carved scenes of the unicorn's capture on medieval misericords. Although the distinction between mystic and secular hunts is not always clear, a fourteenth-century misericord from Ely Cathedral depicts a maiden clasping a unicorn with hunters carved on the supporters against a background of oak leaves and acorns. As symbols of strength and fidelity, these plants carried both secular and religious meaning.[25] In the thirteenth-century *Bestiare d'amour* by Richard de Fournival, the unicorn is a human, courtly lover who submits to a chaste maiden in order to be tamed and transformed by love. Similarly, the troubadour poet, Theobald king of Navarre, identified himself with the unicorn conquered by love.[26] The theme of the unicorn as a tamed lover may also underpin a marginal illustration in which a woman tenderly arrays a unicorn in an embroidered saddlecloth.[27] The love aspect of the hunt was a popular topic for *Minnekastchen*, ivory caskets given as love tokens.[28] The unicorn makes brief appearances in late medieval romances. A somewhat bizarre Arthurian adventure occurs in *Le Chevalier du Papegau*, in which a shipwrecked king Arthur meets a giant who has been suckled by a unicorn, and in *Le Roman de la dame à la lycorne et du biau chevalier au lyon*, it swims across a moat with a lady on its back.[29]

The multiple meanings of the unicorn, sacred, secular, erotic and mystical, come together in two sets of tapestries woven about 1500, which, poignantly, reflect the flowering of unicorn symbolism at the point at which it was about to change. Elaborate tapestries reflected the status of the owners. Since the figures were life-size or larger, the sense of inhabiting a richly coloured, symbolic world undoubtedly added to the impact. The rediscovery of a set of medieval tapestries in a provincial French town in the nineteenth century renewed interest in traditions about the unicorn. In 1841, the novelist Prosper Mérimée, an accomplished amateur archaeologist and inspector-general of historic monuments, visited the Château de Boussac in the Limousin district of central France with his friend, the writer George Sand (aka Lucile Aurore Dupin). Sand herself wrote about the tapestries as an image of the lost courtliness of the past, most notably and somewhat fancifully, in her novel *Jeanne*.[30] The tapestries, now on display in the Cluny Museum in Paris, may present an allegory of the five senses with a sixth, called *A mon seul desir* after the words inscribed on a banner. Both a unicorn and a lion appear in each tapestry as companions to a beautifully dressed lady. There is no hunt or huntsmen, rather the unicorn and its imagery seem to reflect a courtly world of lavish images. The lady in the 'Sight' tapestry holds a mirror in which the unicorn admires itself. This was a popular motif in French courtly interpretations of the legend. However, the monkey, so often a symbol for human frailty, appears as a tame pet. The antagonism attributed to the lion and the unicorn elsewhere appears to be lacking here. The lion is as much the lady's companion as the unicorn. The two beasts appear on the arms of the Le Viste family who may have originally commissioned the tapestries, perhaps as a wedding present for the 'lady'.[31]

The complex sensual allegories of the tapestries, and their very survival as examples of medieval art, have inspired artists and writers, either directly or through renewed interest in the symbolic meanings of the unicorn *topos*. The poet Rainer Maria Rilke referenced this in his *Sonnets to Orpheus* (1923), and Jean Cocteau's scenario for the ballet, *La dame a la licorne* (1953) reflected a personal interpretation of the Cluny tapestries with themes of love, loss and innocence.[32]

Just before the outbreak of the Second World War, The Cloisters, a purpose-built museum overlooking the Hudson River in New York, opened to house the medieval art collection of the Metropolitan Museum of Art. It allowed ordinary Americans, at a time when European travel was not common, to experience the culture of the medieval world. Among its treasures are six tapestries, and fragments of a seventh, depicting a unicorn hunt. Until the French Revolution, the tapestries hung in the de La Rochefoucauld family chateau at Verteuil. They reappeared at the end of the nineteenth century, and eventually John D. Rock-efeller Jr presented them to the Cloisters. The exact meaning of the tapestries, and the identification of the patrons who commissioned them, has not yet been resolved. On one level, the subject is a typical medieval hunt, but with the unicorn replacing the more usual stag. Huntsmen observe the unicorn puri-fying the water by dipping its horn into a stream flowing from a fountain sur-rounded by animals with both courtly and religious meanings. The stag and the panther were associated with Christ; the lion with his lioness represent fidelity. The hare indicated fertility, while the pheasant, jealous of his own reflection, was a warning to married couples. The actual hunt takes place in the next two tapestries. The phrase, *Ave Regina,* inscribed on a hunter's clothing, together with the pomegranate tree, symbol of earthly fertility and heavenly Resurrec-tion, evoke both religious and secular aspects of unicorn symbolism. Only a fragment of the unicorn's capture remains, but a female hand emerging from a sleeve, perhaps leading the animal, can be seen under the unicorn's chin. The double meanings of secular and sacred unicorn symbolism carry over into the next tapestry in which the hunters bring the dead unicorn, with a collar of thorns reminiscent of Christ's Passion, to the castle. Floral symbols associ-ated with love and the Virgin Mary decorate the smallest tapestry in which the unicorn, wearing a jewelled collar and chained to a pomegranate tree, sits in an enclosed garden, reborn and peaceful in its role both as a secular husband and the risen Christ.[33] The most recent theory suggests that the Cloisters tap-estries preserve three versions of the unicorn hunt, the Mystic Hunt of the Incarnation, the Unicorn as Lover, and the Hunt of the Unicorn as an allegory of Christ's Passion. If this is accurate, then these tapestries embody virtually all the elements of medieval unicorn lore.

Occasionally European visitors to the East claimed to have seen tame uni-corns,[34] but most accounts concentrate on the animal's symbolic meaning or the medicinal value of its horn. An unusual variant of the hunt appears in a description of Ethiopia written by a Dominican friar, Luis de Urreta, in 1610. He describes how a trained female monkey lulls the rhinoceros by scratching its belly, so that hunters can shoot it. Intriguingly, Urreta follows this rationalized account of a fierce beast betrayed by a female with a reference to the noble unicorn, symbol of a loving heart, tamed by a virgin.[35] The contrast between the monkey, a symbol of man's barbarous nature, as a way to capture the wild rhinoceros, and the noble unicorn tamed by a virgin provides yet another perspective on how fantastic creatures can be used to construct morality. A thirteenth-century Arabic bestiary influenced by the *Physiologus, Kitāb Na't al-Ḥayawān (Book of the Characteristics of Animals),* (British Library Or.2784), is ascribed, rightly or wrongly, to a famous physician, Ibn Bakhtishu. The sec-tion on the unicorn includes a miniature of a delicate unicorn with its head thrown back so that the long horn seems to project backwards (fol. 197v–198r).

The text describes a method of capturing the unicorn with the help of a pure virgin, although in other Arabic sources the animal is enticed by a girl from a brothel.[36] The *Physica* of Hildegard of Bingen (Bk 8, ch. 5) contains a version of the maiden and the unicorn, which differs significantly from other medieval sources in that the unicorn is attracted to a group of noble maidens that it mistakes for boys, a detail also found in some Eastern stories.

The medieval theme of the unicorn has been compared to the Indian legend of Rsyasrnga and the virgin. Variants of the Rsyasrnga story exist in the *Mahabharata* (3,110–113), the *Ramayana* (1, 8019), in various Buddhist and Chinese texts and in Eastern art.[37] In the *Mahabharata* version, Rsyasrnga is the offspring of a Brahmin and a deer. Although human, he has a single horn on his forehead and lives a wild innocent existence. A king, whose kingdom is suffering from drought, learns that only Rsyasrnga can supply the remedy. A beautiful courtesan seduces the innocent wild creature and brings him to the king who presents him to his daughter. Initially Rsyasrnga's father is angry, but eventually the young man returns home with his princess bride. There is a suggestion that this ancient Eastern tale is the origin of the European unicorn myth. Perhaps it is, but not in a direct or simple way.[38] The European unicorn is a complex amalgam of learned lore, travellers' tales and religious allegory rather than a mythic narrative. The unicorn and maiden motif appeared in the *Physiologus*, which may have been compiled in Alexandria, a cosmopolitan meeting point between East and West. However, there is a fundamental difference between the Rsyasrnga legend and beliefs about an animal with a reputation for wildness. The Eastern versions concern a human with an animal parent. The fact that Rsyasrnga is both a wild and innocent male makes him a powerful force in the story, but he is of use only if he remains alive. By contrast, the death of the unicorn is essential to most European versions, and, while it represents Christ in some interpretations, it is always an animal.

The idea of an ancient source is popular among those who see the unicorn as the embodiment of some eternal truth or as a symbol of a lost world where man and nature lived in harmony. The single horn has been interpreted as a symbol of male power.[39] These are interesting interpretations, but there may be a subtler dynamic at play. The elements, either expressed or implicit, in the Rsyasrnga tales suggest that the drought signifies a failure in governance and the need for the king who lacks a male heir to ensure his succession. As the offspring of a Brahmin and a deer, the one-horned boy living in a liminal state between the wilderness and society is an apt figure to restore the balance between the civil order of kingship and the unpredictability of nature.[40] Structuralist critics, like Claude Levi Strauss, emphasized the contrast between nature and civilization as a fundamental dynamic in narrative.[41] As a human and animal hybrid, Rsyasrnga's single horn resolves cultural opposites and carries the more subtle power of crossed categories, a characteristic shared by many fantastic creatures. A Christian interpretation in which the unicorn's horn represents the unity of Father and Son also reflects the resolution of dynamic opposition. There are other similarities between the Rsyasrnga and Western unicorn lore. For example, the link between unicorn and king, which is a feature of the *Physiologus* account, and the detail recorded in the *Physica* of Hildegard of Bingen that the unicorn admires well-born young women because they appear androgynous. However, correspondences do not necessarily suggest a shared origin, and an important consideration, with arguments of this type, is whether the similarities outweigh the differences. Even one of the translators of the *Mahabharata* admits that the situation is not 'tidy'.[42]

At the start of the play within a play, Hamlet imitates a courtly lover and asks to rest his head on Ophelia's lap (*Hamlet* Act III, sc. ii). The subsequent exchange, full of sexual innuendo, is one of many strands in this scene that reveal the tensions in Shakespeare's drama. There is no mention of the unicorn, but the dialogue calls to mind the complex ironies of the lady and the unicorn, or rather how the interpretations were moving away from an allegory about Christian doctrine, yet retained overtones of chastity and marital fidelity versus promiscuity and deceit. Under the influence of humanist culture, the allegory of the unicorn hunt became more secular. A set of tapestry designs preserved in engravings by Jean Duvet (d. 1571) reflect the fusion of medieval and post-medieval unicorn lore. The tapestries may have been intended as a gift from the French king, Henry II, to his mistress. In this series, the unicorn cleanses the waters of the fountain, but is first captured alive by a maiden and hunters and then led in triumph by the king and queen. The motifs of the maiden leading the unicorn to the king and the animals waiting for the unicorn to cleanse the waters date back at least to the *Physiologus*, but here, the unicorn signifies good governance and reflects a new humanistic aspect to unicorn symbolism.[43]

Renaissance and Mannerist art delighted in multilayered symbolism, but the chaste unicorn remained a favourite motif. Large *cassoni* (wedding chests) for the bride's trousseau began to replace medieval ivory love caskets. Many were painted with scenes based on Petrarch's fourteenth-century allegorical poem, *I Trionfi*, in which the unicorn draws the triumphal carriage of Chastity, the one virtue that triumphs over Death.[44] In one of Raphael's portraits, a chaste young woman cradles a lapdog-sized unicorn (1505) and other artists like Giorgione (1510) and Domenico Zampieri (1602) incorporated this allegorical motif.[45] A unicorn draws the chariot of the faithful wife on the reverse of Piero della Francesca's portrait of Battista Strozzi, while the unicorn approaching the lady in the background of a pair of late-fifteenth-century betrothal portraits (Maestro delle Storie del Pane, New York Metropolitan Museum of Art) symbolizes the future husband's attraction to his chaste bride. Pisanello's medal (1477) for Cecilia Gonzaga, who became a nun, depicts the crescent moon, symbol of chaste Diana, shining on a lady and her unicorn, thereby combining Renaissance interest in classical mythology with unicorn lore. The Renaissance painter known as Moretto, painted a unicorn kneeling at the feet of the martyred virgin St Justina.

Medieval symbolism did not disappear completely or immediately. Unicorns surrounded by symbolic plants, such as Marian flowers and an oak tree, with hunters embedded in the foliage dominate the frontispiece of an early-sixteenth-century printed copy of the Hours of the Blessed Virgin Mary (1504).[46] However, as these new humanistic interpretations of unicorn lore became more prominent, the symbolic contexts in which the unicorn appeared began to change. The lady in Leonardo da Vinci's fifteenth-century drawing of a 'Maiden with a Unicorn', now in the Oxford Ashmolean Museum, points towards a unicorn sitting beside her. Leonardo also composed a little bestiary text that linked the unicorn with indiscretion because its fondness for women made it easy prey for the hunter, and it is tempting to speculate whether Leonardo intended the meaning of one to inform the other.[47] Elaborate and mystical religious symbolism became less popular after the Protestant Reformation and, after the Council of Trent (1545–63), even within the Roman Catholic Church.[48] By the middle of the seventeenth century, the Danish scientist, Thomas Bartholin, felt able to declare that the story of the lady capturing the unicorn was a mere fable.[49]

Fighting unicorns

A bull with a single horn appears on Indus seals. This may be a two-horned beast seen in profile, an Indian rhinoceros, or a unicorn, and it suggests a metaphor for strength. The links between these animals date back to the earliest classical naturalists, and they became further entwined by biblical exegesis and bestiary lore. The Jewish Italian kabbalist, Abraham ben Hananiah Yagel, writing in the sixteenth century, compared the Old Testament re'em to a 'unicorn' given to the king of Portugal. This was actually a live rhinoceros, one of the first to appear in Europe since Roman times, and it provided the basis for Albrecht Dürer's famous 1515 rhinoceros woodcut.[50]

The unicorn as described in classical accounts could be an aggressive animal with a horrible bray, horse-like body, elephant's feet and the tail of a stag. Biblical accounts also reflect its fierce nature. In the Old Testament account of Daniel's vision (Daniel 8, 5–7), Daniel sees a goat with a single horn defeat a two-horned ram in battle, but the single-horned animal is often a unicorn in medieval depictions of this event. Combinations of naturalistic description and biblical commentary, no doubt, influenced bestiary accounts in which fights between the unicorn and the elephant emphasize the strength and cunning of the smaller beast that used its horn to rip open the larger animal's stomach.[51]

Another beast that opposes the unicorn, the lion, is also prevalent in ancient Near Eastern art. A lion attacking a one-horned bull appears on a sculptural frieze from Persepolis (500 BCE), and combats between lions and bulls feature on Sumerian seals.[52] A lion and a unicorn appear to attack the crucified Christ in the ninth-century Stuttgart Psalter, although a chalice-like cup hovers between the two animals to receive the saviour's blood so the process of salvation can begin.[53] Elizabethan writers, among them William Shakespeare, Edmund Spenser and George Chapman, alluded to the fight between the lion and the unicorn. The main character in *Timon of Athens*, one of the darkest of Shakespeare's plays, warns that 'pride and wrath' confounds the unicorn (*Timon of Athens*, Act IV, sc. iii). The proud and arrogant Caesar 'loves to hear that unicorns may be deceived with trees', a flaw that will deliver him into the hands of his assassins (*Julius Caesar* Act II, sc. i), and the poet and dramatist, George Chapman, described an 'Angrie unicorne' who impaled a hunter before he could shelter under a tree (*Bussy D'Ambois*, 1603). As part of the complex allegory of virtue overcoming vice in *The Faerie Queene*, Edmund Spenser compares one character's pride to the rebellious unicorn defying the power of the imperial lion (Bk 2, Canto 5).

The traditional enmity between these two beasts informs a popular rhyme first mentioned in 1709. The verse about the lion chasing the unicorn 'all around the town' reflected the political conflict between the old Stuart monarchy and the new Hanoverian kings, rival claimants to the British throne.[54] In Lewis Carroll's *Through the Looking Glass*, the roles of the nursery rhyme characters are comically reversed. The clever unicorn calmly assures the White King that impaling the sleepy lion with its horn would not hurt him. John Tenniel, one of the best-known illustrators of Carroll's work, updated the political commentary by depicting the pair as caricatures of Gladstone and Disraeli, the dominant rival politicians of the day.

Once Christian commentators had established the unicorn as a symbol of Christ, it was included in the scheme of creation as one of the animals in the Garden of Eden, and its placement relative to other animals underscored its importance. The unicorn and the stag, another symbol of Christ, stand side by side as Adam names the animals on an eleventh-century embroidery from Girona Cathedral in Catalonia, now housed in the Cathedral Museum. In the twelfth-century *Hortus Deliciarum*,[55] the unicorn, placed on God's right, faces his traditional enemy, the lion, on the left. Similarly, in the fourteenth-century Boucicault Hours, the unicorn stands on the right during the creation of Adam and Eve with its horn dipped, and its hoof raised in blessing. Occasionally, the monkey, a symbol of barbarity and sexual promiscuity, opposes the unicorn.[56]

Hieronymus Bosch incorporated several ambiguous unicorns in his painting of 'The Garden of Earthly Delights'. A unicorn dips its horn in the water in the left panel depicting the creation of Adam and Eve, while, at the bottom of this panel, a black unicorn's head on an aquatic body (a version of the narwhal perhaps?) emerges from a dark pool. Since the serpent has not yet appeared in the Garden of Eden, these unicorns may hint at Mankind's imminent Fall, and eventual Salvation. In the central panel, one unicorn has a serrated horn, while another, standing next to a strange beast that resembles male genitalia, balances a pair of sac-shaped fruits on its horn. This rather ominous imagery may echo classical descriptions of the unicorn's fierceness. The god Hades rides a unicorn with a serrated horn in Albrecht Dürer's sixteenth-century rendition of the abduction of Persephone. Here the unicorn and the hunter apparently join forces, and the maiden becomes the victim. Wild men and wild women ride unicorns in medieval art and, even in the context of religious art, the creature never completely loses it aura of ferocity. [57] A medieval Welsh list of the steeds ridden by Arthur's knights gives the name, Korvan, (little horned one) to one of the 'steeds'. Although this usually refers to a young deer, perhaps it too is a unicorn, certainly an appropriate mount for an Arthurian hero.[58]

Because of its association with pure water, the unicorn was a popular watermark, with over five hundred versions identified on paper produced up to the end of the sixteenth century.[59] By contrast, the heraldic unicorn is a symbol of strength, purity and courage. (Figure 1.3) On the Cluny tapestries, it is part of the symbolic narrative, but it also appears on the arms of the Le Viste family who may have commissioned the tapestries. A Scottish coin, called a 'unicorn', bearing a unicorn with its leg on a shield and a crown encircling its

FIGURE 1.3 *A unicorn from a sixteenth-century Manuel of Heraldry strikes a pose described as 'a unicorn tripping'.*

neck, was struck at the beginning of the fifteenth century during the reign of James III. Another Scottish king, James VI, kneels before an altar emblazoned with his arms supported by two white unicorns in a specially commissioned Book of Hours. After he ascended the English throne in 1603, to become James I of England, the Scottish unicorn eventually joined the English lion as a supporter on the royal arms.[60]

Medical unicorns and the curative power of a spiral horn

The unicorn became an established emblem for European pharmacists because of the supposed curative power of its horn, and it was still an important pharmacological product when the arms of the Society of Apothecaries were granted in 1617. The Society's arms have golden unicorns as supporters, and a rhinoceros, another animal whose horn had pharmacological properties, crests them. The medicinal and magical importance of unicorn horn was the result of fusing beliefs about the properties of the horn itself with the unicorn's power to cleanse poisoned water. However, the efficacy of unicorn horn had already proved controversial by the sixteenth century, and the new century brought even more challenges.

The image of a unicorn cleansing the water carved on a fifteenth-century misericord at Cartmel Priory, Cumbria, reflects a long-established belief about the purifying power of unicorn horn.[61] This aspect of unicorn lore became popular in late medieval art. The *Physiologus* noted that the unicorn cleansed water poisoned by serpents by making the sign of the cross with its horn. The medieval traveller, John of Hesse, associated the story of the unicorn purifying water polluted by serpents with 'the bitter waters of the river' purified by Moses (Exod. 15.23),[62] and there is a suggestion that the motif has an even older source in a one-horned beast in Zoroastrian tradition that cleanses water polluted by demonic forces.[63] The unicorn's role as purifier occurs again in the garden of the Medici Villa di Castello near Florence where the unicorn dominates a group of animals that adorn a fountain grotto.[64]

The belief that cups made of unicorn horn were a protection against poison is noted as early as Ctesias, if that section is indeed contemporary with the original work. Philostratus (c. 165–250 CE) in the *Life of Apollonius of Tyana* (*Vita Apollonii*, Bk 3, ch. 2) claims that only kings have the right to hunt the unicorn and that goblets made of unicorn horn protect against disease, wounds, fire and poison. However, the author immediately distances himself from this by having his hero, Apollonius, question the truth of these statements. The *Physica* of Hildegard of Bingen (Bk 8, 5) does not mention the horn. However, unicorn liver offers protection against leprosy, while a belt or shoes made of unicorn hide prevents plague, and perhaps a later hand has added that the hooves cause poisoned food to sweat. A thirteenth-century Arabic bestiary, Kitāb Na't al-Ḥayawān (*Book of the Characteristics of Animals*) (British Library Or.2784), contains information about the unicorn (called both *kardunn* and *dabba*). There is an entry about a two-horned beast (*dabba*) that can purify water and create, in effect, a temporary 'peaceable kingdom' among the animals. The accompanying illustration shows an antelope-like creature surrounded by animals standing under a tree near water, a composition that recalls the unicorn in the Garden of Eden. Another drawing of a delicate prancing unicorn with its head thrown back accompanies a discussion about how the horn is used. The smell exuded by heating unicorn horn protects against magic, and when the horn is sliced, it reveals a black core containing 'shapes' which resemble animals (fol. 197v–198r). The texts assert that they protect against evil and are much prized by the Chinese, especially their kings, who wear belts of unicorn horn, which suggests that the 'figures' in the horn may actually refer to ivory or bone carvings.[65]

References to objects made of unicorn horn are tantalizing, but evidence for medical use in Europe is often difficult to pin down. The increase of whaling and trade no doubt made such products more available, while the existence of actual horns gave the animal more credibility. Twelfth-century drawings of unicorns showed them with long white horns like a narwhal tusk, and a 'unicorn horn' now in Salzburg has a late-twelfth-century dedication. Long spiralled narwhal tusks, actually the whale's tooth, were valued possessions that appear in church and aristocratic inventories in the fourteenth and fifteenth centuries. Elaborate carvings and protective metal caps adorned some of these objects, while their use as ceremonial staffs in churches imply that the whiteness and the spiral markings reinforced ideas of purity and the importance of ecclesiastical spaces. Their frequency in ecclesiastical settings suggests that the objects themselves were important. The numerous scratches on these objects suggest that they were used in medicine. Scratches on cups and pendants believed to be unicorn horn might also indicate medical or magical use, although it is difficult to date when exactly such scratching occurred. Luxuriously carved and silver mounted cups made of narwhal ivory were produced as late as the seventeenth century.[66] Anecdotes about famous unicorn horns, some perhaps more credible than others, reinforce the belief in the horn as both a protection against poison and a symbol of status. Sir Martin Frobisher found one on a Newfoundland beach, and presented it to Queen Elizabeth I. A specimen, now in a Viennese museum, was fashioned into a sword pommel for the Duke of Burgundy, and an English monarch requested a piece of the unicorn horn owned by an Oxford College. Such anecdotes, often repeated in histories of the unicorn, lose nothing in the retelling.[67] In his autobiography,

Benvenuto Cellini recalls a competition with another goldsmith to design a setting for a unicorn horn that Pope Clement VII intended as a gift for King Francis I. Although Cellini's design was never realized, he provided interesting details about the exorbitant cost of such objects. [68]

Where the medieval unicorn drew artists and clerical commentary, the medical unicorn attracted doctors and scientists. As unicorn horn became more available in powdered form, the question of fraud became an issue and, not surprisingly, medical practitioners were keen to distance themselves from quackery. If the Middle Ages were a highpoint for allegorical representations of unicorns in art and literature, then the sixteenth to eighteenth centuries were a time when the source of unicorn horn and beliefs about its medical efficacy came to the fore. Over two-dozen studies on the unicorn appeared between 1500 and 1700.[69] Most accepted the possibility that the animal existed, but the focus had shifted to the medicinal properties of the horn and methods for determining its authenticity. Conrad Gesner in *Historiae animalium* (1551–8) included accounts from friends and correspondents who examined known specimens of unicorn horn. The surgeon, Amboise Paré, although aware of the difficulties arising from lack of first-hand accounts of the animal, was more interested in fraudulent claims for its horn (1582), and Andrea Marini (1566) adopted a similar critical position. Doctors and apothecaries with commercial and professional interest in this medicine defended its use. Andrea Bacci (1573) mounted an elaborate defence of the benefits of *alicorno* (the medical form of unicorn horn). He included anecdotes about successful treatments, some of which sound like traditional legends, such as the man (unnamed) who ate a poisoned cherry, but was cured by unicorn horn dissolved in wine.[70]

The existence of actual horns made the reality of the animal harder to discount, but three professors at Copenhagen University laid the groundwork for a more scientific approach to the subject. Caspar Bartholin, the elder (1585–1629), had seen unicorn horns in apothecary shops, but he was also aware of the trade in narwhal ivory and, in his treatise on the unicorn, *De unicorn ejusque affinibus et succedaneis opusulum*, he distinguished the unicorn and narwhal as two separate one-horned animals. His son, Thomas Bartholin (1616–80), published a study of one-horned animals in *De unicornu observationes novae* (1645). The new edition of 1678 by Thomas's son, Caspar Bartholin the younger (1655–1738), added a frontispiece combining classical imagery and scientific observation. A lady and a unicorn stand in the centre; behind her are a warrior with a rhinoceros horn and a satyr with an antelope whose two horns have been twisted into one. At the bottom, tritons carry narwhal teeth and a fish-like narwhal with its tusk removed.[71] In the 1630s, Danish merchants requested the Danish scientist, Ole Worm, to test the medicinal efficacy of unicorn's horn. Although he never actually denied the possibility that unicorns could exist, he demonstrated that unicorn horn was in reality the tusk (actually tooth) of a narwhal and his tests undermined its pharmacological credibility.[72] The debate began to widen as scientists like Sir Hans Sloane incorporated the work of Bartholin and Ole Worm on narwhals and false unicorn powders,[73] although attitudes changed slowly.

One of the oddest unicorns from this period was undoubtedly the Quedlinburg unicorn, a curiosity created from fossil bones found in the quarries around Magdeburg in Germany. In *Protogaea* (written in 1692 but published in 1749), Gottfried Wilhelm Leibniz discussed the unicorn in the context of the nascent science of geology. The discussion was part of a larger consideration of the significance of fossils in a world with little understanding of geological chronology. Leibniz knew that the Danish scientist Bartholin had demonstrated that unicorn horns came from a 'fish' found in the Northern Ocean.[74] Nevertheless, on the testimony of an unimpeachable observer, he considered whether unicorns did exist. The unimpeachable observer was Otto von Guericke of Magdeburg, a scientific pioneer in the study of vacuums. He described a 'fossil' found by quarrymen in 1663 who disturbed the original intact animal and brought what remained to the Abbess of Magdeburg. Guericke mentions a horn nine feet long and as thick as a man's leg, which suggests that the remains were that of a mastodon skull and tusk. In *Museum Museorum* (1704), an early survey of European fossils, Michael Bernhard Valentini attributes the drawing of the Quedlinburg unicorn to Johann Meyer. Another illustration and description, published by J. A. Wallmann in 1776, asserted that the hind legs were found when the bones were uncovered in the quarry, but later lost, so the skeleton had to be assembled without them. This implies that the animal as originally found would have conformed to the four-legged European idea of a unicorn. It appears below a drawing of a mammoth tooth in the woodcut included in the 1749 edition of Leibniz's book. It has only two legs and its tail (the original spine?) seems to drag on the ground, and this illustration appears to be the source for the one reproduced in books about unicorns.[75]

Although there is consensus that a substance called *khutu* was the source for specimens of unicorn horn and for beliefs about its pharmacological properties, there is less agreement about the exact identification of *khutu* itself. Speculations range from plausible to wishful. Arabic traders refer to 'fish teeth', which could mean walrus or narwhal, since both were classified as 'fishes'. References to a 'thousand-year-old snake' suggest a twisting narwhal tusk, and other sources attribute the horn to various four-footed beasts.[76] The science writer and cryptozoologist, Willy Ley, suggested that unicorns were memories of an extinct genus of giant rhinoceros (Elasmotherium), and recent fossil finds still play into the idea of 'Unicorns Were Real, and a New Fossil Shows When They Lived'.[77] Ley was an early proponent of the theory, currently very popular, that misinterpretations of fossil remains were the source for beliefs about mythological creatures.[78]

The 'Truth behind the Myth'

The wonderful sights on Prospero's island cause one of the shipwrecked aristocrats to exclaim, 'Now I will believe in unicorns' (*The Tempest* Act III, sc. iii). By the latter part of the sixteenth century, when Shakespeare wrote the play, there was probably some doubt about the unicorn's reality. Nevertheless, there have been many attempts to unpick the travellers' tales and traditions that created the European unicorn. The search for the 'truth behind the myth' dates back at least to the fourth century BCE and the writings of the Greek mythographer, Euhemerus, whose mythological method, which became known as euhemerism, rationalized that myths were distorted accounts of historical events or experiences. In the context of the legendary unicorn, this has meant a search for an animal or animals whose characteristics and habits gave rise to the idea of a one-horned beast. Writers as diverse as Tertullian, Luis de Urreta and Abraham Ben Hananiah attempted to distinguish the unicorn from the rhinoceros. In 1825, Baron George Cuvier, in perhaps the first attempt since Aristotle to deal with the problem of a 'real' unicorn in terms of animal anatomy, questioned whether single-horned animals were possible in nature.[79] Odell Shepard, an academic and a specialist in American transcendentalism, published an admirably wide-ranging and common-sense study on the origins of unicorn lore in 1930. It is still very readable and useful; moreover, its availability on the internet has contributed to contemporary unicorn lore since many sites quote or paraphrase this book. For Shepard, the unicorn was a kind of chimaera, a mixture of beasts, including the rhinoceros, oryx, chiru and onager. The Indian rhinoceros has one horn, as opposed to the two-horned African species, and the horn has medical uses. The oryx was a much-hunted animal in ancient Persia. According to Shepard, it could have been the source for the unicorn's equine-like fighting abilities. The central positioning of the unicorn's horn may owe something to observations of the chiru, or Tibetan antelope/goat. The long, upright horns of the males can appear as a single horn in profile, and, when traded as objects detached from an animal skull, could lend further credence to the unicorn myth.[80]

The geographer Chris Lavers has recently presented a comprehensive book called *Natural History of Unicorns*. He concentrates on several animals found on the Tibetan plateau, which reflect different characteristics of the unicorn while preserving the geographical coherence of Ctesias' account. The *kiang*, a large wild ass, is fast and cannot be domesticated, and thus could account for the unicorn's speed and untameable nature. The chiru remains the most likely candidate for the horn, as it was a valuable trade good with pharmaceutical properties, but Lavers considered a third animal, the yak, because of its size and strength. Lavers suggests that the Himalayan plateau provided a 'spiritual home' for the unicorn, but he is never really clear as to whether the idea of the unicorn coalesced there, or whether the elements were reassembled to create a new animal in European sources.[81]

Lavers also records eighteenth- and nineteenth-century descriptions of unicorns, many linked to exploration and colonial expansion. This is his most original contribution to the unicorn's history, since it demonstrates how a search for the marvellous can exist in parallel with other cultural activities. Tibet continued to provide fertile ground for reports of unicorns. It was a contested area between the expanding colonial spheres of the Russian and British empires and, like any liminal space, provided a forum for the dangerous and the marvellous. The Russian explorer of Polish descent Nikolai Przhevalsky, who never saw a unicorn but gave his name to the only extant species of wild horse, became suspicious of reports that claimed that real unicorns were always somewhere over the horizon.[82] One feature of these accounts is the extent to which European perceptions of unicorns were projected onto indigenous belief. A certain Major Latter announced that descriptions in Tibetan manuscripts and first-hand accounts corresponded to 'the unicorn of the ancients', and the unicorn had, in fact, been discovered. A hopeful article appeared in print, followed by another only a few years later reporting the seeker's disappointment.[83] The last of the serious unicorn hunts took place at the beginning of the twentieth century. Harry Johnston, a British colonial administrator, followed up rumours of a strange animal living in the Ituri Rainforest in Central Africa and found, not a unicorn, but the shy and exotic okapi.[84]

If unicorns are not born, occasionally they can be made through the practice of horn manipulation on domestic cattle and sheep. The single-horned Nepalese sheep supposedly presented to a member of the British royal family and exhibited in London's Zoological Gardens in 1906 are somewhat dubious, but Dr W. Franklin Dove conducted a well-documented experiment in the 1930s in which he transplanted the horn buds on a day-old bull calf to produce a 'unicorn' bull.[85] One-horned animals continue to attract public interest, like a deer born with a single horn on an Italian nature reserve in 2008, a natural oddity compared, perhaps inevitably, with the old unicorn myth.[86]

The unicorn's survival

Belief in the medicinal efficacy of unicorn horn died out, but the unicorn itself survived and eventually flourished once again as a subject for art, literature,

FIGURE 1.4 *These fanciful little unicorns are being loaded aboard Pantagruel's ship in a scene from Rabelais's satirical novel as envisaged by the illustrator Albert Robida.*

fantasy and mystical meditation. Not surprisingly, the meaning of the unicorn and its horn departed significantly from the meaning invested in it in the past. About the time it was dropped from the British *Pharmacopia*, William Hogarth included a unicorn horn as a dual symbol of quackery and promiscuity in his satirical series, *Marriage à la mode*.[87] Two centuries earlier, when the unicorn was still taken seriously, Rabelais also exploited the risqué potential of the horn in *Gargantua and Pantagruel*. (Figure 1.4) When the giant Pantagruel visited the 'land of Satin', he described an entire herd of typical unicorns, except for one important feature: their horns dangle, like a cock's comb, so Rabelais informs us, until they need them for some purpose, whereupon they stand rigid as an arrow (Bk 5, ch. xxx). In case the reader misses the point, Gargantua compares his own male member to the unicorn's horn in extensive Rabelaisian detail. Aubrey Beardsley's version of Tannhauser's journey to the Venusberg, *Under the Hill*, is another satirical work in which a unicorn appears. A visitor to the home of Venus finds a pamphlet in her library entitled 'A Plea for the Domestication of the unicorn' and is invited to watch Beardsley's very fin de siècle goddess feed her own domesticated pet unicorn with the somewhat incongruous name of Adolphe.[88] The sexual connotations continue to be reappropriated. According to contemporary urban slang, a bisexual female who is willing to join an existing couple in a long-term, non-demanding relationship is called a 'unicorn'.[89]

Sexuality had been a prominent element in the complex symbolism surrounding the unicorn, and, as religious meaning declined, this aura of romantic sensuality became stronger. The French symbolist artist, Gustave Moreau (1826–98), painted several versions of the lady and the unicorn. The sensuous female figures, some naked, others clothed, in *Ladies and Unicorns* and *The Unicorn* echo the contrast between sacred and profane love in Renaissance art. A similar use of naked and clothed figures feature in Arthur Bowen Davies' *Unicorns* (1906), in which a fully clothed young woman stands apart, while milky white unicorns approach a partially naked female. The painting is unlike the intimate stylized landscapes of medieval scenes. An ethereal landscape, which echoes the sweeping allegorical panoramas depicted by painters such as Giorgione, rather than the figures which were the focus of medieval depictions, dominated the painting. By contrast, Salvador Dali's *The Happy Unicorn* (1977) dances through the sky with neither woman nor hunter to disturb it. Dali inscribed the name of his wife on another unicorn painting, *The Tower of Enigmas* (1981), where the unicorn's rider, whatever the legend may have meant in Dali's personal surrealist mythology, still suggests the world of courtly love.

Writers and artists, far more than have been considered here, continue to revisit the theme of the unicorn and to use it in personal as well as traditional ways. The thirteenth-century *trouvère* poet, Theobald of Navarre, compared himself to a unicorn in his love for his lady, while one of the best-known songs by the contemporary Cuban song-writer, Silvio Rodriguez, 'Mi Unicornio azul' (1982), laments the loss of his blue unicorn, a symbol of friendship, love and truth. Another unicorn, symbolic of lost youth, is one of the fantastic creatures who visits a dying artist in Gian Carlo Menotti's music drama, 'The Unicorn, the Gorgon and the Manticore' (1956).[90]

Poets as diverse as Rainer Maria Rilke, Anne Lindbergh, David Jones and W. B. Yeats incorporated unicorn imagery. Medieval tapestries inspired both Rilke and Lindbergh. Rilke addressed the 'animal that never was' in his *Sonnets to Orpheus* (1922 – Part II, sonnet 4). The tapestries in the Cloisters Museum inspired a poem on 'The Unicorn' (1955) by Anne Morrow Lindbergh, writer, aviator and wife of Charles Lindbergh.[91] The Anglo-Welsh poet and artist, David Jones, designed a woodblock print entitled 'Unicorn in enclosure' as a cover for a religious magazine in the 1920s. As a Roman Catholic convert, Jones frequently incorporated medieval Catholic imagery with special emphasis on the salvation aspect of the Christ story, and this image recalls the final tapestry from the Cloisters series.[92] For W. B. Yeats, the unicorn was both a personal symbol and a cosmic apocalyptic image. In *The Unicorn from the Stars* (1907), a joint venture by Lady Gregory and Yeats, the main character recounts a vision that begins like the *sluagh*, the fairy ride, of Irish folk tradition. A group of white horses appear, one of which is rider-less. The dreamer mounts the horse, and when they arrive at an enclosed garden surrounded by wheat fields and vineyards, the horses turn into unicorns and begin trampling the grain and the grapes. This scene of creative destruction owes something to Nietzsche's Dionysian fantasies, but even more to Yeats's association with the Golden Dawn where the phrase *Monocerus di Astris* (the unicorn from the stars) was his personal motto. For Yeats, this heroic, Dionysian destruction signifies the necessary spiritual transformation at the heart of Golden Dawn occultism. The unicorn was something to which one must surrender in order to overcome. His interpretation is not all that far from the essence of the medieval image, and significantly, when he died in 1939, a winged unicorn decorated his first memorial stone in the cemetery of Roquebrune-cap-Martin.[93]

Traditions about the unicorn, whether secular, religious or pharmacological, appear predominantly in written or visual sources, but they are seldom associated with a particular myth or narrative. By contrast, the unicorn of contemporary art, literature, film and fantasy illustrates the dynamic nature of the symbolism surrounding fantastic creatures, and the increasingly active role of contemporary audiences with access to digital and social media in shaping new meanings. Nevertheless, it is possible to approach this material in terms of traditional unicorn lore and to admire the ways in which authors, artists and filmmakers elaborate well-established themes. James Thurber's story, 'The Unicorn in the Garden' (1939), is a delightful reshuffling of the unicorn legend that plays on the supposed non-existence of this fantastic animal. Ironically, and with typical Thurber flair, it allows the male (a henpecked husband, rather than a medieval hunter), and by implication the unicorn itself, to outwit the lady (a shrewish wife) who is hauled off as insane (a kind of captivity?) because of a unicorn that society insists does not exist.[94] Iris Murdoch's *The Unicorn* (1960) is, on the surface at least, a gothic novel with a typical story line of a young woman who finds herself in a mysterious mansion with mysterious inhabitants behaving in mysterious ways. The name of the central character, Marian, evokes older meanings of the unicorn's companion, while the tormented and trapped married woman she looks after echoes the 'unicorn' of the title. In Tennessee Williams's play, *The Glass Menagerie* (1944), the glass unicorn, which Laura's gentleman caller describes as 'kinda lonely', resonates with Laura's own shy and isolated nature. Peter S. Beagle's *The Last Unicorn* (1968) reworks the unicorn myth as a quest fantasy about a female unicorn who leaves the safety of her wood to find, and eventually free, the rest of her kind. In an interesting twist, the author fuses the figures of the lady and the unicorn, and, for a time, the unicorn becomes a woman. Neil Gaiman's *Stardust* (1999) also incorporates elements of unicorn lore. The hero saves a unicorn from a lion, and subsequently, the unicorn uses its horn to reveal the presence of poison and helps rescue the star girl. While it would be a mistake to push such comparisons too far, or to see these novels solely in terms of traditional unicorn lore, the underlying theme of a marvellous animal lured, hunted, captured or tamed remains important.

An idyllic forest, where the unicorn's horn can empower evil as well as good, is the setting for Ridley Scott's film, *Legend* (1985). Although not a commercial success, *Legend* has achieved cult status largely through internet comment. The plot was an original idea by the film's director and screenwriter who claim that they looked to Grimm's fairy tales for the ideas of good versus evil. The only unicorn in the Brothers Grimm's tales comes from a literary source, while the unicorns in *Legend* belong to a world of romantic purity and nostalgia. Significantly, the main character is named Lily. The relationship between these fantasy creatures and Lily, whose curiosity and pride initially leads the unicorn to its death and then to rebirth, is an interesting reworking of the lady and the unicorn theme.

Carol Reed's film *A Kid for Two Farthings* (1955) was adapted from a novel by Wolf Mankowitz, an English author of Russian Jewish descent.[95] A young boy from the East End of London has heard stories about a lost race of unicorns. He buys a sickly kid with a single horn that he believes is a captured unicorn, which will grant wishes. The lost race of unicorns, in both book and film, has overtones of the Holocaust, not surprising given the author's background. Despite the fact that the story ends with the death of the little unicorn, the message of the film stresses the power of hope amid adversity. The unicorn often acts as a catalyst for a child protagonist's 'coming of age' experiences in modern fantasy novels and films.[96] When Harry Potter and his friends sneak into the Forbidden Forest near Hogwarts, they are warned that drinking unicorn blood will prevent death, but carries with it a curse because something pure has been slain (*Harry Potter and the Philosopher's Stone*, dir. Chris Columbus, 1997). J. K. Rowling's fantasy echoes the medieval bestiary tradition of the pure unicorn, but the focus shifts to the personal moral responsibility of the novel's protagonists. Unicorns play a more varied and active role in Tanith Lee's *Unicorn Trilogy* 'coming of age' fantasy series. In the *Black Unicorn* (1991), the main character, Tanaquil, undergoes a series of adventures with a unicorn that leads her to an understanding of her own nature. In the second novel, she unwittingly activates a giant mechanical war-machine in the form of a *Gold Unicorn* (1994), and, in the final novel, Tanaquil follows the *Red Unicorn* (1998) into a mirror world where she confronts her own alter ego. The three unicorns reflect different stages of the main character's personal growth as she moves towards maturity.

The unicorn, along with many other fantastic creatures, has become a popular subject for internet fantasy art. Romantic pastel-coloured examples abound, but there is a darker side to the modern unicorn, especially in graphic novels, manga comics and video games. The contemporary Japanese artist, Yoshitaka Amano, who designed characters such as the powerful unicorns that appear in the Final Fantasy role-playing game franchise, creates unicorns that are at once futuristic and nostalgic, and owe something to contemporary gothic and steampunk trends.[97] The 'unicorn dream' sequence has become a key scene for fans of Ridley Scott's cyberpunk thriller, *Blade Runner* (The Director's Cut, 1992). Deckard, the 'bladerunner', warns Rachael that her family photographs reflect the implanted memories of a 'replicant' robot, not the experiences of a real woman. After she leaves, Deckard looks at his own photographs and mementoes and begins to daydream about a unicorn galloping in a lush bucolic landscape quite unlike the urban dystopia that forms the background to his (and the film's) world. When Deckard and Rachael make their escape, they step over a twisted origami unicorn of the type made elsewhere in the film by the cynical and enigmatic police officer, Gaff. For some viewers, the unicorn reverie and paper unicorn figure indicate that Deckard himself is a replicant with implanted memories. Director, screenwriter and actors have all expressed their opinion on Deckard's status as a real or artificial human. The 'unicorn reverie' has attracted the kind of attention typical of cult film fans keen to articulate the 'real meaning' of a scene to a like-minded online fan community and illustrates how such commentary can construct new meanings for existing films. So popular has this episode become, that a collectible DVD edition (2009) included a metal casting of the unicorn figure, a somewhat ironic fate for an origami prop.[98]

Damien Hirst's formaldehyde installation of a white foal with a golden horn called 'The Child's Dream 2008' is representative of this new unicorn mythology. The little white unicorn was the showpiece of an exhibition at Tate St Ives called 'The Dark Monarch'. The curator of this exhibition characterized the unicorn as 'a powerful symbol of good in early pagan mythology and is still associated with fairy tales and the mystical landscapes of King Arthur in Britain and Cornwall'. In fact, none of these statements is accurate. The unicorn is not a creature of pagan mythology. Classical sources debated whether the unicorn was a real animal, and, unlike Pegasus for example, it does not appear in any myth. It is an infrequent character in fairy tales, and it has only a tangential role in Arthurian tradition. The exhibition's aim was to demonstrate how art can restore the sense of magic to a modern world and function as a counterpoint to rationality.[99] In this sense, the curatorial comments encapsulate one of the most intriguing new developments in unicorn mythology – the unicorn as an embodiment of an ideal eternal truth.

Unicorn lore has often served the aims of advertising, merchandizing and humour. A perfume advertisement from the 1960s for Helena Rubenstein's *Herbessence* projected an updated view of the unicorn as a symbol of 'legendary beauty'. It featured a model seated on a unicorn surrounded by a background of flowers based on The Cloisters Unicorn tapestries. At the beginning of the twenty-first century, unicorns seem to be having a moment with a significant amount of merchandizing aimed at young girls. The 'My Little Pony' brand, created by the Hasbro Toy Company, in the 1980s included cuddly lavender unicorns, later endowed with wings. Although often dismissed as merchandizing ploys, they inspired several animated television and film spin-offs. An anthropomorphized unicorn pony in lavender plush may seem a long way from the elegant companion in the *A mon seul desir* tapestry, but the toys have been immensely popular, and the power of popular culture is not to be dismissed lightly. The image projected is one of sparkling, pastel-tinted optimism that ranges from Barbie's companion unicorn (*Barbie and the Secret Door*, 2014) to the cuddly toy with pink mane, tail and hooves, owned by the unicorn-loving Agnes Gru from the *Despicable Me films*. Walt Disney anticipated these child-like unicorn characters in his 1940 animation *Fantasia* in which Beethoven's Pastoral Symphony provided mood music for a classical world of gods and fantastic creatures. Silenus rides a comical unicorn donkey who gets as drunk as his master, while another vignette echoes the earliest description of the unicorn's fierce defence of its young by the Greek physician, Ctesias. In the Disney film, a diminutive mother unicorn bravely shields her brood from the gathering storm. Thurber's tale of 'The Unicorn in the Garden' exploits the unicorn's humorous potential. Numerous cartoons account for the 'scarcity' of unicorns because they missed the departure of Noah's Ark. One does not need a detailed knowledge of Talmudic teaching to appreciate cartoons in which two unicorns gaze at the departing Ark saying 'I could have sworn he said next Thursday' or 'A free 40-day cruise, there must be a catch', but it requires considerable cultural information for the point to make sense.

A final word might be added about the 'Chinese unicorn'.[100] Animals in traditional Chinese cosmology were often classified in terms of their auspiciousness, none more so than the *qilin*, and its Japanese cousin the *kirin*. The qilin appears at times of great significance, such as the beginning of the reign of an important ruler. As the cult of Confucius developed during the late Ming period (fifteenth to seventeenth centuries), woodblock print biographies of Confucius became popular and over time fantastic episodes were introduced, among them the supposed appearance of a qilin before the birth of Confucius and the death of a qilin in anticipation of the sage's passing.[101]

The qilin, unlike the Western unicorn, usually has a set of branched deer-like horns and is associated with a different set of traditions. The interpretation of this creature as a 'Chinese' unicorn could be seen as an attempt to bridge the idea of 'otherness' by finding parallels for Western beasts in other cultures. The drawing of a qilin presented to a Chinese emperor in the fifteenth century has the long neck and two small horns of a giraffe, while Western candidates for the 'real unicorn' were invariably single-horned animals.[102] However, a striking hybrid of Western and Eastern 'unicorn' elements has emerged in the syncretic world of contemporary fantasy writing, specifically manga. Fuyumi Ono's *The Twelve Kingdoms* illustrated by Akihiro Yamada is an elaborate multi-novel alternate-world fantasy. The first novel, *The Shadow of the Moon, The Sea of Shadow* (1992) introduced the basic structure of this alternate reality of twelve island worlds centred on a divine island kingdom. An important theme throughout the stories is the kirin, a supernatural creature with both human and animal form that serves the ruler of each kingdom. They are born from a special tree located on a mountain in the central kingdom, and their animal form fuses elements of a Western unicorn with a branched horn characteristic of the Oriental qilin/kirin.[103]

The sea unicorn and the corpse whale

The source of the unicorn's horn, its most marvellous and valuable feature, is not a land animal, but a species of small Arctic whale, *Monodon Monoceros*, commonly called the narwhal or the 'sea unicorn'. The animal, known to Canadian and Greenlandic Inuit groups as *qilalugaq tuugaalik* (toothed white whale), is found in the Arctic waters of Canada and Greenland. Male narwhals typically develop the spirally twisted tooth that became identified with the unicorn's horn. Its specialized habitat makes it vulnerable to changes in climate, and consequently, the animal has begun to work its way into ecological rhetoric with its increasingly reverential concern for the environment and nostalgia for a simpler, less commercial, less industrialized way of life.

Denmark was pivotal in the narwhal trade, and the word probably entered European languages from Danish, *narhval*. Citations are surprisingly late, mostly seventeenth and eighteenth centuries, and may reflect the medical trade in unicorn horn more than the earlier visual realizations, which make the unicorn myth so attractive and lasting. The meaning of 'narwhal' is not entirely clear. It may be cognate with Old Icelandic *náhvalr*, for which the first element might be *nár*, a corpse, hence 'corpse-whale'. The earliest reference to the narwhal is probably a mid-thirteenth-century Icelandic law code, *Grágás*, which forbids eating its flesh. The *King's Mirror* (*Konungs skuggsjá*) warns that eating narwhal flesh will cause sickness and death.[104] Perhaps the whale's mottled greyish skin gave the appearance of a corpse, but this is just speculation. For indigenous Canadian and Greenlandic Inuit groups, *mattaq* (whale blubber) from the narwhal is a prized and valued food source. Another confusing description from a saga text, *Sigurðar saga þögla* compares a monstrous figure with a horn four ells long on his forehead and teeth to a narwhal.[105] Single-horned sea monsters are not unknown. Heracles faces such a creature when he rescues Hesione, and some sources describe the New England sea serpent as horned.[106] However, no source explains exactly why the narwhal is associated with a corpse, or why some writers considered the flesh of a creature whose horn was valued for its curative properties, deadly to eat.[107]

As the complex trade in various ivories has become better understood, it is clear that objects of 'unicorn horn' were made from a variety of material. The ninth-century account of Ohtere the Dane is evidence for trade in walrus ivory in Europe, and there is similar evidence for China.[108] It is less clear how or when the narwhal ivory was traded, but unicorns in art began to sport long delicate appendages about 1200. Information about narwhal trade before the fourteenth century is scarce, but from that period onwards, aristocratic inventories mention 'unicorn horns' and reflect the demand for luxury, high-status ivory products, which were valued for their rarity and as protection against poison.[109] King Charles the Bold of France may have owned a sword decorated with narwhal ivory and an ivory piece specifically to test for poison. Queen Elizabeth also owned unicorn horn (i.e. narwhal) objects, which were supposedly passed on to her successor James I.[110] Editions of works by Olaus Magnus (1555) and Konrad Gesner (1558) included woodcut prints of rather fanciful narwhal-like beasts. Olaus Magnus noted 'a sea-monster that has in its brow a very large horn wherewith it can pierce and wreck vessels and destroy many men', which is also reminiscent of the creature described as a narwhal in the sixteenth-century saga. Samuel Purchas recorded details of a narwhal/unicorn horn recovered from an individual stranded on a Norfolk beach in 1588. Once the line between unicorns and narwhals began to blur, sources began to question the reality of unicorn horn.[111] Thomas Browne, writing in the seventeenth century, may have been referring to specimens in the then fashionable 'cabinet of curiosity' collections when he identified 'those long horns preserved in many places' as 'the teeth of Narhwales'.[112]

Later in that century, the newly powerful Danish monarchs commissioned a throne, now in Rosenberg Castle, made of narwhal teeth and other types of ivory. The Danish Royal Treasury contains a cup of narwhal ivory surmounted with a silver figure of an Inuit hunter, from whom presumably the Danes acquired the valuable trading commodity. Medieval wall paintings in Danish churches display unicorns in a context that reflects the religious meanings associated with the sacred unicorn hunt, and it is possible that the popularity of this theme was reinforced by Denmark's role in the ivory trade.[113] The Danish throne was constructed at a time when this elaborate medieval symbolism and belief in unicorns was on the wane. However, the trade in medicinal unicorn horn and objects of narwhal ivory decorated with unicorn motifs continued to flourish during the seventeenth century, while scratches on what were obviously high-status and expensive objects suggest that the ivory was still being used medicinally.[114]

The idea of a unicorn in the sea reflected the widespread belief, which appears in Pliny (Bk 9, ch. 2.7–8, ch. 4.10–11), that land animals had their equivalent in the oceans. A marginal illustration in the Luttrell Psalter (British Library, Additional Manuscript 42130, fol. 179r) depicts a fanciful unicorn with webbed feet, but this is not yet a narwhal. Ambrose Paré (1582) described a sea unicorn 'with a horn on his forehead like a saw', while Pierre Pomet in *Histoire Generale des Drogues* (1694) included a picture of a 'sea unicorn' with a horse-like head and centrally placed spiral horn, together with a more or less accurate drawing of a narwhal. Descriptions and illustrations of the narwhal as sea unicorn sometimes overlap with whales or sea monsters, but one early map has a beautiful 'sea unicorn' based on the classical hippocampus with the addition of the delicate narwhal tooth horn, a form found in other medieval illustrations.[115] The sixteenth-century Dutchman, Adriaen Coenen, wrote of the many curiosities he encountered in his years as a fish merchant. One of the charming illustrations in his *Visboek* (1578) shows a scene from the Apocryphal Book of Tobit in which an angel warns Tobias against a very unicorn-looking narwhal lurking in the water.[116] By the eighteenth century, this view of the parallel between land and sea animals had largely died out. The narwhal, although still called a 'sea-unicorn', joined the toothed whales.[117] Descriptions of its behaviour, however, continued to depend on rumoured reports, which stressed its size and aggressive nature towards ships and other whales, rather than actual experience.[118] A narwhal attacks a whale on the frontispiece of an illustrated edition of Jules Verne's novel, *Twenty Thousand Leagues Under the Sea*, and a fanciful natural history about a giant narwhal is presented as an explanation for the then unseen Nautilus:

> The ordinary narwhal, or unicorn fish, is a kind of whale which grows to a length of sixty feet .... [It] is armed with a kind of ivory sword, or halberd, as some naturalists put it. It is a tusk as hard as steel. Occasionally these tusks are found embedded in the bodies of other kinds of whales, against which the narwhal always wins. Others have been removed, not without difficulty, from the hulls of ships which they had pierced clean through as easily as a drill pierces a barrel.[119]

The eco-narwhal and the atheist unicorn

The oceanic world of Jules Verne was one of monsters in need of Captain Nemo's enlightened science, but the sea unicorn, once a mirror of the land unicorn, has come to embody a modern ecological need to rebalance our relation with nature. Fiction and art reflect these changing attitudes. Michael Morpurgo's novel *Why the Whales Came* (1985) and the subsequent film (*When the Whales Came*, Clive Rees, 1989) are set in the Scilly Isles at the start of the First World War. Two children befriend the mysterious resident of the supposedly cursed nearby island. The plot hinges on the slaughter of a beached pod of narwhals many years ago and on the islanders' reaction to the appearance of another pod. The Danish artist Jørn Rønnau created a series of land art sculptures in the woods around his native Aarhus in the 1990s. One of them, a tree trunk carved to evoke both the spiral unicorn horn and the narwhal tooth, is called 'The Tooth (*Tanden*), a unicorn's horn growing up from the hidden world'. The artist's work reflects the popularity of the unicorn and the narwhal as ecological symbols for the natural world as a reality, in the case of the narwhal, and, as part of an imaginary landscape, in the case of the unicorn. An important aspect of this environmental art is that the sculptures will eventually re-enter the cycle of nature through decay.[120]

Although science and myth appear in opposition to one another, there is a significant degree of interpenetration between these two modes of apprehending the world. As inhabitants of a fragile environment threatened with exploitation, narwhals have become part of a complex modern discourse about our relationship to, and responsibility for, the earth and its resources. The title of a *New Scientist* report on a study to monitor the temperature of the fragile Arctic Seas reads, 'Enlisted "sea unicorns" reveal unexpected sea warming' with the cooperation with Inuit groups.[121] It may not be clear why Nordic peoples called these creatures 'corpse whales', but it is certainly striking that centuries later we have enlisted them as allies in our struggle to save the planet.

Invisible pink unicorns, on the other hand, would seem to belong to the world of Disney cartoons and Barbie doll accessories. Somewhat surprisingly, they have become an online symbol for modern atheist and humanist movements as a way to comment on religious belief. To this end, they feature in learning activities aimed at encouraging rational thinking and scepticism in children raised outside a religious-based ethics system. The free-thought *Camp Quest* movement began in the United States in the 1990s. The 'unicorn problem' challenges children to disprove the existence of an invisible unicorn that 'lives' in the woods.[122]

The unicorn is one of a comparatively small number of fantastic creatures without a precursor in Greek mythology. Classical naturalists and historians, biblical commentators and writers of medieval bestiaries defined its meaning, and subsequently, poets and artists put these ideas into literary or visual form. Alchemists and physicians, and eventually scientists and naturalists, reclassified the world to exclude the unicorn as a species, but kept the narwhal, the source of its unique feature. The unicorn legend absorbed travellers' tales about various animals such as the rhinoceros, mythical and semi-mythical ones like the Arabic *karkodann*,[123] and eastern motifs about the seduction of a wildman. Simultaneously, Christian, Jewish and Islamic exegesis of sacred texts, as well as commentaries on classical sources, developed the complex allegory of the unicorn hunt. The unicorn has become popular again in contemporary fantasy writing and in the virtual world of the internet. This has added a new dimension to a creature whose meaning was stabilized, although not necessarily created, in a European context. In contemporary culture, the unicorn and its meaning have been defined by new users of this tradition, namely readers of modern fantasy, participants in video and RPGs, fans of modern cult films and creators of unicorn web sites.

Man-eaters and half men

Other four-footed beasts with classical roots and didactic potential like the bonnacon, the yale and the manticore have not achieved the splendid after life of creatures like the unicorn. Both the bonnacon and the yale are horned, four-footed beasts regularly included in medieval bestiaries, but with little or no didactic elaboration. The bonnacon is an unsavoury equine/bovine hybrid that Pliny locates in Paonia (Northern Greece). He comments that while its tightly curled horns are useless for defence, it expels particularly obnoxious dung (*Natural History* Bk 8, 16). The Hereford *mappa mundi* also notes the intricately twisted horns and superheated excrement, but locates it in Phrygia.[124] Bestiary illustrations show the bonnacon fleeing from hunters who raise their shields against a spray of dung.[125] At least one dragon uses the same technique to repel More of More-Hall, but this occurs in a seventeenth-century burlesque ballad, 'The Dragon of Wantley'.[126]

Pliny's description of an exotic animal called the yale (eale) combines elements of hippopotamus, boar and elephant. Its defining characteristic is that its horns can move in any direction (*Natural History*, Bk 8, 30). This description, as adapted by the third-century Latin grammarian, Solinus (*Poly-historia*, ch. 58), influenced medieval bestiaries. The illustrations in bestiaries vary, but the yale is usually hoofed with spreading antlers.[127] The Hereford *mappa mundi*, like other early maps, placed it in India.[128] It is quite rare in other manuscripts, although a small example, possibly copied from a bestiary illustration, sits atop the foliage in a medieval psalter (Pierpont Morgan Library MS. M. 796 fol. 35r). As with so many fantastic creatures, attempts have been made to identify the real animal behind Pliny's description. Various types of antelope are the most common suggestions.[129] The yale survived as a heraldic beast. The best-known example is the Yale of Beaufort, a supporter of the arms of Margaret Beaufort, mother of Henry VII. It is also a prominent decorative motif in Horace Walpole's gothic folly at Strawberry Hill, since Walpole claimed Margaret Beaufort as an ancestor.[130]

Among the beautiful carvings that adorn a twelfth-century arch from a church in Narbonne, France is a crowned lion, whose crown signifies that, as king of the beasts, he is a symbol of Christ the King. He sits at the lower right of the arch, and, unlike the other creatures, faces the viewer directly. On the extreme left, a manticore looks towards the lion. This hybrid man-eating beast has a lion's body, human head, scorpion's tail and cannibalistic temperament. Its nature and its placement in the sacred space of ecclesiastical architecture present a direct contrast to the positive qualities of the lion.[131] Ctesias, according to the summary of his works by the ninth-century scholar Photius, may be the earliest source for the manticore, but Aelian gives a more elaborate description (*On Animals*, Bk 4, 21). Its name, manticore or martichore, may derive from a Persian term for man-eater. Aristotle, quoting Ctesias, says it lives in Asia and has large teeth, lion-like body, a human face and a sting in its tail. The Elizabethan writer Arthur Golding translated a description given by Solinus.

> Wyth three sette of téeth in his head checkquerwise one against another, faced like a man, gray eyed, sanguine coloured bodied like a Lyon, tayled like a Scorpion wyth a stinging pricke in the ende, with so shrill a voyce that it counterfetteth the tunes of pypes, and the harmony of Trumpets. Hée séeketh most gréedilie after mans flesh. He is so swift of foote, and so nimble in leaping, that there is no space so long that may forslowe hym, nor anie thing so broade that can let him of hys way. (*Polyhistoria* ch. 58)

By comparing the yellow–orange coat of the manticore to a tiger, Pausanias offers a rational explanation of its origins (*Description of Greece*, Bk 9, ch. 21, 4–5). The prominent teeth and strange cry of the manticore suggested to some classical and early modern writers that its origin might lie in reports of the African hyena. To others, the long tail, speed and spots suggested a cheetah, while its alleged cannibalism may simply express the fear of that which is both fierce and foreign.[132]

As early as the second century, the Greek writer, Flavius Philostratus, in his *Life of Apollonius of Tyana*, suggested that the manticore was a 'tall story' (Bk 3, 45). However, Pliny's description, although itself based on an earlier account, seems to accept its reality, and this influenced later writers (*Natural History*, Bk 8, 75). In the thirteenth century, Bartholomew Anglicus compared the manticore to a bear and located it in India (*De Proprietatibus Rerum*, Bk 18), and Brunetto Latini's encyclopaedia, *Li Livres dou Trésor*, classified it with other rapacious beasts such as the hyena and the wolf (Bk I, 192). Based on these descriptions, it is not surprising that illustrations of the manticore in bestiaries vary widely. It always has a human face on a lion-like body, and sometimes wears a Phrygian cap to emphasize its exotic nature.[133] On the Hereford *mappa mundi*, the manticore and a tiger (lion?) face one another on either side of a tree. The explanatory text, based on the writings of the Latin grammarian Solinus, claims that it makes a hissing sound (*voce sibilla*).[134] One of Arthur's knights confronts a manticore in a, now damaged, mural in Runkelstein Castle near Bolzano, although it is unclear whether this is linked to any narrative episode.[135] An unusual and naively drawn graffito, possibly sixteenth century, on the outside wall of All Saints Church, North Cerney in Gloucestershire may be intended to depict a manticore (or possibly the half-ass, half-human onocentaur), together with another carnivore, perhaps a leopard (lion?).[136] The plethora of teeth, which Pliny compares to a comb, is noticeable in the woodcut that illustrates Edward Topsell's description in his *History of Four-Footed Beasts*, although the illustration from a later version has a more lion-like beast.[137]

Outside these sources, the manticore is not very common, but it reappears in contemporary fantasy novels and video games as a character in the *Warhammer* table top games first released in 1983, in the earliest edition of *Dungeons & Dragons* (1974), and in the trading card game, *Magic: The Gathering* (1993). Often these fantasy-game manticores have wings as well as lion-like bodies and spiked tails.[138] The game manticore is part of the playing environment rather than a developed character, which means that the players have a considerable degree of input into how the creature acts, and this pattern continues in the numerous spinoff RPG, video and trading card games that have developed. Elsewhere, Manticore is the name given to the semi-occult secret facility from which the genetically altered humans escape in the cyberpunk television series *Dark Angel* (James Cameron and Charles H. Eglee, 2000–3). Dr Thorn, the shape-shifting opponent of the teenage Olympian hero, Percy Jackson, can change into a manticore with a deadly scorpion's tail, hence his name (Rick Riordan, *Percy Jackson and the Olympians* 2005–9).

Two of the protagonists, Lord Juss and his cousin Brandoch Daha, fight a more traditional 'mantichore' in E. R. Eddison's fantasy-novel *The Worm Ouroboros* (1922). The beast is described in the author's ringing faux-Shakespearean prose as having 'a man's face, if aught so hideous might be conceived of human kind, with staring eyeballs, low wrinkled brow, elephant ears, some wispy mangy likeness of a lion's mane, huge bony chaps, brown bloodstained gubber-tushes grinning betwixt bristly lips'. Eventually the creature is driven over a cliff where it 'smote an edge of rock near the bottom, and that strook out its brains'.[139] Not all fantasy manticores are fierce and dangerous. In a story from her collection *The Book of Dragons*, one of E. Nesbit's young heroes helps a shy manticore escape temporarily from a bestiary.[140] Gian Carlo Menotti also introduces a non-traditional manticore, one who represents the central character's shyness in old age, in his madrigal opera, 'The Unicorn, the Gorgon and the Manticore' (1956). The witch-like Mommy Fortuna captures the unicorn of the title in Peter S. Beagles' *The Last Unicorn*. The character can use her magic to make ordinary animals appear like their mythical counterparts, and thus the poor circus lion takes on the appearance of a manticore.

A late Hellenistic mosaic depicting the River Nile, now in the Italian city of Palestrina, reflects the Roman fascination with Egypt as an exotic landscape. A hybrid animal with a quadruped's body and a human face, identified as a female onocentaur, occupies a rocky outcrop in the upper right-hand corner. In illustrated copies of the *Physiologus*,[141] the onocentaur has a man's upper torso fused to the body of an ass. Although bestiaries distinguish between the onocentaur and the more common (hippo)centaur, which is half human and half horse, the two are often indistinguishable in medieval iconography.

Centaurs have a history in the fantastic imagery of Western civilization almost as complex as that of the unicorn. According to Greek sources, they inhabited the mountainous region of Thessaly. Their drunkenness and promiscuous behaviour made them the antithesis of civilized man, a quality reflected in accounts of their origin in which the drunken Ixion assaulted the cloud nymph, Nephele, thinking it was Hera. The offspring of this odd union was either a single monstrous being, Centaurus, or the entire race of centaurs who mated with the wild mares of Thessaly. During the wedding of the Lapith king, drunken centaurs attempted to abduct the bride and the female guests, but the Greeks defeated them in battle, an incident famously recorded on the Parthenon frieze.[142] The behaviour of these half-animal, half-human hybrids violated important notions of hospitality and the institution of marriage. The defeat of centaurs that lived in wild and marginalized regions symbolized the triumph of civilization embodied by the ordered, male-dominated world of the Greek *polis*. The clash between nature and culture became a persistent theme in centaur lore from their appearance in Greek art and literature, through the medieval period and into the Renaissance. As early as the eighth century BCE, the centaur appeared in Greek art with a horse's body attached to a standing male figure, or as a male torso fused to an equine body. The latter form eventually became the accepted image of this half-human hybrid that embodied both the power and the bestial nature of the horse. The adventures of Heracles illustrate this characteristic mixture of power and beastliness. The hospitable centaur, Pholos, offered the hero cooked meat, although he ate his own food raw. On another occasion, Heracles rescued his wife from the lustful advances of the centaur, Nessos, although the hero was eventually poisoned by the centaur's blood.[143]

The polarities between nature and culture, savagery and civilization underpin the conflicts between hybrid centaurs and the Greeks, but these polarities are more nuanced in the relationship between the immortal and skilled Cheiron and the young Greek heroes whom he teaches. This centaur instructs Achilles in the art of hunting which he, Cheiron, pursues with bow and arrow, rather than the sticks and stones of his fellow centaurs.[144] As a hybrid being who inhabits two physical categories, his liminal nature makes him appropriate for nurturing young men in transition from boyhood to adulthood, and his role as teacher to Greek heroes was established in the Homeric epics by the eighth century BCE.[145] This wise centaur, who is skilled in the civilized arts of hunting and medicine, also teaches the young Heracles, and when Heracles accidentally wounds the immortal Cheiron, he becomes the constellation known as Sagittarius or Centaurus.

The dichotomies of beastliness and intelligence continued to dominate interpretations of the centaur's mixed physiology. In Jerome's fourth-century account of the *Life of St Paul the Hermit*, a centaur directs St Anthony to Paul's hermitage. This creature lacked the power of human speech and could only point the saint in the right direction. Later medieval sources such as *The Golden Legend* of Jacobus de Voragine and Walter Map's *De Nugis curialium* incorporated the incident.[146] The wildness of the centaur stood in opposition to the social organization of civic life that differentiated men from beasts, but paradoxically, the wilderness abode of the hermit saint had a redemptive power that contrasted with the perceived decadence of urban life. The Sienese painter known as Sassetta is among the artists who have interpreted this incident. In his fifteenth-century painting of Anthony's journey to meet St Paul, now in the National Gallery, London, Anthony sets out on his journey in the top left corner and meets the centaur at a bend in the road that will eventually bring him to Paul's hermitage. A near contemporary of St Jerome, the Greek writer, Aelian, considered the possible reality of the centaur.

> Anybody who has seen one would never have doubted that the race of Kentauroi (Centaurs) once existed, and that artificers did not falsify nature, but that time produced these creatures by blending dissimilar bodies into one. But whether in fact they came into being and visited us at one and the same period, or whether rumour, more ductile than any wax and too credulous, fashioned them and by some miraculous combination fused the halves of horse and a man while endowing them with a single soul. (Aelian, *On Animals* 17. 9)

Centaurs continued to embody the negative overtones of barbarity they acquired in Greek mythology. Christian commentators like St Jerome and St Gregory linked them with Jews, and occasionally centaurs in manuscripts wear Jewish headgear.[147] They appear on church architecture, in the margins of manuscripts and on other decorated objects. Later examples, unlike their classical forbears, usually carry bows and arrows. Dante and Virgil meet bow-carrying centaurs, including Cheiron and Nessos, in Hell (Bodleian Library, Holkham Misc. 48. p. 18). Nessos's attempt to abduct Heracles's wife was also a popular incident for illustration.[148] However, Sagittarius, a bow-carrying centaur was the zodiac sign for November, and centaurs in bestiaries often hold medicinal plants, reflecting Cheiron's skill.[149] The link between centaurs and medicine underpins depictions of centaurs killing or battling poisonous serpents and dragons. An aquamanile was a vessel that held water for washing hands before secular and religious events. A thirteenth-century example in the form of a crowned centaur fighting a serpent-like dragon is on display in the New York Metropolitan Museum of Art. Some renditions are quite fanciful, such as the female centaur bending over her cooking pot, or the male centaur balancing plates in the margin of a thirteenth-century bible.[150]

Female centaurides were not mentioned in early classical sources, although they appeared later in both art and literature. In a second-century mosaic from Hadrian's Villa, probably a copy of an earlier work, a centaur holding a large boulder attacks a tiger who has killed his wife and child. Another lost classical painting apparently depicted an idyllic world filled with lush springs and fruitful trees in which centaurs lived with their wives and offspring.[151] The description might have served as the pattern for the world conjured by the Disney animators for Beethoven's Pastoral in *Fantasia* (Samuel Armstrong, 1940) with its fashion conscious centaurides preparing to entertain the local centaur lads. C. S. Lewis populates his *Narnia Chronicles* (1950–6) with extremely civilized centaurs who can also be formidable warriors. The warrior-like centaur Glenstorm counsels Caspian in his efforts to liberate Narnia, while the wise centaur, Roonwit, foresees danger in the stars. The latter's name, perhaps from Anglo-Saxon *runwita* meaning counsellor, reflects his role as a learned astronomer and prophet. In the final chapter of *The Silver Chair*, two centaurs transport Jill and Eustace. Like idealized classical scholars from Lewis's own university world, they impart all manner of interesting knowledge to the children as they journey across Narnia. Although the centaurs are considerably wilder in J. K. Rowling's Harry Potter universe, a centaur named Firenze saves the young Harry and later teaches the art of divination to Hogwarts's pupils.

Conclusion

The fantastic creatures that walked the earth, if only in imagination, were many and varied. The centaur, manticore, bonnacon, yale and unicorn are rooted in European travellers' tales and in accounts of classical natural history and continue to appear in medieval art and the bestiary tradition. The centaur was prominent in classical and Renaissance myth, and centaurs have existed, at least in the imagination, as long as the unicorn. The contrast between drunken, lascivious centaurs, the hospitable Pholos, and the wise Cheiron suggests that the apparently opposed categories embodied in these hybrids have helped define ideas of what it means to be human by establishing, and occasionally testing, the boundaries between ideas of human and non-human, civilized and untamed. The gentle yale and the fierce manticore, although less widely known, also have the potential to create and challenge boundaries on many levels.

This chapter has concentrated on perhaps the most famous of this group of fantastic creatures, the unicorn. It became an important heraldic beast, but it also adorns toys and T-shirts. The unicorn has symbolized everything from the doctrine of the Incarnation to the smell of sophisticated perfume. When Ctesias first described it, he had in mind a real animal in the natural world. In his influential study of the unicorn legend, Odell Shepard concluded with an appropriate sentiment for a specialist in American transcendental philosophy, which favoured imagination as a way to balance the dry intellectualism of fact and science.[152] He presented the unicorn as somehow embodying an eternal transcendental truth over and above the mere fact of whether it is real or not. More than any other creature discussed in this book, the unicorn has been the object of serious exploration, and the search for an actual animal that inspired the legend added a further layer of mythologizing about its meaning and function. Once a powerful religious symbol, it now inhabits 'popular' genres such as fantasy novels and especially children's literature. This new role has given the unicorn something it lacked in the classical sources, namely a voice which can express emotion. The unicorn has been used to deconstruct myths and legends and, conversely, to restore their spiritual potential. Although it is no longer a potential inhabitant of the world of nature as Ctesias thought, it now exists in cyberspace, that pervasive and modern objective correlative of our imagination.

2

Lingering in sea caves: The world of the mermaid

Who would be
A mermaid fair,
Singing alone,
Combing her hair
Under the sea,
In a golden curl
With a comb of pearl,
On a throne?

ALFRED LORD TENNYSON

In the year 1723, John Nott, celebrity chef to the English aristocracy, included a recipe in his cookbook that required a boned and scalded suckling pig baked in a crust to produce a culinary delight called *Mermaid Pye*. The recipe is not listed under either mermaid or pie in Nott's book, but appears under 'the letter *t*' as in 'To make a Mermaid Pye'.[1] Thankfully, this recipe does not grace modern cookbooks, but its position in Nott's culinary scheme illustrates a feature of fantastic-beast traditions already noted, namely the frequency with which they defy neat and tidy classification. This is certainly true of the rich complexity demonstrated by the many manifestations of mermaids, mermen and their relatives considered in this chapter.

Sea-dwelling creatures, both aquatic and partly human, are known by a variety of names, and they grace the mythology, folklore, literature and popular traditions of many cultures. The world that such creatures inhabit – seas, rivers, lakes, deep pools and wells – is a mirror image of ours. On one level, the idea of beings that resemble humans, but live in a world closed to us, does not need any explanation other than a human desire to explore an unfamiliar environment. Western traditions about mermaids and mermen, collectively known as merfolk, travelled along with merchants, tourists, invaders and immigrants. However, not all mythic sea creatures conform to European ideas. Numerous beings with aquatic characteristics have developed independently of European cultural influence. The waters of the earth also contain a vast range of fantastic sea life such as sea serpents, talking whales and other strange creatures that can threaten or protect those who venture away from land. Human attitudes to 'real' animals, especially whales and dolphins, can also vary dramatically. If any feature characterizes these beings, it is that they evoke the intrinsic ambiguity of the water world, while, at the same time, providing apt metaphors for the mixture of fear and awe that the sea inspires.

Because creatures like mermaids appear partly human, they can function, if only by contrast, as a way of defining essential human characteristics. The juxtaposition of human and non-human qualities allows us to define this 'otherness' in terms of similarities as well as differences. When a bestial aspect predominates, mermaids embody destructive forces – natural ones, like storms, or moral ones, like promiscuity. Their family and social organization reflect human society, but with a crucial difference that prevents the two from mingling completely. The obvious boundary of water versus land creates an obstacle for humans who cannot breathe under water and for merfolk who cannot walk on land. By crossing, or at least challenging, these boundaries, hybrid creatures provide a means to consider our own customs and moral codes, while the strategies adopted to overcome this barrier lend themselves to further interpretations of a mythic, social, psychological and fantastic nature.

Origins: From siren to mermaid

The origin of mermaids is, like so many imaginative concepts, a fusion of elements. The Mesopotamian deity, Oannes, embodied the sea itself, and traditions about him may date back to 5000 BCE. Matsya, the fish Incarnation of the Hindu god, Vishnu, and Levantine moon deities, such as Atargatis and Derceto, mixed both human and piscine elements. These sea-dwelling deities in Near Eastern and Indian mythology, who could be benevolent or violent, were important in formulating ideas about water dwellers. Triton, son of the sea god in Greek and Roman tradition, was, like many sea deities and maritime spirits, associated with storms, abundant fish and shipbuilding. He was usually a benevolent presence to those who treated the sea with respect. Not every sea deity possessed obvious piscine characteristics. Fishtailed Nereids and the horse-headed hippocampus accompanied Neptune, but the classical sea god retains a human form. Writing in the first century BCE, the Greek historian

Diodorus of Sicily claimed that Derceto, mother to Semiramis, the semi-mythical queen of classical legend, threw herself into a lake when she discovered she was pregnant and became half fish (Diodorus, Bk 2.1-28 based on Ctesias *Persica* Bk 1, 6). The Inuit supernatural being, commonly known as Sedna, embodied the bounty and peril of the sea, and in one version of her myth, her father chopped off her fingers while she clung to a kayak, and all manner of creatures, fish, whales, sea birds and the like flow from her bleeding hands.

Classical sources provide a basis for understanding both fantastic and scientific ideas about sea dwellers. Greek and Roman writers refer to mythical creatures called sirens whose beautiful voices lured sailors to their death. Beliefs about the classical siren formed an important source for ideas about mermaids and mermen, and many European languages have adopted what was originally a Greek term to describe the sea-dwelling, fishtailed being. However, these creatures with beguiling voices, which is what *siren* means, were originally winged and bird-like, and they were not particularly seductive; their parents were the river god Achelous and one of the Muses in Greek tradition, while Roman tradition favoured Phorcus, an 'old man of the sea', as their father. The names Parthenope (splendid or maiden voice) and Ligea (clear/shrill? toned) relate to the idea of vocalizing, while Leucosia (white substance) may refer to the appearance of white caps on waves in windy weather. The names link the sirens and water, a connection that influenced their development into mermaids. The sirens' home was an island near Sicily. Mariners, who heard their song, threw themselves into the sea or pined away. Individual sirens became the focus for local cults such as Parthenope's tomb near Naples and Leucosia's island (Pliny the Elder, *Natural History* Bk 3, ch. 85). Despite some doubts, Pliny locates the sirens in India, an area much favoured as a repository for all things strange, and says that they attacked men after charming them with song (*Natural History*, Bk 10, 70). The heroes Odysseus (Ulysses) and Jason, leaders of famous Greek voyages, both outwit sirens. Ulysses has his men tie him to the mast in order to hear their song (Homer, *Odyssey*, Bk 12), and Jason's shipmate, Orpheus, overpowers their fatal music with his own. Eventually the sirens themselves drown because a hero remains unaffected by their singing. Although they live near the sea and drown themselves after their defeat, classical sirens are winged (Apollonius of Rhodes, *Argonautica*, Bk 4, 885–991).[2] The range of traditions associated with them from seventh-century BCE Greek sources to tenth-century Byzantine history suggests that they were not rooted in a specific myth. Rather they were associated with a common traditional motif in which an individual or a group must perform a task until some circumstance disrupted its execution, which brought about the sirens' death.

Classical sirens with their avian attributes and their water-dwelling mermaid cousins existed side by side for a considerable period. With the appearance of the *Physiologus*, a Greek didactic text compiled about the fourth century, descriptions of real and imaginary animals, accompanied by a homiletic exposition of their moral and symbolic qualities, became more prominent.[3] For example, Chaucer's *The Nun's Priest Tale*, written in the fourteenth century, quoted this text ('Phisiologus seith sikerly') to the effect that mermaids sing (*Physiologus* VII, 3271–2). Another important source for changing attitudes was one of the most influential books of the medieval period, the work of the seventh-century archbishop, Isidore of Seville whose *Etymologiae* summarized all the knowledge of the ancient world that would be useful to a contemporary Christian scholar. Isidore's work described classical winged and clawed sirens (Bk 11, ch. 3, 30–1). The tenth-century Byzantine encyclopaedia, *the Suda*, characterized sirens as women with bird heads, who sang lewd songs. The compiler added a 'rational' explanation that their 'song' was just the sound of water rushing through a narrow channel at a place (the island of Anthemoussa) associated with these classical creatures (*Suidas* s.v. Seirenas). Under the influence of Isidore's work, medieval bestiaries of the twelfth and thirteenth centuries, presented allegorical interpretations of animal behaviour to encourage Christian virtue. Sometimes the siren appears with claws, like its classical predecessor, but retains a mermaid's fish tail. In Guillaume le Clerc's thirteenth-century *Bestiaire*, the siren is a 'monster of strange fashion' beautiful only from the waist up.[4] The rest resembles a fish or a bird. Her song lulls sailors to sleep, whereupon she kills them. Another thirteenth-century work, *De Proprietatibus Rerum* by Bartholomew Anglicus mentions three sirens whom he denounces as evil women who tempt men. One siren sings, while the others play the pipe and the harp (Bk 18).

The fishtailed mermaids eventually came to dominate European art and literature. Within the sacred space of ecclesiastical buildings, mermaid carvings often occupy peripheral areas, which underline their liminal natures. They appear on the borders surrounding doorways, on misericords, external surfaces and at the edges and corners of choir stalls, columns and roof bosses as symbols of the dangers of worldly pleasures in general and of women in particular (Figure 2.1). They include winged and clawed as well as double-tailed sirens and fishtailed mermaids, some holding a comb and a mirror (pride), playing an instrument (temptation), or clutching a fish in one hand (a sinner in the grasp of sin). A lovely mermaid suckles her young in the thirteenth-century Alphonso Psalter (British Library Additional 24686, fol.13r), but a monkey (a symbol for the bestial in human nature) sits on her tail. Mermaids also appear in the company of centaurs, and this motif, which combines the bestial aspects of both land and sea, may go back through Isidore to classical writers who claimed that the centaurs fell victim to the sirens' song.[5]

The variety of descriptions in classical sources provided inspiration for writers, especially during the Renaissance when interest in the classics revived.

FIGURE 2.1 *This mermaid occupies the same marginal space that she would in a medieval manuscript in this illustrated Victorian version of Tennyson's* Idylls of the King.

Emblem books were an indispensable reference for humanist culture, and the most influential was *Andrea Alciato's Book of Emblems*, first published in 1531. The emblem relating to the sirens (Emblem 116) combined both classical and medieval material. Ulysses is strapped to his ship's mast in the accompanying illustration and faces avian sirens playing instruments, while a fishtailed mermaid appears in the background. The text highlights the monstrous, that is to say unnatural, nature of 'maidens without legs and fish without snouts'. It associates them with lust and seduction and alludes to their defeat by the Muses and by Ulysses. While emblem books retained the moral significance of particular fantastic creatures, they also introduced the notion that they were metaphors for complex ideas. This is also reflected in elaborate Renaissance ornaments made from pearls and jewels shaped like mermaids and other fantastical sea creatures. In keeping with humanist Renaissance sentiment, the subjects tended to be secular or fantastic rather than devotional, and provided a medium through which the individual artisan could challenge and surpass the limits of nature. Mermaids also abound in the greatest of seaports, Venice. The double-tailed sirens and fishtailed women with lovely torsos that adorn secular and religious buildings have an added layer of meaning in a city whose very identity depended on the sea.[6]

A siren is among the monsters that Edmund Spenser's questing knight must overcome in his allegorical poem, *The Faerie Queene* (1596). The poem echoes Homer's suggestion that the sirens were once privileged beings that plunged into the sea after the angry Muses plucked their wings, where they became fish-like, sea-swimming mermaids. Spenser frames his allegory as a quest in which a hero negotiates dangerous obstacles to obtain his goal. The young hero is warned against the piteous cries of this 'doleful maid' (Canto 12). The siren/mermaid is an example of an unnatural monstrosity, evidence not of the richness of God's creation, but how it can be distorted. The same pattern, although without Spenser's complex allegory, underlies a sub-genre of modern horror fiction and film in which the 'monster' embodies a distorted version of human nature. In the kitsch horror film *She Creature* (Edward L. Cahn, 1956), a sinister hypnotist regresses a beautiful woman into the prehistoric sea monster she was in a past life.

Continuity and adaptation

In Spenser's Elizabethan allegory, the mermaid represents moral danger; in the horror film, the danger is internalized as part of the main character's inner being. Despite the lapse of several centuries, the mermaid's nature is still the focus. Folk narratives, popular culture and literary writing intertwine to produce evermore intriguing interpretations, and the continuing adaptation of the lore surrounding mermaids, as well as other fantastic creatures, is one of its most fascinating aspects.

A theme, which illustrates this diversity across time and culture, underpins accounts of romantic or sexual encounters between mer-people and their human counterparts. The medieval romance traditions surrounding Mélusine, the Inuit myths about Sedna, the Amazonian Serek-A, the South American *boto* and the Chinese Madam White Snake[7] illustrate both the varieties of form and the similarities in narratives from different cultures about liaisons between humans and water dwellers. Such narratives draw on common international folklore themes, as well as the classical heritage of sirens and mermaids. Traditions about the otter people among North American first nations, and the shark gods of the Pacific, as well as the finnfolk of the North Atlantic, occur in so many cultural contexts that a comprehensive survey would be overwhelming. This section examines a few significant examples and highlights some representative themes.

In Hesiod's poem, the *Theogony* (c. 700 BCE), the Olympian gods bring order and balance to a chaotic world. The sea, with its hybrid deities and monsters, plays a significant role in the emergence of a stable cosmos. Pontus, a primordial Greek sea god, is both the offspring and the mate of the earth-goddess, Gaia, with whom he fathers Oceanos, the embodiment of the salt waters, who is pictured with a serpentine tail. Oceanos and Tethys are the progenitors of deities who in turn embody rivers and streams. Phorcys, a god with crab legs and fish tail, fathered sea monsters, such as Scylla, with his sister/wife, Keto, who is associated with whales. The sea deity, Achelous, fathered the sirens, while Thaumas and Electra (possible embodiments of sea and weather) gave birth to the harpies. In these cosmological matings, one partner has a connection with the sea and the other with weather, a factor linking them to the unchecked power of the elements and with monsters, whose very existence challenged the ordered world.[8]

In many ways, mermaid brides and merman husbands resemble Greek and Roman demi-gods like the Nereids and tritons and their land-dwelling cousins, the nymphs and satyrs. Mélusine was popular in medieval romance, and she retains her popularity in contemporary literature. When she bathes, Mélusine metamorphoses into a creature like Scylla, half woman with a serpentine lower body. Tales about water brides appeared in early collections of folktales, and in literary *Märchen* like Frederick de la Motte Fouqué's *Undine* (1811). These tales form a sub-class of a widely known folk narrative about a supernatural spouse with both human and non-human forms. There are several possible outcomes for marital/sexual attachments between these creatures and mortals. Some event (a broken taboo or the rediscovery of a hidden talisman) may force the supernatural partner to return to its original environment, or, alternatively, break a spell and free the supernatural being.

In some variants of this legend, a man steals an essential possession from a mermaid. She stays with him, and they have a family until she recovers the stolen possession and returns to her natural home, the sea. The tale is well known in coastal areas of Ireland, Scotland, the Faroe Islands and Scandinavia.[9] In other variants, the supernatural bride imposes conditions on her husband. These legends, most conveniently referred to as the *melusina* legends after the most famous literary example, occur in Ireland and Wales.[10] The association with water is a constant, even when the brides are not actual mermaids. Melusina narratives are often attached to inland lakes rather than the sea, and the woman fulfils the role of mythical family ancestor. An early Irish example dates to the eleventh century, although the most popular Irish narrative, published in 1840, concerns the O'Quinn family of Inchiquin.[11] In the Welsh *melusina* legends, the fairy bride may return to tend her children, and in the most famous Welsh example, she endows her sons, the Physicians of Myddfai, with medical knowledge.[12]

The beautiful Mélusine of medieval romance promises to marry a young nobleman, as long as he does not interrupt her Saturday bath.[13] He discovers her true nature when curiosity gets the better of him, and he realizes that his beautiful wife has wings and a sea serpent's tail. Mélusine is a complex creation who returns periodically to herald a death in the family with her 'prophetic' cries. The terms of her marriage suggest a connection with the supernatural bride motif; the scaly serpent-like tail associates her with the dragon, while her wings and her connection with water and death seem to echo the siren. However, the marriage is disrupted, not by the rediscovery of a talisman, but by the revelation of the wife's ambiguous supernatural nature.[14]

In Irish tradition, Liban has an altogether more gentle history. Ninth-century Irish chronicles noted that a giant mermaid washed up on the coast. While this was probably a partially decomposed basking shark or whale, one account associates it with Liban, the mermaid who converted to Christianity and became a saint. The eleventh-century *Book of the Dun Cow* recounts how Liban was transformed into a mermaid after Lough Neath overflowed and drowned her father's palace. Her dog became an otter, and together they swam in the lake for many years. Eventually Liban gave up the longevity of a supernatural creature and was baptized as Muirgen (sea-born), a Christian saint.[15]

Not surprisingly, the mermaid is an important signifier for the complex relationship between fishing communities and the sea (Figure 2.2). The Irish Liban tradition appropriates the potential dangers of the mermaid's nature to the service of the Christian world, but in the romantic era, she became a metaphor for the conflicts of duty and desire. However, mismatched marriages that ultimately lead to separation feature prominently in *melusina* legends in which the wife embodies a dangerous otherness. Contemporary interpretations of mermaid lore continue to draw on literary and folk discourse in different ways to allow the mermaid's significance to take on new meanings. Nevertheless, understanding the structure of these traditional tales is essential in order to appreciate literary reinterpretations of these narratives. The outcome of marriages with a water being in legends is usually negative. The dynamics of the tale create a series of oppositions – supernatural versus human, water versus land, the constraints of marriage versus the freedom demanded by the wife.[16] Irish versions of the mermaid bride shape the work of two twentieth-century poets, Seamus Heaney and Nuala Ní Dhomhnaill. In 'Maighdean Mara', Heaney frames his poem with the image of a mermaid who, although returned to the sea, cannot forget her life on land. Mermaids appear in Nuala Ní Dhomhnaill's poems as a means to explore contemporary themes of femininity, sexuality and cultural identity. The character in *The Fifty Minute Mermaid* is a conflicted figure only able to live on land if she forgets the sea, while the female authorial voice and the mermaid in 'An Mhaighdean Mhara' seem to fuse in a more personal interpretation.[17]

" Well, well," said the mermaid, "you may keep him four years more to see if it be easier to part with him. See, here is his like for age. Is yours as fine as mine ? " and she held up a big bouncing baby.

FIGURE 2.2 *A mermaid shows her son to a fisherman in a scene from a Gaelic tale painted by Rachel Ainslie Duff.*

Two of the most famous mermaids in European literary tradition are *Undine* (1811), the female protagonist of Friedrich de la Motte Fouqué's German romantic novella, and the unnamed protagonist of Hans Christian Andersen's *The Little Mermaid* (*Den lille havfrue*, 1837). Although these literary works mimic the simplicity of the folktale and ballad forms, they carry very different messages. Fouqué's *Undine*, a water nymph, lacks a traditional mermaid tail, but she hopes to gain a soul by marrying a mortal. Although she returns to her world after her lover weds a human bride, her curse brings about his death. The author adapted a traditional folk narrative motif, a supernatural being who hopes to obtain an immortal soul, to express important concerns in romantic literature about femininity, mutability, death and desire. This story with all its romantic nuances plus elements of Danish mermaid folklore influenced Hans Christian Andersen. *The Little Mermaid* is a more conventional mermaid in appearance, but she too desires a soul and a husband. Like Undine, she loses her lover to a human bride, but, unlike Undine, she sacrifices herself to save him. Oscar Wilde's literary fairy tale, *The Fisherman and His Soul* (1888), draws on similar sources, but Wilde inverted the motif of an otherworld being seeking a human soul. The fisherman sells his soul to a witch in order to live with a mermaid. Ultimately, the fisherman, in losing his humanity, pays a terrible price.

The dramatic possibilities of merfolk and mortal unions struck a chord with numerous writers. Jane Yolen's *The Lady and the Merman* (1977) focuses on female self-doubt rather than seductiveness. A seemingly unattractive young woman longs for the love of a merman, and eventually, she follows him into the sea, beautiful at last in death. A. S. Byatt's time-shift novel, *Possession: A Romance* (1990), returns to the Mélusine theme. The novel exploits the richness and complexity of the medieval tale in order to explore issues of freedom and dominance in the relationships of two pairs of lovers. In the medieval tale, the husband's gaze exposes the wife's demonic nature, while the issue for the women in Byatt's novel is whether to accept the expectations of a patriarchal male gaze in the very different contexts of Victorian and twentieth-century society. Pierre Loti's *Pêcheur d'Islande* (*An Iceland Fisherman*, 1886) used the conflict between a fisherman's love for a beautiful woman and his fatal attraction to the mysterious sea to express the quintessential romantic tension between necessity and desire. The setting is Brittany and, although there is no actual mermaid, the sea itself is personified as an all-absorbing feminine force.

Folksongs also provide inspiration for remaking stories about the mermaid and her kin. Among the ballads collected and published by American folklorist Francis James Child in the latter part of the nineteenth century, 'The Mermaid' (Child Ballad 289) concerns a shipwreck in which the mermaid's appearance heralds the approaching disaster.[18] Although the ballad probably originated in the late seventeenth century, the association of a mermaid with bad luck has a history that extends from the classical sirens to medieval images in bestiaries and beyond. The Lorelei sat high above the Rhine combing her hair and distracting sailors with her song. Clemens Brentano (1778–1842) first composed the story of a betrayed maiden accused of witchcraft, who gazes – romantic heroines never merely look at something – on the Rhine one last time before she dies. Although not a mermaid, the flowing hair, plangent song and fatal beauty resonate with elements of mermaid lore. Brentano's version (1801) owes as much to his interest in the alleged ancient roots of Germanic identity and to Ovid's classical story of Echo, as it does to German folklore, but he created a compelling tale of supernatural femininity, which is at once poignant and destructive. Heinrich Heine's famous poem *Die Lorelei* (1824), based on

Brentano's version, was set to music in 1837. The musical version remained popular with German soldiers, who were encouraged during the Second World War to regard it as an authentic German 'folksong' in an attempt to obscure Heine's Jewish heritage.

Another poem inspired by folk tradition, Matthew Arnold's 'The Forsaken Merman' (1849), drew on a Danish ballad about a human wife who abandons her merman husband and their children. Although the subject matter and rhyme scheme echo the ballad metre, the poem is firmly rooted in Arnold's concern with the stifling moral norms of Victorian society. The wife rejects the freedom of the merman's aquatic world for a sterile, unfulfilling Christianity dominated by 'bells and books'.[19] The poet Anne Hunter (1742–1821) was wife of the surgeon John Hunter, founder of the Hunterian Museum collection, and sister to the scientist/biologist Sir Everard Home. Anne's most famous poem, 'The Mermaid's Song', was set to music by her friend, the composer Joseph Haydn. The refrain 'Follow, Follow, Follow me' are the words of a sea maiden luring mortals to a beautiful, coralline undersea world. Not all mermaid songs are tragic. 'Married to a Mermaid' with music by Dr Thomas Arne was featured in the 'Masque of Britannia' produced in 1755. This is a more playful use of mermaid lore, since the mermaid does not drown the sailor who falls overboard; rather they live happily 'at the bottom of the sea'. 'The Eddystone Light' also presents a light-hearted view of mermaid/human relationships. The context, however, apparently refers to the famous Lighthouse built to John Smeaton's revolutionary engineering design, which was constructed in the eighteenth century on the treacherous Eddystone Rock off Cornwall.

However varied the dynamic between sea dwellers and their human counterparts, at its core are the tensions and the disruptions that result from crossed boundaries. The mermaid's nature evolved from the prophetic powers of the siren to the seductive voices of medieval mermaids and into the complex voices, silences and anxieties of female literary protagonists like Andersen's mermaid who gave up her voice to win her lover or Byatt's women who attempt to resolve the conflicting demands of love and personal freedom. Rooted in traditional legend motifs, the plight of a mermaid or merman forever caught between the sea and the human world has attracted writers for centuries, and the tragic outcome of mermaid tales continues to attract contemporary authors.

Sedna, the sea woman

Nineteenth-century missionaries and ethnographers recorded traditions about an Artic 'sea woman' who dwells at the bottom of the ocean. In some variants, the Inuit woman, called Sedna, takes a dog or a bird as a husband. Her father, angered by this marriage, throws his daughter out of the kayak. As she clings to its side, he cuts off her fingers, which turn into sea creatures. She then descends to the bottom of the sea where she lives with her animal husband and controls the availability of both land and sea animals. Shamans undertake the dangerous journey to her house to free game animals and human souls trapped in her long, tangled hair.[20] In some accounts, her storm-spirit husband raises a storm at sea when her male relatives attempt to rescue her. Her frightened relatives cast her overboard, and her grandfather cuts off the hand with which she continues to grasp the boat.

Although known throughout the polar region, she is prominent in the Central Artic and Greenland where the ethnographers Knud Rasmussen (1879–1933) and Franz Boas (1858–1942), who made significant contributions to the understanding of Artic cultures, collected traditions about her. Rasmussen concentrated on the area in and around Greenland, where he was born, while Boas worked closely with the inhabitants of Baffin Island and Hudson Bay. From the latter comes the most frequently anthologized version of the Sedna tale, the story of her marriage to a fulmar and the creation of sea creatures from her severed fingers.[21] Sedna has become more widely known as a result of renewed interest in Inuit art and culture, and also as an Inuit 'mistress of the animals' in the context of contemporary goddess and shamanic studies. The name, Sedna, comes from a southern Baffin Island tradition. However, other names like Arnakuagsak (old mother of the sea) and Nulijuk Takanakapsuluk ('she down there') reflect her undersea location from where she controls the availability of animals.[22]

Other hybrid creatures, some with horns resembling caribou or with fish tails, occur in Inuit cosmology. They can be helping spirits, like the shaman's ancestors who take sea mammal form when he undertakes his trance journeys, or monstrous creatures who kidnap children. Qalupalik collects drowned humans in his parka hood and has a human shape, although eider duck feathers cover his clothing. Sometimes he functions as a warning for children playing on the ice, as does the gigantic female *amajurjuit*, who is fond of stealing children. *Palraiyuk* has the form of a sea serpent, while other sea-dwelling creatures like the *tuutalit* exist in both seal and human form, whereas the *taliillajunt* will save people from drowning as long as they are treated with respect.[23]

Missionaries, explorers and early ethnographers, working within their own Western religious framework, assumed that Sedna was the primary deity in Inuit cosmology.[24] The notion of Sedna as a goddess reflects external views of Inuit culture, as does the notion that a shamanic hunting culture like the Inuit, ipso facto, live in harmony with the forces of nature. Inuit shamanic activity concerns the availability of game, the control of weather, protection against evil spirits and illness, and the dangers of social transgression. It is based on a relationship between human and non-human beings supported by a complex system of taboos, rather than a direct sense of connectedness to the natural world. If proper conduct and ritual are not observed, these non-human beings (*inuunngattut*) can withhold game. The shaman (*angakkuit*) undertakes a journey to the home of the sea woman, sometimes with the aid of helping spirits (*tuurngait*), to free the animals or rescue a sick soul. Accounts of shamanic séances emphasize the importance of taboo as a concept for maintaining the relationship between human beings and 'others', namely the non-human beings who populate the Inuit cosmos. The sea woman is part of this non-human world rather than an actual deity.[25] An autumnal festival marked the link between human and non-human in Inuit society in relation to the availability of animals for hunting. The practices associated with the celebration varied, but the role of the sea woman reflects her importance in maintaining a balanced society through cultural ritual and the avoidance of taboo behaviour.[26]

Shamans helped maintain the stability of the cosmos and of society. Traditional cosmology still influences Inuit culture despite the prevalence of Christianity, especially in the field of Inuit art, which has provided an alternative to traditional shamanism. The changing role of Sedna reflects this complex interplay between Western influences and contemporary Inuit culture. Unsurprisingly, there is a marked contrast between the attitudes to Sedna, and other figures like her, within Inuit culture and among ethnographers and art collectors. With the rise of artist cooperatives and guilds in the 1950s, there has been ever-increasing interest in the meaning and function of Inuit art, as well as an expanding commercial market. Neither the concept of a goddess in a Western-style hierarchical pantheon, nor the notion of a 'mistress of the animals' in harmony with natural forces, which characterizes the eco-spirituality of some forms of modern goddess culture, fits comfortably into Inuit world views. Sedna is not a mermaid. Her fingers and hair form the locus for creation and control of hunting animals. However, with the changing focus of Inuit art as a representation of the world of non-human beings, and as a conduit for interaction with the outside world, the sea woman has acquired 'mermaid'-like attributes and is increasingly called 'Sedna'.[27]

Serek-A the mermaid

Indigenous tribes in the Amazonian river basin have a myth about a supernatural female who resembles, at least superficially, the Mélusine figures of European tradition. The Arua and Makurap tribes inhabit the Rio Branco and Guapore area of the Amazonian rainforest in the Brazilian state of Rondonia, located in the northwestern part of the country bordering Bolivia. The myth of Serek-A concerns an unhappy wife whose husband covers her with an irritating substance. She dives into the river to relieve the itching and becomes half woman, half snake. When her brother finds her, she swallows him, and whenever he wishes to re-emerge, he urinates inside her and reappears covered with a beautiful body painting that attracts all the young women. She is reconciled with her husband, but he becomes trapped when he forgets to urinate inside his snake-wife. Eventually he too becomes a snake, and they become the parents of anacondas and boa constrictors. The swallowing and regurgitation motif reflects the role of these powerful creatures in Amazonian mythology as a bridge between life and death, and like the mythic husband and wife, they inhabit both water and dry land. Another striking feature of the myth is the implied brother–sister incest. While incest violates the normal order, as a mythic theme, it can resolve fundamental conflicts between natural and non-natural cultural spheres. Although definitely not a mermaid in the usually accepted sense, Serek-A's dual nature combines elements of both land and water. She and her husband become, through an apparent violation of societal norms, the mythic progenitors of powerful beings who bridge the seemingly unresolvable dichotomies of land and water and life and death.[28]

The Boto and the Aumakua, shape-shifters and ancestors

River dolphins (*Inia geoffrensis*) are native to the Orinoco, Amazon and Tocantins river systems that flow through the South American countries of Brazil, Bolivia, Ecuador and Venezuela. Common names for these mammals include *bouto vermelho* (red dolphin) or *boto*. Legends about a mer-creature, an *encantado* or shape-shifter that changes from a dolphin (the boto) into a handsome man, are prominent in the northern region of Brazil, which encompasses the Amazon rainforest and several Brazilian states. At the time of the full moon, the boto becomes human in order to seduce young women. The mysterious lover wears a hat to cover the dolphin's breathing hole, which, even in his human form, would reveal his true nature. The 'children of the *boto*' is a term still used for children born out of wedlock. Nineteenth-century sources suggested that the boto was sometimes half male and half dolphin, like a merman, and that there were female botos as well. The Brazilian writer, José Veríssimo, drew on native Brazilian and Amazonian folklore and wrote about the boto as both male and female. During the nineteenth century, the naturalist Henry Walter Bates undertook an expedition to the Amazonian rainforest with his friend and pioneer in the theory of natural selection, Alfred Russell Wallace. Bates collected intensively in the area of the Tocantins River where these pink dolphins were plentiful and traditions about the supernatural boto found their way into his account of his travels, *The Naturalist on the River Amazons*.[29]

Sightings of river dolphins are associated with prophetic dreams, successful fishing and luck in love. As a result, fetish objects, ostensibly made from river dolphin eyeballs and genitalia, are traded along the Amazon River where local *curanderos* consecrate these organic embodiments of 'sight' and 'potency'. Since river dolphins are a threatened species, a group of South American biologists examined the supposed boto body parts sold in Amazonian markets in order to establish whether they derive from river dolphins. Fortunately, most of the objects sold, and apparently accepted as real, came from domestic animals.[30]

The trade in fetish objects demonstrates the importance of belief in structuring reality. In the context of Brazilian folk and popular culture, legends attached to the boto illustrate how traditions about fabulous creatures can forge new cultural identities. As part of native Amazonian tradition, the boto appears uniquely Brazilian in contrast to European cultural forms imported by the Portuguese colonialists. As such, this supernatural being appealed to nineteenth-century writers seeking to create a national Brazilian identity after the country's independence from Portugal in 1822. The film *Ele, o Boto* (*He, The Boto*, Walter Lima Jr, 1987), a supernatural romance featuring a boto who seduces the daughter of a fisherman, reflects the continued interest in the boto and its role in maintaining cultural identity. While it is possible that there has been some European influence on boto traditions, what is important is that these traditions are perceived as part of indigenous lore. Whatever the actual source, this bestows uniqueness, antiquity and dignity on notions of cultural identity. The populations of river dolphin species are declining due to habitat loss and fishing, common causes of concern in contemporary eco-consciousness regarding the Amazonian rainforest. As elsewhere, these cetaceans feature not just as shape-shifters or luck-bringers, but also as symbols of a new ecological hierarchy, which embodies a concern with the stewardship of the environment and the vulnerability of animal species in the face of exploitation.[31]

In Hawaiian mythology, sharks are among the most powerful forms taken by the *aumakua*, which were family gods or deified ancestors. Sometimes the aumakua associated with Hawaiian family clans were the offspring of a god and a human, or they were stillborn and premature children, in other words, individuals who never became members of a normal family. Martha Beckwith, an anthropologist and the first woman professor of folklore at Vassar, lists over three dozen examples of shark aumakua associated with particular families and places in the Hawaiian Islands.[32] She also notes a tale comparable to the boto traditions concerning Nanaue, the son of a human woman and the shark-god Kamohoali, brother of Pele the powerful fire-goddess. The boy child has a shark's mouth on his back, which he conceals beneath his clothing. Unlike the boto, however, this is not a charming seducer of women. His father warns the family not to feed the child any meat, but this taboo is broken, and he becomes a man-eating shape-shifter.[33]

Jumanja, Lasirène and Mami Wata

The popularity of the boto outside a relatively restricted traditional belief area in northern Brazil reflects a widening national identity, which incorporates influences from indigenous Portuguese and African traditions. The religions of the African diaspora, which include Haitian vodou, Cuban santeria, candomblé and Bahia in Brazil, combine elements of African religion, Roman Catholicism and local traditions. This fusion embraces a range of figures that include the iura, Jumanja, Lasirène and Mami Wata.

The aquatic associations of the beautiful *iura* (*yara*) draw on aspects of snake-mother creators, like Serek-A, and they reflect interest in Brazil's indigenous heritage. The influential Brazilian romantic poet Antônio Gonçalves Dias (1823–64) was particularly interested in the traditions of the Tupi people, one of the largest indigenous ethnic groups, and his writings helped create a romanticized fusion of European mermaid traditions and the mythological Tupi snake-mother creator known as iura (yara). Like the boto, a 'blowhole', which persists even in her human form, reveals her true nature.[34]

Yemoja, mother of the fishes of the sea who was originally a Yoruba water spirit, has also absorbed qualities of the European mermaid. She is called Yemanja among practitioners of candomblé, a syncretic religion that originated in the Brazilian state of Bahia, but retains close links with the Yoruba *orisha* tradition. She protects sailors and functions as bringer of wealth and children. As the most popular *orisha* in Brazil, Yemanja appears as a woman rising from the water, often with a mermaid's tail.[35]

Lasirène, an important *lwa* (spirit) in Haitian vodou who brings wealth, love and children, is pictured with the mirror, comb and fishtail of the European mermaid. Water is an important component of vodou cosmology, and the mermaid's mirror is an appropriate metaphor for the reflective surface of water that both divides and allows communication with other worlds. Elements of the mermaid's ambiguity have also been absorbed into this complex figure. Lasirène displays characteristics of two classes of vodou deities, the gentle Rada and the volatile Petwo, and she appears sometimes with her long hair, coloured blond on one side and black on the other. The cult of another African water spirit, Mami Wata, has spread rapidly in Central and Southern

Africa, the Caribbean and parts of North and South America. Like Lasirène, she brings wealth and romance, but, in addition to mermaid features, Mami Wata is associated with snakes, especially the rainbow python. Snakes, as is evident from the stories of Amazonian figures such as Serek-A, link the water and the land and serve as a metaphorical bridge between life and death.[36] Combining aspects of mermaid and snake mother, these syncretic images and ideas acquire new meanings to serve changing social, spiritual and aesthetic needs.

Mermaids and the landscape

Caves, beaches and rocks are common sites for mermaid narratives, and these, often specific and identifiable, places root traditions in the local environment and provide a matrix for belief. A tale seems so much more believable when one can point to the actual rock on which a mermaid sat combing her hair. Details add credibility to 'sightings', while the reliability of eyewitnesses is an added factor that can reassure an audience of readers or listeners. A pamphlet recorded such an event near Pendine in Wales in 1603: 'Most strange and true report of a monsterous fish, that appeared in the forme of a woman, from her waste upwards: seene in the sea by diuers men of good reputation'. The person who first sighted it called others to witness the event, and a reliable judge examined these witnesses later. The pamphlet illustration is not a first-hand rendition of the sighting, but a generic image of a creature with a fish tail, human arms and leonine head, which suggests that the 'mermaid' might have been a sea lion. These mistaken observations interested scientists and naturalists like C. J. S. Thompson, but the important factor here is the supposed reliability of the observers, all of whom were carefully questioned.[37] Another mermaid, trapped in a fisherman's net near Neath in South Wales, was displayed in the town. Unfortunately, the captured creature (perhaps an injured sea mammal?) soon died out of water. A Dutch mermaid fared somewhat better when, in 1403, the dykes near Edam in the Netherlands broke during a storm. A group of young girls found a 'mermaid' floundering in shallow water and took her home, although there is no mention of a fish tail. She wore women's clothing, became adept at spinning and weaving, but never learnt to speak. The lost girl is not a conventional mermaid according to the fish merchant Adriaen Coenen in his *Visboek* (1578); she is one of a strange race of sea-dwelling people,[38] rather like the finnfolk of Shetland and Orcadian folklore, who are covered with weed and moss, and therefore green like the sea.

The belief that mer-creatures, like fish, cannot live out of water underpins a series of medieval legends localized in southern Italy about Colá Pesce

(Colapesce, Nicolas/Nicoló the fish, or Nicholas Pipe), who, though human in appearance, had a preternatural affinity with water and could not survive away from it. The name recalls St Nicholas of Bari, the patron saint of sailors throughout the Mediterranean. Legends about Colá Pesce link him to the important hero/king, the thirteenth-century Frederick II of Sicily. Once, when the king wanted to test Colá Pesce's powers, he threw objects into the sea for him to retrieve. Twice Colá Pesce retrieved the lost object, but the third time, he did not return and disappeared forever. The well-travelled courtier, Walter Map, who undertook diplomatic missions for King Henry II, recorded a legend about him in *De Nugis Curialium* (The Courtier's Trifles). Colá Pesce could dive deep into the sea by attaching weights to his belt, but he would not survive if he was away from water. The king of Sicily (probably Frederick II, although not named in this account) had this marvellous diver brought to the court. Alas, despite being constantly drenched with water, Colá Pesce died. Map's story fuses real and legendary motifs. Weights help pearl divers, like the ones drawn on an early Catalan map, descend into deep water,[39] while stranded marine mammals, the source of many sightings, die when their skin dries out.[40] Shetland and Orkney water dwellers called finnfolk typically suffer a less gruesome fate. Like the girl caught in the dyke, they do not seem to have fish tails, but their behaviour marks them as non-human. These visitors from the sea cry at christenings and laugh at funerals because they have preternatural knowledge of a person's fate. This unsettles the land-dwellers, and eventually the uncanny visitor returns to the underwater world.[41]

A similar ambiguity towards sea dwellers underlies an episode in the medieval *Romance of Alexander* about the king and a mermaid, which remains popular in Greek folklore, literature and in the traditional Karagiozis shadow-puppet plays. Alexander's daughter drinks the Water of Life that Alexander had obtained from a well that was guarded by a dragon. The daughter became a mermaid, usually depicted in the double-tailed siren form popular in Greece. Like other mermaids, she caused storms, but she also appears, usually on a Saturday, to ask sailors 'Where is Alexander the Great?' If the answer is 'Alexander lives and reigns,' the sea becomes calm and the ship sails on.[42]

An implied moral perspective often underpins narratives about humans and merfolk. The royal power of the king of Sicily has tragic results for the mysterious aquatic being, Colá Pesce, but captured mermaids reward fisherman who set them free. When a fishing fleet puts out to sea, only one fisherman, who once released a captive mermaid, heeds the mermaid's warning and avoids the sudden tempest. Such localized mermaid narratives reflect the concerns of fishing communities about storms and the availability of fish. The Breton *Mari Morgan* inhabits a beautiful land beneath a mysterious island. Like Andersen's mermaid, she desires a mortal husband, but sailors who listen to her singing either drown, or, euphemistically, live forever in her underwater domain. A fisherman's fatal attraction to this legendary sea creature provides the framework for a contemporary exploration of the conflicts between external force and inner desire in Roparz Hemon's Breton-language novel, *Mari-Vorgan* (1971). Some mermaids are associated with particular families and appear, or sing, before births and deaths. Mermaids on the Isle of Man were called *ben varre* meaning 'woman of the sea'. A tale retold by Sophia Morrison, a key figure in the Manx cultural revival, attributes the prosperity of a local family to its association with a mermaid after one of the sons planted an apple tree near the place where she appeared.[43] Traditions about the Danish *havfrue* (sea woman) illustrate their links with seemingly uncontrollable forces. A *havfrue* foretold the birth of King Christian IV (1577–1648), one of Denmark's most important kings. When the *havfrue* drives her white cattle across the water (a reference to the white wave caps in a turbulent sea), it is a sign of stormy weather. She sometimes visits fishermen in the guise of a beautiful woman apparently wet and shivering from cold. Anyone unwary enough to allow a *havfrue* close to the fire will be dragged into the water and drowned, and the victim's liver and lungs will be found the next day floating in the surf.[44]

Lakes can serve as settings for mermaid traditions. In local legends from Cheshire and Shropshire, a disapproving figure, such as a Puritan, or even Oliver Cromwell himself, hurls a church bell into a lake. The angry mermaid refuses to release the sunken bell, so the townspeople attempt to reclaim it while she sleeps. Someone inadvertently speaks (or swears), causing the mermaid to drag the bell back into the depths, where it rings once a year or just before a disaster. A late-eighteenth-century example from Child Ercall in Shropshire concerns a lake-dwelling mermaid who offered to show two men a golden treasure at the bottom of the pool. When one of them swore, the mermaid seized the treasure and vanished.[45]

The Karoo desert region of South Africa has a local tradition about a *watermeid* who haunts waterfalls and mineral springs. She resembles other hybrid creatures located at the periphery, but the context, a mermaid in a desert, is unusual. However, local accounts incorporate familiar motifs. The watermeid sometimes steals clothes left by bathers, or acts as a bogey-figure to scare children away from dangerous waterholes. She is even the object of a P. T. Barnum-like joke involving a painted mannequin displayed as a mermaid supposedly washed up during a flood. Occasionally, she drowns the unwary. Traditions among the San people, the dominant culture of the region, describe supernatural beings that drag young girls under water. However, these are different from the Western concept of mermaids. Narratives about this South African mermaid date to the late nineteenth century at the earliest. Nevertheless, the Karoo mermaid inspires local artists and contributes to local identity. Recent accounts have begun to reflect contemporary attitudes to environmentalism and spirituality. Rock paintings have been reinterpreted in this uncertain and harsh environment as water-bringing 'mermaids' (water-meids) who have been compared to a pre-patriarchal goddess, a remnant of the lost harmony between humans and the natural environment. For others, fossil shells from an earlier geological period suggest that the mermaid might have been a 'real' creature, an archetypal memory from the time when the Karoo was not a desert.[46]

Mermaids in art

The ninth-century *Book of Kells* depicts a fishtailed figure swimming up the centre of a genealogy, which is unique among the illustrations in this manuscript. [47] This early example anticipates the popularity of the mermaid, the sirens' fishtailed descendant, in medieval art. Lavishly illustrated medieval bestiaries presented these sea dwellers as allegories of human moral behaviour. Mermaids and sirens occur together in these texts. Sometimes the siren takes bird form; sometimes she is an aquatic mermaid or a composite figure with wings, claws and a fishtail.[48]

Images of mermaids, and less frequently mermen, appear on columns, misericords and friezes, and the frequency with which carvings occur on peripheral surfaces within the sacred space of the church is a visual embodiment of their otherness. Mermaids appear on the carved blocks supporting the shelf-like misericord seat, on which weary monks could rest, and yet remain upright, during prayers. Details varied, but there was always an implied moral message in the activities of mermaids and mermen. Sometimes they play instruments, a reference to the deceptive songs of the sirens, hold fish, the sign of an unredeemed sinner, or tempt sailors out of their boats to drown. The mermaid's comb and mirror that appear in medieval church carvings and marginalia are attributes of Venus in classical art, but they came to symbolize feminine vanity and are now essential features of the mermaid in popular culture. A fifteenth-century carving of a mermaid with comb and mirror on a wooden bench in Zennor Church in Cornwall is the source of a local legend about a mysterious woman who seduced a handsome chorister and then disappeared forever. The folklorist William Bottrell recorded this legend, which is a version of the seductive siren, in the nineteenth century.[49] Nevertheless, the link between the fifteenth-century mermaid carving and the tale has become part of romantic Cornish lore, and the church, with its bench, is a popular tourist attraction.

Although intended as visual reminders of moral principles, after the Reformation, many mermaid carvings were removed or defaced as inappropriate in a sacred context. This seems to have been the fate of the mermaid on the fourteenth-century Easter sepulchre in St Andrew's Church in Heckington,

Lincolnshire, where a mermaid carved on its edge, an appropriately peripheral space, has been partially chipped away. Contemporary popular interpretations of these ecclesiastical carvings classify them, along with other fantastic creatures, as 'pagan survivals' in church art, although there is no convincing evidence for this speculation. Perhaps a middle way might suggest that there is nothing essentially pagan about mermaids; they are just 'other', an expression of the inherent contrasts of the natural world. Just as the iconoclasts of the past removed material they considered unchristian, now there is a fashion for 'restoring' this material as symbols of a benevolent pagan world.

The famous bronze 'Little Mermaid' statue by Edvard Eriksen was placed on its rock in Copenhagen harbour in 1913. The oft-abused word 'iconic' aptly describes this poignant embodiment of Hans Christian Andersen's creation. A very different mermaid appears in a Renaissance painting, *St Nicholas of Bari Rebuking the Storm* by Bicci di Lorenzo. The painting, now in the Ashmolean Museum in Oxford, shows the patron saint of mariners bringing clear skies and calm weather to a foundering ship. Below him, a mermaid, surrounded by storm clouds and rough seas, swims away. The metaphor is clear. The mermaid in the painting is a symbolic embodiment of the dangers of the deep, a painted contrast to the sacred power of St Nicholas. A similar theme of human frailty and the power of salvation informs the positioning of a mermaid in a medieval floor mosaic in Otranto Cathedral. This classical double-tailed siren, who occupies the left side of the mosaic floor, is an indication of nature in its unredeemed state. Mermaids became a staple of Victorian art, as popular for their long hair and well-endowed torsos as their symbolic associations. Yet even here, they have a darker side. The mermaids in a series of paintings by the Swiss symbolist painter Arnold Böcklin (1827–1901) have an unsettling earthiness, while the mermaid in the Edward Burne-Jones painting *In the Depths of the Sea* (1886), now in the Spencer Museum of Art, Kansas, lovingly clutches a sailor whom she has inadvertently drowned.

The capacity for such creatures as mermaids to embody a multiplicity of meanings has made them popular in a variety of contexts, and their changing significance in art demonstrates this. Ulysses's sirens may have promised knowledge rather than sex, but their nature became more overtly sexual as time went on. The sirens' fish tails turn into lithe female legs as they clamber onto Ulysses's ship in Herbert Draper's early twentieth-century painting; a neat solution to the potential problem of sex with a mermaid. This creature bestows meaning from the periphery, and, as a creature of the margins, placed beneath the misericord shelf or literally in the margin of a medieval manuscript, her presence provides a tacit commentary that, presumably, onlookers were able to understand. A spectacular hand-illustrated copy of Tennyson's *Idylls of the King* that consciously mimics medieval manuscripts places the Lady of the Lake and a beautiful mermaid at opposite corners of the page.

The mermaid, just like her medieval predecessor, occupies the bottom left-hand corner: a comment on the mysterious, magical and aquatic associations of the Arthurian character (Figure 2.1).

Mermaid spectacles: Theatre, film, music

Classical mythological sea creatures featured in European public spectacles from the Renaissance onwards. The imagery woven into these allegorical set pieces, in true Renaissance style, reinforced the power of the monarchs through continuity with the classical world. As Queen Mother from 1559 to her death in 1589, Catherine de Medici employed court spectacles to bolster the influence of the Valois monarchy of France. The grandiose allegories presented at these elaborate events incorporated mythological figures into a royal narrative of power and prestige. As they involved members of the court, and thus kept them occupied, undoubtedly they provided an additional political benefit. Neptune in a chariot drawn by sea horses accompanied by singing sirens processed past King Charles IX, Catherine's son, in a spectacle presented at Fontainebleau in 1564. The link between the classical Neptune and his retinue and the aspirations of the Valois dynasty to become a great naval power was hardly subtle, but splendour, not subtlety, was the point. An equally elaborate spectacle accompanied Catherine's meeting with her daughter Elizabeth, third wife of Phillip II of Spain, at Bayonne in 1559. Catherine's need to impress the Spanish, coupled with Bayonne's location at the confluence of the rivers between France and Spain made the use of water mythology especially appropriate. Guests were ferried past set pieces depicting tritons sitting on a giant turtle, an artificial whale that spouted wine, and gods riding dolphins, the latter a subtle play on the title 'dauphin', heir to the French throne. Drawings by the festival's designer, Antoine Caron, now in the Pierpont Morgan Library, New York, record the Bayonne water festival, as do the Valois tapestries, woven to commemorate the event, in the Florentine Uffizi Gallery. A similar allegorical theme was evident in the *Ballet Comique de la Reine Louise*, dedicated to Catherine's sister, which took place in Paris 1581. Here too, classical mythology supported the French monarchy. Tritons and Naiads danced around a stage machine consisting of a fountain in the shape of a chariot in which Queen Louise sat among her attendants. Ulysses (rational man) escaped from Circe (symbol of the untamed world of nature) and presented himself to the queen and her court.[50]

In the following centuries, new theatrical and ballet performances succeeded these expensive court rituals. Friedrich de la Motte Fouqué's romantic mermaid novella, *Undine*, was staged for Fanny Cerito in 1843 and Marie

Taglioni in 1847; both were superstars of the new art of classical ballet. A century later, George Balanchine choreographed an Undine sequence for Vera Zorina (*Goldwyn Follies of 1938*, dir. George Marshall), and Frederick Ashton recreated the part for Margot Fonteyn as *Ondine* in 1958. Both E. T. A. Hoffmann (1814) and Peter Tchaikovsky (1869) adapted the story for opera, while Jean Giraudoux wrote a play *Ondine* for the stage (1938). Anton Dvořák incorporated the theme of a water nymph who falls in love with a human into his opera *Rusalka*, first performed in 1901, which drew on Slavic traditions about female river spirits.

A very different mermaid appears in the *Ramayana*, an epic account of the adventures of Rama, the heroic avatar of Vishnu. Translations and adaptations in drama and dance of this enormous and complex work exist throughout Central and Southeast Asia. King Rama I (1736–1809) of Thailand adopted the name of the hero-avatar, and the Thai version, the *Ramakien*, was adapted to this new context. Although the sources are very different from the court performances of the Valois monarchs, the Ramayana provided an origin myth, and by extension legitimacy, for the Thai royal dynasty. Details of topography, clothing and weaponry were reworked to fit the new context, and its legacy is enshrined in the *Ramakien* murals painted on the walls of Bangkok's Temple of the Emerald Buddha (Wat Phra Kaew). The forces of Rama and Hanuman battle against the army of the demon king, Ravana, who has imprisoned Rama's wife in his island fortress, Lanka. Hanuman and his monkey army attempt to build a causeway bridge to the island, but Ravana's mermaid daughter, who controls the denizens of the sea, causes the stones to be dispersed every night. Hanuman courts the mermaid in an attempt to convince her to support Rama's forces, and the courtship results in a son, Machanu, a fishtailed being with a monkey's body. In the *Ramakien* murals, Hanuman, fittingly dressed in royal Siamese attire, whispers in the ear of the beautiful mermaid, Suvannamaccha (whose name may mean 'golden fish'), while balancing on her tail as she swims through the water. The courtship is a favourite episode in the masked court dance dramas of Thailand and Cambodia and in the shadow-puppet theatres popular throughout Malaysia.[51]

Mermaids appeared as commercial ventures such as the 'Fiji' mermaid, a famous sideshow attraction presented by the American circus impresario, P. T. Barnum. This strange and compelling creature was, in all likelihood, an example of a made-for-tourist item produced in nineteenth-century Japan. Exhibitions of rarities were popular fairground attractions in America and Europe, where the exhibits reflected exotic places newly accessible to Western influence and trade.[52] Sideshows were, in many ways, descendants of the 'cabinets of curiosities' owned by scholars and aristocrats, and the accounts of freaks and rarities printed on broadsides and pamphlets from the fifteenth century onwards. They were exotic and outlandish and embodied colonial sensibilities. These 'mermaids' consisted of a skeletal frame composed of wire or animal bones grafted onto a fish tail covered with a papier-mâché outer-shell. A number survive in museums and private collections. They are usually about two feet long and quite compellingly grotesque. The folklorist, Jacqueline Simpson, kindly supplied the following account of one of these mermaid souvenirs.

> There was one in a glass case in the bar of a Worthing hotel when I was a child, which my father took me to see. He explained how sailors made mermaids, half fish and half monkey. The hotel was Warnes Hotel, a fine establishment on Worthing seafront. Haile Sailassie and his wife stayed there in the 1930s not that that's relevant, but just to tell you it was posh! Since the hotel closed temporarily for the war, it must have been in 1938 or 1939 that my father persuaded the barman to let him take me into the bar briefly to see the mermaid, at a time when nobody was drinking there. Alas, she vanished post-war. Legend says the wife of a later hotel manager was convinced the top half was a human baby and had it given a Christian burial. I can't recall who told me about her having been buried. It was probably when I went back in the hope of seeing her again, at the time I was doing the 'Dragons' book, but she was gone.[53]

Court spectacles and theatrical productions with mermaids sometimes called for human actors to wear fish tails, and no discussion of mermaids would be complete without reference to the two aquatic actors Esther Williams and Annette Kellerman. In the film *Million Dollar Mermaid* (Mervyn LeRoy, 1952), Williams, star of the lavish 'aquamusicals' of the 1940s, dived into the role of Annette Kellerman, the Australian swimming star and silent film actress who made a career out of being a mermaid at the beginning of the twentieth century. Born in Australia in 1887, Kellerman, a successful long-distance swimmer and vaudeville performer in the newly popular aquacades of the early 1900s, starred in water ballet spectaculars in new venues like the New York Hippodrome Theatre. She was an advocate of exercise for women and pioneered a one-piece swimming costume, which gave women more freedom to participate in athletics. Her appearance in this attire led to her arrest for public indecency in Boston in 1907. The charge was dropped, and the notoriety did her image no harm. A superb show-woman, she devised her own choreography and created costumes which enhanced her athletic figure, contributing to the persona of a stage and screen goddess alternating between mermaid and woman. She donned a mermaid's tail for the underwater sequences in a number of silent 'fairy tale films' inspired by Hans Christian Andersen's story. *The Mermaid* (1911) may be the first film to feature an actor actually swimming in a mermaid costume, and Kellerman repeated this winning formula in other films including *Neptune's Daughter* (1914), *Queen of the Sea* (1918) and *Venus of the South*

Seas (1924).[54] Not only did her one-piece bathing costumes challenge the restrictions placed on women's participation in sport at the beginning of the twentieth century, but she also lectured and wrote books on exercise and physical fitness and maintained her personal healthy lifestyle to the ripe age of ninety.

The choreographed swimming choruses in aquacades and Esther Williams' musicals seldom included women imitating mermaids. However, in 1947, an ex-navy diver created a roadside attraction at Weeki Wachee Springs, a natural spring in Hernando County, Florida, that featured an unusual underwater show. Roadside attractions became popular after the Second World War as more Americans bought cars and travelled on family vacations. The show at Weeki Wachee featured swimmers performing underwater using air-hose breathing techniques pioneered by the American Navy. Not long after the attraction opened, the underwater sequences for the film *Mr Peabody and the Mermaid* (1948) were filmed there with the actress Anne Blyth in a mermaid costume, and soon the original 'Aquabelles' donned mermaid tails as part of their routines. The rise of theme parks in the 1970s threatened the popularity of roadside attractions, but, in 2008, Weeki Wachee Springs became part of the Florida State Park System, and the underwater aquacade found a new audience.[55] A few mermen have been added to the show, but it is still the mermaids who rule.

Mermaids also featured in stage plays and film productions that highlighted the conflicts, comic, tragic or surreal, inherent in relationships between beings from two such different environments. Films exploited the comic possibilities of the mermaid's tail for farcical episodes of misunderstanding and drew on her amorous reputation for romantic plot lines. Glynis Johns played a flirtatious Cornish mermaid in two comedy films, *Miranda* (Ken Annakin, 1948) and *Mad About Men* (Ralph Thomas, 1954), based on Peter Blackmore's 1948 stage play. Both films hinge on the mermaid's desire for human experience. Miranda captivates a married doctor on a fishing trip in Cornwall in the first film and she refuses to release him until he takes her to London. In the sequel, she trades places with a prim lookalike human relative. Eventually, the human girl, now less prim thanks to Miranda's antics, marries the hero. The first film ends with Miranda sitting on a rock with a not-quite human child, but the extramarital offspring does not feature in the much less daring sequel where mermaid and human lookalikes change places, and the human girl, conveniently single, merely trades a dull fiancé for a handsome one.

William Powell starred in a fantasy comedy, *Mr Peabody and the Mermaid* (Irving Pichel, 1948), as a man undergoing a midlife crisis pursued by three women – his wife, a mermaid and a nightclub singer. The use of mermaid lore is straightforward. Mr Peabody hears mysterious singing, although the mermaid herself is mute. The mermaid is unaware of the social and moral conventions of human society, which precipitates all the narrow escapes, mis-understandings and sight gags that are the staple of this genre. The sexual politics, which involved the man with three women, were rather daring for its time, but the film ended with a reconciliation at which point Powell presents his wife with the mermaid's comb, the only proof of her existence. In *Splash* (Ron Howard, 1984), another take on the screwball comedy genre, a mermaid (Daryl Hannah), whose tail conveniently becomes legs when she dries out, saves a young boy (Tom Hanks) from drowning. The film revolves around a series of comic crises, as the mermaid adjusts to life in New York City, and ends happily, with the couple swimming off towards an underwater paradise.

These are light-hearted films, but the tone of Curtis Harrington's *Night Tide* (1961) is an altogether darker reworking of the siren myth. A naive young sailor (Dennis Hopper) falls in love with a strange girl called Mara who lives above the carousel at Venice Beach, California and who works as a mermaid at a carnival. The actor, Linda Lawson, who played Mara, has a memorable line. In response to Hopper's innocent chat-up question 'What do you do?' she replies 'I'm a mermaid.' The idea that she is a real siren who kills the men who love her torments Mara, but tragically, it is she, not the Hopper character, who drowns during a storm. The film, like Andersen's *Little Mermaid*, pits the mermaid against a human woman, the daughter of the carnival owner who is suspicious of the 'siren' and, at least by implication, ultimately wins the young sailor's affections.

The mermaid's ultimately tragic desire to transcend her nature is a more durable cultural theme than the antics of comic mermaids, and Hans Christian Andersen's *Little Mermaid*, itself influenced by Fouqué's *Undine*, provides a perennial source of inspiration. The mermaid in Andersen's story falls in love with a prince whom she saves from drowning. She gains legs at the cost of her beautiful voice and experiences constant pain as she walks among human beings. Ultimately, she sacrifices herself to save the man she loves. Unable to be a wife, she becomes an aerial sylph who watches over human infants in order to gain the immortal soul she craves. At the core of this literary tale is the common folk belief that supernatural beings desire salvation. The mer-maid's journey from water to land to air is a morality tale for the redemptive power of true love and self-sacrifice. Such moral themes were fashionable in these literary fairy tales, although they can seem somewhat sentimental to modern audiences. Perhaps it is not surprising that when the Walt Dis-ney Company animated the tale (Ron Clements and John Musker, 1989), it replaced the sombre morality of Andersen's story with an upbeat Disney mes-sage. A cheeky red-haired adolescent, Ariel, desires adventure rather than a soul. The film replaces Andersen's long-suffering mermaid with a strong-willed teenager and adds an array of improbably voluble sea life and a happy end-ing. The Disney version also changed Andersen's sinister undersea witch to a more comical love-rival, Ursula, an inversion of the traditional mermaid with octopus tentacles rather than a fishtail.

In the fictionalized musical film biography of *Hans Christian Andersen* (Charles Vidor, 1952), the Andersen character (played by Danny Kaye) suffers from unrequited love for a ballerina (Zizi Jeanmaire) who dances as the mermaid in 'The Little Mermaid' ballet sequence. This subplot reverses the gender dynamics, but retains the poignancy of unrequited love. The Russian fantasy film *Rusalochka/ The Little Mermaid* (Vladimir Bychkov, 1976) follows the general structure of the Danish tale. The same actor played Hans Christian Andersen, the film's narrator, and a character in the tale who attempts to help the little mermaid, which underscored the similarities of moral choice in both real and narrative worlds. In a Japanese anime version, *Ponyo on the Cliff by the Sea* (Hayao Miyazaki, 2008), Ponyo is a goldfish with a little girl's face. Her desire to become human to be with a human boy, Sosuke unbalances the worlds of land and sea. The controlling supernatural force here is not a witch, but a figure called Granmamare, an anime version of Guanyin, Japanese goddess of mercy. At the end, the children's love is tested and Ponyo jumps into the air and turns, not into sea foam as in the Andersen source tale, but into a real little girl.[56] These variations and modifications demonstrate the power of Andersen's mythical creature – her ability to evolve and adapt to continually changing circumstances.

Marine life and mythic perception

Many sightings of so-called mermaids are no doubt real sea mammals, such as seals, whales, crocodiles or the perennial favourite, the manatee. Although the crocodile was the subject of intense interest in the classical period and distinct from a mermaid or siren, it may lie behind Pliny's account of male and female sirens swimming in the Nile (*Natural History*, Bk 10, ch. 70). This famous incident was still being cited and illustrated as a warning prodigy centuries later by writers such as Ulisse Aldrovandi in *History of Marvellous Creatures* (1581). Amboise Paré linked the unknown with the marvellous in his 1573 treatise in which he comments on the plethora of 'wondrous' creatures from the sea whose 'secret corners and receptacles are not previous [i.e. known] to men'. From the sixteenth century onwards, marine monsters were displayed to the public in exhibitions as well in as broadsheets and pamphlets. As curator of the Royal College of Surgeons Museum, C. J. S. Thompson gathered a number of these printed accounts. Such curiosities were particularly striking when, like the mermaid, they resembled humans. The details of the sightings and capture are often as interesting as the descriptions, since they help place the creatures in a physical context. A scaly, talking fish caught after the death of a pope was given to his successor, but it soon died 'being destitute of its own natural place and nourishment'. Another, taken off the coast of Denmark, was a popular exhibit during the reign of Queen Anne.[57] A fish that resembled a monk was caught 'in tempestuous seas' near Norway in 1531.[58] John Swan's *Speculum Mundi* takes a critical look at the reality of some fabulous beasts, but accepts the oft-repeated account of a mermaid washed through the dyke near Edam in the Netherlands in 1402 who became a Christian and learnt to spin, but never spoke. Some 'mermaids' caught in Ceylon (modern Sri Lanka) about 1560 were dissected by a famous 'doctor' who declared that they were just like humans inside and out.[59]

Careful observation and rational explanation are techniques intended to dispel old myths, but the misinterpretations that produced descriptions of marvellous beings reveal the importance of tradition in constructing meaning through our perception of the real world. Reliable witnesses were often the only basis for evaluating the authenticity of sightings, and so-called rational explanations are sometimes so fantastic as to be more folk discourse than science. The distorted, partially decayed, carcases that have washed up on beaches or been caught in fishing nets present an interesting interface between observation and belief. The so-called Stronsay Beast washed up on the island of Stronsay, off the Scottish coast in 1808. Measurements given at the time, by three reliable witnesses, indicated that it was fifty-five feet long. Contemporary drawings of the carcase show appendages and a mane of bristles, features regularly ascribed to sea serpents or the Loch Ness Monster, and some commentators suggested the possibility that it could be a new species. Rather prosaically however, scientists – among them the British surgeon, Everard Home, and John Goodsir, professor of anatomy at Edinburgh University – identified the beast as the decaying carcase of a basking shark.[60] The identification of such creatures as natural occurrences rather than prodigies reflected the growing interest in prehistoric and exotic beasts that continues to this day.[61] Sir Everard Home (1756–1832), for example, also described a fossil ichthyosaur at Lyme Regis and undertook early studies on the platypus. His expertise was even sought concerning the authenticity of a mermaid curiosity, although he rather blotted his copybook by appropriating some of the research contained in the notebooks of his brother-in-law John Hunter, founder of the Hunterian collection and husband of Home's sister and writer of a famous mermaid poem, the poet, Anne Hunter.[62]

Advertisements provide another source of traditional motifs in popular culture. In the 1997 Levi's advertisement for its 'Shrink to Fit' jeans, a sailor falls overboard to the song 'Underwater Love' (Smoke City, 1997), but the mermaids are more interested in his clothing than in him. Although the advertisement plays on the notion that mermaids unwittingly drowned the sailors with whom they fell in love, Levi's mermaids prefer the product to the person. Whatever this may say about our consumerist values, it assumes, quite correctly, that the target audience will know something about traditional mermaid behaviour. *Chicken of the Sea* tuna introduced a smiling blond mermaid in the 1950s. She carried a golden wand, and her 'tail' extended modestly upwards to cover her breasts. The logo became a trademark that has continued to evolve with the company. As television advertising became increasingly important in the 1960s, the company added a new jingle 'Ask any Mermaid You Happen to See ... What's the Best Tuna? Chicken of the Sea'. Customers in the 1970s could purchase a souvenir mermaid doll, and the company has responded to public concern about dolphins drowning in tuna nets with another slogan, 'The Mermaid Cares – Dolphin-Safe Policy'.[63]

A crowned double-tailed siren was associated with the powerful Colonna family, and a beautiful bronze example from the sixteenth century, now in the New York Metropolitan Museum of Art, may have been a bridal gift.[64] Today a double-tailed crowned mermaid graces Starbucks coffee shops and company merchandise. The origin of the crowned-siren logo has become a subject for internet blogging, as well as a symbol of this ubiquitous chain. The official explanation cites a sixteenth-century Norse woodcut that embodies the seductiveness of the product and the seafaring tradition of the early coffee traders (which overlooks the fact that the Norse never traded coffee!). However, indefatigable bloggers have traced the crowned siren to a book of symbols published in America about the time Starbucks became popular and, because of its distinctive crown, to fifteenth-century editions of the medieval French romance, Mélusine.[65]

In the cyberpunk TV series *Sanctuary* (2008–12), a telepathic mermaid is one of the creatures protected from the evil designs of the villains. The idea of the mermaid as 'rare but real' continues to inform sightings and hoaxes. Recently, a reward was offered to anyone who could supply proof of a 'real' mermaid sighted off the Israeli coast.[66] Some early- nineteenth-century taxonomists admitted the possibility of an 'amphibious primate' that would correspond with land examples and explain the tales of mermaids, and the 'aquatic ape' hypothesis remains a subject for popular science.[67] Two bizarre 'docufictions' aired by the Discovery Network's 'Animal Planet' series, apparently showed actual footage of mermaids. Although there was a vaguely worded disclaimer identifying this as 'science fiction' and the so-called researchers as actors, the programme proceeded to push all the right buttons, presenting mermaids as a peaceful society cooperating with dolphins and prepared to sacrifice themselves to a shark-like Predator X in order to protect their young. It even produced a mermaid skeleton. P. T. Barnum would have loved it, but the National Oceanic and Atmospheric Administration (NOAA) felt obliged to post a rebuttal.[68] In Shakespeare's *Midsummer Night's Dream*, the song of a mermaid riding a dolphin is so sweet that the sea becomes calm and the stars fall from heaven. In the twenty-first century, such poetic rhetoric has given way to internet conspiracy theorists who assume that if an official body like NOAA issues a disclaimer, somebody must be hiding something!

What then is the truth in the mermaid story? Classical sirens possessed wings and claws rather than the fish tails now associated with mermaids. Their voices promised knowledge, but led men to their death. With the advent of printing in the fifteenth century, illustrated broadsides and chapbooks were printed and sold widely. They were the sensational tabloids of the day, and the illustrations of aquatic creatures began to look ever more human in subsequent copies. There are male and female fishes, monkfish (a term still used for an edible whitefish) and bishop fish. Every possible type of human seemed to have a 'fish' counterpart, and these visual images contributed to wider traditions about mermaids. The transformation from suicide-inducing winged siren into sexually alluring fishtailed mermaid demonstrates how complex our desire is to populate the universe with creatures against which we can measure ourselves. Nor is it surprising that we attempt to rationalize our imaginative creations to make them seem more real by suggesting that sea mammals, like manatees and dugongs who nurse their young, have been mistaken for mermaids.

The whale, the dolphin and the sea serpent

'Very like a whale' says Polonius to Hamlet as he tries to humour the cloud-gazing prince (*Hamlet* Act III, sc. ii), and with these words, we come to a creature that inhabits the world of myth as readily as it does the ocean itself. Examples of sightings and strandings, accounts of being swallowed or of mistaking a whale for an island, and tales of whale riding reflect differing perceptions of this marine mammal. Attitudes to the whale encompass economics and ecology as well as myth and legend, and the changes through time and across cultures illustrate a network of interactions that bind together a number of themes in this book (Figure 2.3).

Whales and whale products, likely acquired by drift whaling or from beached animals, have been identified at ancient Greek sites.[69] Classical Greece mythologized many of the fearsome sea creatures of the Mediterranean as *ketea* (sea monsters). The sea goddess Keto gave her name to cetacean mammals, and her husband Phorcys, whose name may be associated with the seal (*phokes*), presided over the ocean depths. They controlled the creatures that inhabited the depths of the sea, and their offspring included the monstrous Scylla (crab), who devoured passing sailors.

FIGURE 2.3 *A bizarre double-spouting whale nurses two equally bizarre offspring from Ulisse Aldrovandi's sixteenth-century description of the aquatic world.*

While Jonah's whale was more mythic than real, Pliny's negative characterization of the orca (*Orcinus orca*), given the popularity of his work in constructing Western ideas about the natural world, provided an influential description (*Historia Naturalis*, Bk 9.5, 12). The medieval whale became associated with the devil, while still providing a source of food and useful products.[70] When, in 1558, Konrad Gessner described the whale based on a description of one stranded a few years earlier in the Bay of Greifswald between the island of Rügen and Germany's Baltic coast, the link between animal and devil was no doubt fading. However, a drawing of the beached creature still occupies a significant ecclesiastical space on the wall of St Mary's Church in Greifswald.

Moby Dick may be the most famous named whale, but he was not the first. Pliny mentions a huge fish that lies, like an island on the surface of the water, to lure unwary sailors who drown when the monster dives into the deep. Pliny calls the creature 'Pistis', although this may be a reference to the whale's ability to spout water rather than a personal name (*Historia Naturalis*, Bk 9, ch. 4). *The Exeter Book* (Exeter Cathedral Library MS 3501), a tenth-century collection of Anglo-Saxon poems, compares the whale that sailors mistake for an island to the devil who seeks the destruction of Christian souls. This 'swimmer of the oceans streams' is named Fastitocolan (*þam is noma cenned, fyrnstreama geflotan, Fastitocalon*, 'The Whale', fol 96b–97b). The whale in the *Physiologus*, called *aspidochelone*, helpfully translated as 'asp-turtle', gives much the same account of the whale's propensity to mimic a false island and draws much the same moral lesson about sinners and the devil.[71] Bestiaries, which ultimately derived from this seminal text, usually call the creature *Cetus* (whale), but the description and the warning, remain. The whale also emits a sweet smell from its mouth to lure unsuspecting fish and resembles the biblical Leviathan. It may ultimately have influenced the idea of Hellmouth, which was depicted as a monstrous head with a giant set of jaws that swallowed hapless sinners whole.

Illustrations of whale-islands appear in medieval bestiaries, although the creatures depicted are usually fish-like and nothing like a whale. The story, however, had a considerable heritage before it entered medieval didactic zoology. The Pseudo-Callisthenes, written in the third century CE, but set in the time of Alexander the Great, describes a disappearing island.[72] St Brendan and his Irish monks land on such an island. The whale, called Jasconius, is so large it cannot find its own tail. Although initially disturbed by the heat of the fire, it allows the voyagers to celebrate their annual Easter mass on its back. Jasconius may also be the 'fysse … out of the west' (according to the Caxton translation) who saves them from a sea monster, and, Brendan's monks give thanks to God when this aquatic convert leaves them for the final time.[73] That other great seafarer, Sinbad the Sailor, also had an encounter with a similarly named whale, and he too emerged unscathed.[74] Traveller's tales and fantasy blend with scientific observation in Al-Kazwini's *The Wonders of the World* (thirteenth century) in which sailors land on a monster turtle, which recalls the name of the 'asp-turtle' from other sources.[75] The early-sixteenth-century world map of the Arab explorer, Piri Reis, depicts two sailors lighting a fire on a giant fish-like creature. The accompanying text refers to the St Brendan episode (here called Savolfandan).[76] Milton restores the link between the whale as monster and the devil: 'There leviathan, Hugest of living creatures, on the deep/ Stretched like a promontory, sleeps or swims And seems a moving land' (*Paradise Lost*, VII, 412–15). In a curious modern replay of this old tale, a seaplane making a seemingly ordinary landing in an Alaskan inlet had to pull up sharply to avoid a breaching whale. Fortunately, it suffered nothing more serious from the spouting whale than a drenched windshield.[77]

Almost as common as the false island, is a tale about men and women swallowed by whales. The most famous is undoubtedly the biblical story of Jonah. His miraculous recovery from a *piscis grandis*, variously depicted in art as a large fish, a whale or a sea serpent, was a warning against sin and became symbolic of salvation through Christ's Resurrection. This tradition, which is more a widespread legend than a myth, concerns someone who after being swallowed by a whale, kills it, and emerges bleached, blind and hairless because of the heat inside the monster. In the earliest recorded European version, Hercules dives into the mouth of a sea monster to save Hesione, and then hacks his way out. He is unharmed, but the intense heat of the monster's guts causes him to lose his hair.[78] A huge whale swallows the author and his companions in Lucian's satirical *True History* (second century CE). Inside its belly is an entire society, a microcosm of the world outside. Eventually Lucian and his men destroy the whale by digging an escape tunnel in its side and lighting a fire (Bk 1, 31–41, Bk 2, 1–2). A dramatic medieval version of this legend is the subject of a tenth-century poem by a French monk Letaldus, *De quodam piscatore quem ballena absorbuit* in which a whale swallows an English fisherman and his boat. The fisherman, named Within, sets fire to the boat and stabs the whale, which beaches near his home port of Rochester. He calls out to the townspeople who fear that the animal is possessed. Eventually, Within emerges, temporarily blind, bleached white and hairless.[79] This marvellous tale combines several aspects of whale lore: the economic reality of drift whaling, the whales' supposed demonic nature, and a set of folk motifs about being swallowed and regurgitated by monsters.

The puppet who wants to be a boy in Carlo Collodi's *The Adventures of Pinocchio* (1883) rescues his father from an asthmatic sea monster called 'Il Terribile Pescecane' (The Terrible Dogfish). Collodi's sources included Ariosto's late chivalric *Cinque Canti* and Lucian's satirical *True History*.[80] Disney reimagined the creature as Monstro the Whale for his animated version of *Pinocchio* (Ben Sharpsteen and Hamilton Luske, 1940), in which the puppet hero still uses Lucian's escape technique by lighting a fire inside the whale's belly. Despite the abundance of these swallowing tales in literature and folklore, there have been those who looked for a reality behind the biblical version of this incident, Jonah and the fish. In 1891, James Bartley apparently emerged alive, but blind and bleached, from inside a whale. Newspapers and biblical apologists opposed to modern scientific theories recounted Bartley's adventure, and some writers even claimed to have met him. Unfortunately, the tale of his swallowing and survival is a contemporary legend whose sources may lie in sensational newspaper reports, popular sideshow exhibits that spawned curiosities like the Fiji mermaid, and the traditional motifs that underpin earlier monster-swallowings.[81]

The Orcadian tale of 'Assipattle and the Great Stour Worm', collected in the 1880s by the folklorist Walter Traill Dennison, contains a number of typical motifs. The huge Stour Worm has elements of the world serpent in its size and in the fact that the dead serpent became part of the landscape. Like the cockatrice,[82] it hatches from an egg and has poisonous breath and, like the monster in the Andromeda story, only a royal virgin sacrifice can appease its hunger. The unpromising hero, Assipattle, sails his boat into the monster's mouth and sets its liver on fire, but seems to escape without blindness or bleaching.[83] In the *Gesta romanorum*, a medieval compendium of moralized popular tales, a whale ('*cete grande*') swallows and regurgitates a princess.[84] She, however, retains her hair and her sight, as does Ninnella who escapes a monstrous fish in a tale from Basile's *Pentamerone*.[85] St Margaret of Antioch has a similar adventure with a dragon, and she too emerges hairstyle intact.[86] Evidently, ladies could withstand the heated insides of monsters better than men.

At least forty instances of whales beached along the Dutch coast, many recorded in etchings and prints, occurred during the sixteenth and seventeenth centuries. Some of these regarded the whale as an omen, and all showed the local population harvesting the animals. Although the medieval fondness for moral comparison between the whale and demonic forces had begun to change, contact remained violent, and mixed attitudes continued during the centuries when whaling was an important industry.[87] Sea monsters attacking ships appear together with scenes of whaling on Olaus Magnus's *Carta Marina* (1539) and on other maps of this period.[88] The moral argument today, at least in non-whaling nations, favours the whale as a symbol of an environment in peril, and as a creature whose mammalian nature, complex social structure and human-seeming behavioural capacities deserve respect. The film *Free Willy* and its sequels (director Simon Wincer, 1993, 1995, 1997) illustrate the controversies which still colour our attitudes to these marine mammals. The original film concerns a troubled boy who bonds with an orca in a marine park and eventually helps it escape to the accompaniment of a stirring soundtrack. The feel-good message of the films contrasts with the unhappy real-life story of the orca, Keiko, who played Willy in the films. Keiko was eventually rescued from a marine park, rehabilitated and released in 1998 into the waters around Iceland where it had been captured. Unfortunately, the orca died of pneumonia in 2003. The controversy surrounding Keiko continues, and now centres on the appropriateness of orca shows in marine parks. Unresolved issues include the rising economic value of whale tourism, environmental protection and arguments about the relation between human and non-human species.[89]

Whales as bringers of knowledge

Although disappearing islands and swallowed seafarers are among the dangers that whales posed to seafarers, accounts about whales as guides and protectors reveal complex attitudes to these huge creatures. The monks in the Latin poem, the *Voyage of St Brendan*, mistake a huge whale for an island, but far from harming Brendan and his companions, the whale apparently saves them from another great fish that is pursuing them with its hungry mouth wide open.[90] Witi Ihimaera's novel *Whale Rider* is the story of Kahu, a young Maori girl descended from a legendary 'whale rider'. Traditionally, the title of chief belongs to a male heir, so Kahu, despite being the only surviving great-grandchild of the ageing chief, is, by virtue of her gender, excluded. When a mass beaching of whales threatens the livelihood, as well as the spiritual continuity, of the tribe, Kahu 'speaks' to the bull whale whom she rides out to sea, thereby leading the pod away from danger and saving her people. The novel and the film *Whale Rider* (1987, filmed in 2002, directed by Niki Caro) concern very modern themes of gender, coming of age and the positive cultural value of contact with the environment. The film brought the whale-riding traditions of Maori culture to a wider public. Such traditions are associated with tribal ancestors who arrived on the back of a whale from the mythical homeland of the Maori. Descent from the whale-rider creates a genealogical link with other members of the community and through the whale, who often merges with the landscape, a link with the land itself.

Among the fantastic adventures attributed to Miyamoto Musashi, a famous seventeenth-century Japanese samurai and swordsman, is a fight with an enormous whale, which was immortalized by the artist Utagawa Kuniyoshi (1798–1861) in which the samurai stands astride the whale's back and plunges his sword into it. The tradition of the whale-rider Kahutia-te-rangi, the ancestor of Maori tribes inhabiting South Island and the east coast of New Zealand's North Island, presents a striking contrast to the heroic battle between samurai and whale. A humpback whale rescued this Maori hero after his jealous half-brother attempted to drown him. The word *pai-kea* applies to humpback whales generally, and the whale-rider assumes the name Paikea from the whale that rescued him and carried him to New Zealand. According to Maori tradition, the rules of hospitality compelled Chief Tinirau to offer his whale companion Tutunui as transport for a rather sinister guest, who kills and eats the whale. The story illustrates the close relationship between the Maori and whales – as friends, guardians and food, and similar versions exist in other Pacific cultures. Whales can also become part of the landscape. A group of hills near Welcome Bay in Tauranga Harbour, a coastline where whale strandings occur regularly, are said to be a family of stranded whales. Such stranding events were important, as whales provided a rich source of protein as well as the whalebone used for objects associated with ritual, social status and combat. Whales guarded and guided the canoes that, according to tradition, brought the original inhabitants to Aotearoa (New Zealand) from the mythical homeland of Hawaiki, and images of whale-riders adorn the beams of storage houses where foods, like whale meat, were stored.[91]

The complex relationships between a society and an animal that is both a source of food and possesses cultural or spiritual meaning permeate many traditions. Two tales collected by the linguist and anthropologist Edward Sapir recount how the ancestor chiefs of particular families among peoples living on the Northwestern coast of America and Canada received the supernatural power to hunt whales, as well as the rituals and songs for a successful hunt, from the whales themselves. The first tale concerns two powerful whalers from rival families who possess the ability to 'see' whales before anyone else. One of the whalers, himself a chief, accompanies his enemies who send him to cut off the dorsal fin of a drifting dead whale, which rightfully belongs to the chief, and then abandon him. Although marooned on the drifting carcase, the whale's spirit, which dwells in the dorsal fin, leads him safely to land.[92] In the second legend, a chief is in possession of a whale's dorsal fin when a great flood overtakes the whaling party. They survive by eating whale meat while the whale spirit in the dorsal fin sings to them, imparting the knowledge to make the family successful whalers, and leading them to safety.[93]

Whaling involved the entire community, and whalers were high-status individuals, often a chief or his close relatives. A successful hunt not only provided food, it also consolidated power. Preparation for the hunt involved complex rituals and taboos. The uses of whaling equipment, as well as the special songs and incantations, were carefully guarded and passed down through clans. The feast that accompanied a successful hunt honoured both the whale and the hunters, while the special rituals and ceremonial treatment of whale parts insured that the whale's spirit returned to the sea.[94]

Dolphins

Dolphins drew the chariot of Poseidon's consort, Amphitrite, and, of all the creatures of the sea, the dolphin has attracted the most consistently positive response from land-based humans. Greek and Roman writers stress the dolphin's speed, close communal links, love of music and sympathy with humans. Mediterranean dolphins allegedly responded to the nickname Simo (fat-nose) and helped fisherman catch fish. Classical sources present these stories as reliable observations of actual events, although they read like variants of a legend.[95] Cross-species friendships are prominent among these accounts. A dolphin is said to have mourned the death of a boy whom he ferried to and from school on its back. Dolphins protected a man who freed their captive comrades and mourned his death, and they played with children at the port of Hippo. Two famous dolphin incidents concern thwarted piracy. The famous musician, Arion, was thrown overboard by pirates, but dolphins, attracted by his singing, carried him to safety. The story of Dionysius and the Tyrrhenian pirates first appeared in a Homeric Hymn (seventh to fourth century BCE). Pirates attempted to kidnap the young god who caused vines to entwine the ship's oars. As the terrified pirates jumped into the water, Dionysius, belatedly merciful, turned them into dolphins. A black figure vase from sixth century BCE, now in the Toledo Museum, shows the sailors in the midst of transformation. In Lucian's *Dialogue of the Sea Gods* (Dialogue 8), dolphins tell Poseidon that they sympathized with Arion because they were once men themselves.

In addition to this broadly consistent characterization of their behaviour, dolphins fulfil a symbolic function. Their ability to dive and rise above the waters suggested renewal, resurrection and the safe passage of the soul into the afterlife. For this reason, carved dolphins appear on both pagan and Christian tombs and sarcophagi. A Renaissance mapmaker, in 1500, depicted Venice as a dolphin-shaped city evoking in one humanistic sweep the implications of speed, trade, renewal and all aspects of classical and Christian allusions that this creature embodied.[96]

Accounts of dolphins interacting with humans continue. A Risso's dolphin (*Grampus griseus*) named Pelorus Jack escorted ships through Cook Strait, New Zealand at the beginning of the twentieth century and was protected by law. In the 1950s, Opo, a bottlenose dolphin, the most common member of the family *Delphinidae*, played with children around the New Zealand town of Opononi. The affinity between dolphin and child informs the film and subsequent television series, *Flipper* (Ivan Tor, 1964–7), in which a dolphin befriends a young boy living on a Marine Preserve in Florida. Beautifully smiling dolphins do not enchant everyone. An old sailor in Shakespeare's *Pericles* refers to the longstanding belief that leaping dolphins are a sign of rain and complains that 'they (dolphins) never come but I look to be washed' (*Pericles* Act III, sc. i). The medieval chronicle-writer Gervase of Tilbury also linked dolphins to storms. When a storm arose after a young sailor wounded a dolphin, a figure like a mounted knight galloping over the sea appeared and demanded retribution. The sailor followed the knight to a strange country where he was obliged to remove his weapon from the wounded dolphin.[97] This human/dolphin transformation is somewhat unusual. However, Adriaen Coenen's *Visboek* has a drawing of the author in the guise of a sea knight.[98]

Interest increased sharply in dolphin/human interaction with the rise of the environmental movement of the 1960s. John Lilly, a doctor interested in consciousness, conducted controversial experiments with the aim of establishing meaningful communication with dolphins.[99] Mike Nichols's film *The Day of the Dolphin* (1973), based on Robert Merle's Cold War novel about military research on animals, incorporated elements of Lilly's work. Contemporary research has re-evaluated the idea of dolphin intelligence and criticized their use as performers in aqua displays. Nevertheless, our fascination with this creature continues. The Clearwater Marine Aquarium in Florida adopted a badly injured bottle-nosed dolphin, which was fitted with a prosthetic tail. It was featured in a film stressing ecological issues, *Dolphin Tale* (2011), and attracts many visitors.[100]

Sea serpents and sea monsters

In 1864, the American symbolist artist Elihu Vedder exhibited a painting, *In the Lair of the Sea Serpent*. It was in many ways a typical New England coastal scene with one significant difference. A huge, realistic-looking sea serpent rested among the sand dunes. The painting was eventually gifted to the Boston Fine Arts Museum by the art connoisseur Thomas Gold Appleton who may have suggested the subject, namely, the famous New England (or Gloucester) sea serpent which had been sighted intermittently from 1817 onwards.[101] Interest in this particular phenomenon reflected more than just the possible existence of such a creature. The regional identity of New England was changing in a country that was rapidly expanding westwards, and there was a new interest in the 'coast' as a place of recreation. Many of the sightings were viewed by people on land rather than in ships; witnesses, according to newspapers, were interviewed by respected authorities. The writer Eugene Batcheldor published a 'docufiction' account in 1849, although earlier, in 1819, Charles Crafts, a playwright from the rival port of Charleston, denounced the entire episode as a hoax.[102]

The nineteenth century was a good time for sea serpents, and serious biologists considered whether this *animalia incognita* should be included in the scientific classificatory systems taking shape. New animal species were being identified in what were then remote parts of the globe, so the depths of the sea, which covered so much of the planet, seemed a likely place to find new species. Drawings appeared in popular sources like the *Illustrated London News*, and reputable ships' captains reported a surprising number of sightings. Fossils of ancient animals challenged attitudes to the age of the earth, and it seemed reasonable to search the ocean depths for possible survivals of prehistoric ichthyosaurs and their kin.[103] Attitudes were shifting away from the moralistic view of the animal world contained in bestiaries and broadsides. Visits to the seaside, with the added possibility of encountering 'real' sea serpents, as well as sideshows, which invited people to marvel at oddities, became popular. These factors influenced the very mixed views of sea serpents that ranged from serious scientific enquiry to equally serious scepticism. With the waning of the nineteenth century, explaining monstrous creatures in terms of real species became less common, and, although sightings of sea serpents still occur,[104] the heyday of this particular fantastic beast seems to have passed (Figure 2.4).

The description of the kraken in the thirteenth-century *King's Mirror* echoes traditions about the monstrous medieval whale. The kraken resembles an island, sailors drown in the whirlpool created when it dives, and it belches to attract unwary fish that swim into its open mouth (*King's Mirror*, Bk 12). In

FIGURE 2.4 *A sea serpent spouting water catches an unwary seal while a sea turtle looks on. This mix of real and imagined animals is from Ulisse Aldrovandi's treatise on* De Piscibus.

The Natural History of Norway (1752–3), Erik Pontoppidan, bishop of Bergen, drew on accounts from 'reliable' witnesses that likened the kraken to an island and claimed that it had tentacles, could sink a ship, but, overall, was peaceful.[105] The tentacles suggest a giant squid or octopus, while the disappearing island references whale/island traditions. However, as no one has ever caught a kraken or found a dead specimen, this brings the description closer to the interface between mythological animals and real ones. The nineteenth-century Danish biologist Japetus Steenstrup identified the kraken as a giant squid by examining actual specimens and historical accounts, and the American scientist A. E. Verrill explained another cryptid, the 'Florida Sea Monster', in this way.[106] Melville's hero Ishmael makes a similar comment about the origin of the kraken in *Moby Dick* (1851).[107] Fantastic creatures like the kraken and sea serpents have been the subject of intense, and often intensely contested, attempts to classify them scientifically. The kraken is an interesting cryptid in that the discovery of real marine species has seemingly validated its existence. From these 'monster' accounts, supported by the identification of actual specimens of giant cephalopods, has emerged evidence for species such as a giant squid (*Architeuthis*), a giant octopus (*Enteroctopus*) and, as late as 2007, a colossal squid (*Mesonychoteuthis hamiltoni*) currently on display in a museum in New Zealand.[108] Since the 1960s, cryptozoology circles apply the term 'globster' to unidentified organic specimens that wash up on coasts, although DNA testing has regularly identified these mysterious beached specimens as nothing more than masses of blubber from decaying whale carcasses.[109] Discussions about the possible existence of sea serpents still rely on observations by 'reliable' witnesses, but proof of the existence of water monsters living in Loch Ness, Lake Champlain and elsewhere are the, as yet, unattained holy grail of cryptozoology.

Fearsome monsters lurk beneath the unexplored waters of the earth on early maps and embody the uncertainty of humans who penetrate an unknown environment. However, identifying them and lodging them safely within a scientific framework fails to explain away the fear of many-tentacled monsters appearing from the deep. Scylla and Charybdis, primordial monsters mentioned by Hesiod, predate kraken sightings, yet the descriptions of sailors plucked almost at random by long snake-like appendages or sucked into whirl-pools are remarkably similar. Tennyson described the latent horrific power of the kraken's 'ancient, dreamless uninvaded sleep' beneath the 'abysmal sea' (1830), and illustrations of an outsized, but often realistically drawn, cephalo-pod attacking the Nautilus appeared in editions of Jules Verne's novel, *Twenty Thousand Leagues Under the Sea* (1870–1972).[110] Although early sources were keen to point out that, like the biblical Leviathans, there were never more than two krakens; they resurface in horror films, science fiction, fantasy, role play and computer games in ever-greater numbers. In *Lovecraft*'s Cthulu mythos, they are peculiarly nasty elder gods, while Tolkien's 'Watcher in the Water' preserves the nameless undefined horror of the original beast. The evil, cephalopod-headed Davy Jones releases and eventually kills a kraken in the *Pirates of the Caribbean* films, *Dead Man's Chest* and *At World's End* (Gore Verbinski, 2006, 2007). A kraken-like squid attacks San Francisco when the earth's ecological balance is disturbed by a nuclear blast in *It Came from Beneath the Sea* (Robert Gordon, 1955). The anxieties of the Cold War perme-ate John Wyndham's novel, *The Kraken Wakes* (1953), in which alien invaders emerge from the vastness of outer space to inspire the same fear as ancient sea monsters. China Miéville's *Kraken* (2010) updates the horror with disap-pearing museum exhibits, cyberpunk villains, strange squid-worshipping cults and assaults on the integrity of science. Without stretching the comparisons too far, one can surely see the kraken's tentacled descendants in the machines operated by H. G. Wells's Martians in *War of the Worlds* (1898), the sentient robots of *The Matrix* (The Wachowski Brothers, 1999) and the parasitic crea-tures of the *Alien* films. No doubt, the kraken and its fellows will continue to embody our primeval fear of all that is squishy, malevolent and tentacled.[111]

In the context of the Jonah story, however, accurate identification of the creatures is less important than the meaning of the story itself. A ship carrying the soul to the afterlife attended by dolphins, symbols of renewal, gambolling in the water was a popular motif on Roman sarcophagi, and the story of Jonah with its promise of the Resurrection appeared on Christian tombs from Italy and North Africa.[112] In many early Christian depictions, a sea monster with a serpentine tail swallows Jonah, while Islamic illustrations typically depict a scaled fish. The Gerona *Beatus*, a tenth-century commentary on the Apocalypse, contains one of the earliest maps depicting sea monsters whose watery environment marks the boundary of the world. In this dangerous space, Jonah remains trapped inside the fish.[113] The Greek translation of the Bible used the general term *ketos* for the swallowing monster, but whale-like characteristics begin to emerge in Jan Brueghel the Elder's rendition of Jonah, painted about 1600, and a spouting, if rather ambiguous creature, raises it head in Carlo Antonio Tavella's version a century later (National Maritime Museum, Greenwich). In *Jonah and the Sea* (Smithsonian Institute Museum, Washington DC), painted by the nineteenth-century American artist Albert Pinkerton Ryder, the outline of the whale, although accurate, blends mysteriously with the sea itself.

The Irish hero Fráech, the son of a sidhe-woman, accepts a challenge to retrieve a branch from a rowen tree guarded by a serpentine water monster.[114] This beastly lake dweller is one of several that inhabit the deep lochs of Ireland and Scotland. Pliny links Keto, goddess of sea monsters and whales, with the story of Andromeda. He located the cult centre at Joppa (modern Jaffa), and claimed that visitors were shown the marks made by the chains with which Andromeda was bound to the rocks (*Natural History*, Bk 5, 69). Greek and Latin authors from the first to the fifth centuries CE identified various rocky promontories with the petrified remains of the monster, but the texts give few details about its appearance. There are numerous artistic renditions of this popular tale on Greek vases, Roman mosaics, paintings and statues from the Renaissance onwards. The monster may have a serpentine tail, webbed forelegs and either a snout or a horse-like head. Piero di Cosimo's version, now in the Uffizi, has mastodon-like tusks, while Edward Burne-Jones opts for a particularly sinuous sea serpent.

The final water-dwelling beast considered in this chapter is a curious hybrid creature. The heraldic *enfield* appears on the arms of the O'Kellys of Ui Maine. The origin tale concerns a strange animal that emerged from the sea to protect the corpse of an ancestor who died at the Battle of Clontarf. The enfield is a relatively rare armorial beast, which may be linked to the Irish word 'onchu' meaning water dog or otter. Even without this etymological link, a tradition about a protective water beast added prestige to the founding of an important Irish family.[115] A similar creature appears on tombstones in Co. Leitrim and may have subsequently become associated with local tales about women killed by a dobhar-chu (otter) while they washed clothes at the edge of the lake.[116] As a creature that lives on land and in water, the otter frequently has a double nature. When the land-dwelling princess Liban became a mermaid, her faithful hound became an otter, although, according to another Irish folktale, the off-spring of the otter-king and a human princess is an evil being who is eventually destroyed by its equally evil father.[117] The Tlingit, a North American tribe living on the western coast of Canada and the United States, fear the Kushtaka, the land-otter people, shape-shifters who captured mortals and held them in a kind of limbo where they slowly morphed into otter form. Children and victims of drowning were most at risk. Only a shaman could rescue these captives and shamanic rattles often included carvings of such beings.[118] Despite the cultural differences of these traditions, they reflect the obvious liminal and ambiguous nature of a creature that inhabits two environments.

Conclusion

The medieval map of Britain by Matthew Paris dismisses the Atlantic Ocean as a vast expanse containing nothing but sea monsters.[119] Despite his distinctly land-based perspective, traditions about the sea creatures, monstrous or not, demonstrate a dynamism that is characteristic of fantastic creatures, and they fulfil a multitude of functions. The changing perception of Sedna is a case in point. Traditional Inuit cosmology continues to shape contemporary renditions of this figure, but in contemporary art, Sedna has become increasingly mermaid-like. Both Mélusine and Serek-A are ancestor figures, one operating within the context of European romance, and the other in the mythology of indigenous South American cultures. The qualities passed by the siren to the mermaid include song, knowledge of the future, a link with the sea and an ambiguous relationship with all who use it. Mami Wata has absorbed some mermaid characteristics, and a growing body of material, particularly on internet sites associated with goddess culture and other forms of modern spirituality, reinterpret these figures in terms of a universal 'goddess'. These developments have provided a wealth of new meanings and metaphors to enrich the traditions surrounding mythical sea creatures.

We continue to believe that legendary beings such as mermaids, iara and the boto can interact with humans, affect the weather and bring good or bad luck. Authors like Pliny questioned the existence of some of these creatures, while repeating what are essentially legends about others. During the nineteenth century, the sea serpent was simultaneously the focus of serious consideration about its place in a developing hierarchy of animal species, and a target for satire and disbelief. Changes in our perception of the environment have made the relations between human and non-human worlds more contentious in several important ways. From our modern perspective of environmental concern and mistrust of industrial exploitation, it would be too easy to underestimate the complexity of the discourse surrounding our response to creatures that never existed or to real animals whose nature has been mythologized. It would also be a mistake to give the impression that Western thinking has eliminated the fabulous in favour of the scientific or that non-Western cultures automatically view the world in a more holistic way.

This chapter has considered a range of water-dwelling denizens. Significant themes and patterns have emerged, although by no means all the extensive folklore of aquatic shape-shifters, encounters with sea monsters and sightings of sea serpents could be included. Contemporary attitudes have added new layers rather than destroyed old ones. Whale hunting continues, but Pliny's fierce killer whale has given way to a greater appreciation of the complex mammal that is the orca. Marvellous creatures were once a symbol of God's ordered world, but monstrous ones went against nature. Later these creatures were explained in terms of natural phenomena as part of a rational appreciation, and ultimate control, of the world around us. This disenchantment of nature, for some at least, created a void and some of us still search for sea serpents and hope to hear the mermaid's song.

3

Things with wings: The creatures of the air

All foutherly this Griffeth horse doth flie
ORLANDO FURIOSO, TRANSLATED BY SR. JOHN HARRINGTON (1634)

Leonardo da Vinci's design for an elegant bird-like flying machine embodies the forward-looking genius of the iconic Renaissance engineer, but the tantalizing legend that he actually tried to fly his machine appeals to our earthbound fascination with flight. According to medieval legend, Alexander the Great anticipated Leonardo by several centuries by chaining griffins to his chair, thereby creating an ingenious flying machine. Legends such as these remind us that wings provide access to an environment that humans cannot reach without artificial aid.

Fabulous birds and bird-like hybrids are a universal cultural phenomenon. The biblical Psalms briefly mention a gigantic bird, the Ziz, whose wings, like those of its cousins, the Persian *simurgh* and the gigantic Roc, enable it to overcome the boundaries of earth. Elsewhere, culture heroes in bird form create the world, and travellers' tales about harpies, griffins and other winged beings inhabiting exotic places abound. The wings of the harpy, the siren and the serpent add to the terrifying appearance of these fabulous creatures, while the phoenix and the halcyon symbolize new life and peace. Winged creatures can serve as protectors for those they guard. The winged Pegasus adds the power of flight to the swiftness and power of the horse. Equine–eagle hybrids, like griffins, are especially impressive where the economic and military power of the horse has important cultural value, and the fierceness of predator birds adds to their impact. The hippogriff, who combined the power of both horse and griffin, was the favoured mount of the heroes in Ariosto's *Orlando furioso*.

Angels of course are winged and fairies have been able to fly at least since the nineteenth century, but neither of these are hybrid animals. Many dragons have wings, but some of them also breathe fire and live under the earth or in the oceans, and they have been given a chapter of their own.

Harpies and sirens

Odysseus and Jason, leaders of famous voyages, encounter and outwit sirens. Odysseus has his men stop their ears with wax, while the ever-curious wanderer straps himself to the mast so he can safely hear the sirens' song (Homer, *The Odyssey*, Bk 12). The siren incident in *The Odyssey* was a popular subject in art, and these Greek sirens are always of the winged type. A Greek vase from c. 500 BCE shows Odysseus tied to the ship's mast listening to two sirens playing instruments while a dolphin (a symbol for death and resurrection) dives downwards. On another ancient Greek vase, the sirens themselves are diving into the sea, presumably in the throes of suicidal despair because the hero has escaped. *The Argonautica*, a third-century BCE epic by Apollonius of Rhodes, recounts the adventures of Jason and his companions, the Argonauts, as they search for the Golden Fleece. They pass the home of the half-bird and half-female sirens that prey, vulture-like, on the ships that sail beneath their rocks. Fortunately, for the Argonauts, Orpheus' sweet music drowns out the sirens' song, demonstrating that the civilized and harmonious music of Greek civilization is stronger than the raucous sounds of untamed nature. Apollonius included a motif, common in other traditional voyage tales, namely the death of someone who ignores a warning. One of the Argonauts foolishly listens to the sirens' song rather than to Orpheus, which causes him to leap into the sea and drown (Bk 4, lines 892 ff.).

The song of the winged sirens promised knowledge, and singing is their cosmological function in the Myth of Er that occurs at the end of Plato's *The Republic* (Bk 10). A Roman wall painting from Pompeii (first century CE) in which Odysseus sails past winged sirens playing music atop a high cliff, while the shattered skeletons of their victims litter the rocks below, hints at the inherent danger of prophetic knowledge. Men died after listening to the sirens because they forgot their real lives, so it is fitting that death was the sirens' eventual fate after Odysseus escaped.

A bird with a female head obligingly identifies herself as 'Siren Eimi' ('I am a siren') on a Greek vase painting, and a small human figure rides a sixth-century BCE *askos*, a kind of oil lamp, which is shaped like a winged siren holding a pomegranate and pan pipes. The object, possibly intended as a tomb offering, evokes the ideas of death, music and a spirit being who conveys souls to the afterlife. The connection with a funeral votive such as this suggests that one of the sirens' functions was that of a psychopomp who leads souls into the afterlife.[1] Classical sirens with their bird-like attributes have something in common with another supernatural bird-woman, the harpy. Both are associated with storms at sea, but one sings melodiously, while the other has a harsh voice. The similarities can cause confusion in visual contexts. An elaborate tomb from Lycia in Asia Minor, often called the 'Harpy tomb', dates back to the fifth century BCE. It is adorned with bird-like creatures with women's breasts and faces that carry small, female figures. One interpretation of this monument suggests that the scene depicts the harpies who, according to Homer, carried off the daughters of King Pandareus to become handmaidens to the Furies. However, the appearance of these bird-like creatures on a tomb suggests that they are not the devouring creatures of Greek epic, but benevolent sirens cradling the dead as they carry them into the afterlife.[2]

A key feature of the sirens is the sound of their singing. Homer's account of how Odysseus stopped his men's ears with wax (*Odyssey* Bk 12) is perhaps the most widely known tradition about them. The Argonauts in Apollonius' Greek epic (*Argonautica*, Bk 4) escaped the sirens because Orpheus drowned out their singing with his music, suggesting perhaps that his music is stronger than death. Plato echoes this when he places the sirens in the cosmic sphere as singers of pure music. Other traditions, however, focus on their wings and their connection with water. Originally, they received the power of flight as handmaidens of Persephone to help them search for the young goddess kidnapped by Hades. Eventually the sirens lost their wings, either because they drowned themselves in despair when Odysseus escaped, or lost their feathers after they challenged the Muses to a singing contest, and, shorn of their plumage, they plunged into the sea (Ovid, *Metamorphoses* Bk 5, 294–331). In these accounts, the sirens are originally creatures of the air who become creatures of the sea, namely mermaids.

Both sirens and harpies reflect the violence of stormy seas, although the harpy screeches, the siren's song is beautiful. The latter feature in the *Argonautica* as tormentors of Phineus, king of Thrace, a prophet who revealed too much. The angry gods blinded him and exiled him to an island where harpies tormented him and stole the food laid out for him. Another winged pair, the *Boreads* Calaïs and Zetes, were the sons of Boreas, the North Wind. They were among the Argonauts who accompanied Jason on his voyage. When they arrived at Phineus's island, Calaïs and Zetes drove the harpies from their feast and threatened them with destruction. The Argonauts spared the harpies' lives because their sister, Iris, goddess of the rainbow, promised that the torment would cease. The grateful Phineus tells the Argonauts how to avoid further dangers on their journey, and the harpies finally settled on the Strophades Islands in the Ionian Sea (*Argonautica*, Bk 2, l. 262–300).

Originally, harpies were the offspring of sea and weather deities, and they personified winds and storms, although their name derives from the Greek word *harpezein* meaning 'snatcher'. Thaumas, an ancient sea god, and his wife Electra, who was associated with clouds, are appropriate parents for the stormy whirlwind aspect of the harpies and for their sister, the rainbow goddess Iris, since rainbows typically follow storms. The conflict between the winged Boreads and the harpies further emphasizes the connection with violent weather. Harpies appeared as female-headed birds of prey, or as winged women with unbound hair. This is the form they take on a piece of Greek pottery from the fifth century BCE which shows Phineus being tormented by winged female harpies on the one side and acknowledging the Boreads as his saviours on the other.

Harpies are linked with another set of female supernatural beings associated with retribution and the dead, namely the Furies. Sometimes the harpies were a trio of women with avian attributes, called Aello (Storm Swift), Celaeno (Dark) and Podarge (Fleet Foot). In this guise, they were known as the 'hounds of Zeus'. Over time, however, they took on the more monstrous appearance of carrion birds with women's faces. They were insatiably hungry, constantly screeching and filthy in both their appearance and personal habits. In short, they polluted everything they touched. Virgil described them as vultures with women's faces. Even so, they retained some of the prophetic ability they shared with the sirens. After disrupting the Trojans' feast on the Strophades Islands, Celaeno, the leader of the harpies, prophesied that the Trojans would suffer hunger and tribulation before they reached Italy (*Aeneid*, Bk 3). Renaissance literature, as one would expect, followed the classical model of harpies as monstrous creatures with female heads and torsos, and with the clawed talons and the bodies of birds. According to Dante's description of the wood of the suicides in the *Inferno* (canto XIII), harpies make their nests in the trees that enclose the bodies of those who have taken their own lives. Prospero comments ironically on the gracefulness of Ariel's harpy disguise as he torments the scheming, shipwrecked nobles in Shakespeare's *The Tempest* 'Bravely the figure of this harpy hast thou Perform'd, my Ariel; a grace it had, devouring:' (Act III, sc. iii).

Male and female harpies appear in medieval church carvings as warnings against greed, or as embodiments of monstrosity and all that deviated from the natural order. A gargoyle in the form of a male harpy, probably dating back to the thirteenth century, adorns Cologne Cathedral, while a demonic harpy shoots a dragon in a marginal drollery in the Hours of Charles the Bold.[3] Occasionally, angels appear with feather-covered bodies as well as wings, rather like benevolent male harpies, in medieval ecclesiastical art.[4] Male sirens in bird form appear in bestiaries, as does an extraordinary harpy-like creature called the *serra* or *sawfish*, a destructive, winged sea monster that destroyed ships.[5] Links between harpies, sirens and extreme weather seem to provide the context for this identification, which continued even after the bestiaries ceased to be an important source for meaning. As late as the eighteenth century, a pamphlet identified an amphibious monster seen off the coast of Spain as a 'harpy'.[6]

An illustration of a human-headed harpy with an eagle's body appeared in a late fifteenth-century edition of *Hortus sanitatis* (The Garden of Health), the most popular herbal of its time, and two influential seventeenth-century works, Ulisse Aldrovandi's history of monsters, *Monstrorum Historia* and John Johnston's *Historiae naturalis* similarly depict harpies with human female heads on realistic eagle bodies.[7] Male harpies were common on Sasanian seals as symbols of the power of the Sasanian kings. The Sasanian Empire covered a vast area stretching from what is now Iran and Iraq, northwards to Afghanistan and westwards into Central Asia. Zoroastrianism was the dominant religion in a culture that flourished from the third to the seventh centuries CE and witnessed the flowering of Persian civilization. Like so many fantastic creatures, the harpy absorbed elements from a variety of sources and carried a range of meanings. Harpies were usually female in medieval Islamic art and literature. They shared a talent for music and prophecy with their Western counterparts and carried a generally positive message.[8] The *kinnarris*, half woman and half bird, was associated with divine music, and is noted for wisdom. Harpy-like creatures playing instruments appear in Islamic manuscripts with crowned female heads on colourful peacock-like bodies. In the Alexander legends, which were popular throughout Europe and Asia, the great king asks these wise creatures for advice. They were a common decorative device as bringers of luck on a variety of objects such as ceramics, and they adorn the walls of palaces and other important buildings, especially during the Seljuk period (eleventh to thirteenth centuries), in Turkey and elsewhere in the Middle East. A woodcut based on the drawings of Turkish life and customs by the sixteenth-century Danish artist and traveller, Melchior Lorck, depicts an elaborate version of a peacock harpy.[9]

Literary accounts of harpies recorded in classical and medieval epics provided inspiration for later artists. The *Boreads Chasing the Harpies* by Jan Erasmus Quellinus (1630) hangs in the Prado Museum, Spain. A fourteenth-century copy of Dante's *Divine Comedy,* owned by the Earls of Leicester, contains an illustration of Dante and Virgil's encounter with the harpies, which are birds with female heads.[10] The confrontation between Dante, Virgil and the harpies inspired illustrators of the *Divine Comedy* as divergent as Sandro Botticelli, Gustave Doré and Salvador Dali. Illustrations such as these show the harpies as opponents of the heroes, but they also had symbolic, as well as narrative, associations. In the 1820s, William Blake drew them as owl-like creatures with human faces and women's breasts. The harpies evoke greed in all its aspects in the satirical drawings that make up Francisco Goya's *Los Caprichos* (1868). The image of the harpy, as drawn by both Blake and Goya, takes on aspects of the witch haunting the night in company with other demonic forces rather than classical avengers stealing food. In the sixteenth century, Andrea del Sarto painted a striking altarpiece, now in the Uffizi Gallery, known as the *Madonna of the Harpies* in which the Virgin and Child stand on a classical pedestal adorned with carved harpies. In this context, they may be a symbol of the triumph of Christianity over death. The legendary special effects creator Ray Harryhausen gave the harpies cinematic life in *Jason and the Argonauts* (Don Chaffey, 1963). His dramatic stop-motion animation figures with their bat-wings and dark bodies anticipate the more gothic nature and appearance of both the harpy and the siren in contemporary culture.

In art, film and literature, the harpy appears as a monstrous female creature with some of the sexual overtones of the siren. For Norwegian artist Edvard Munch, the harpy, as drawn in a lithograph of 1898, signified a death-like sexual predation. The Belgian filmmaker Raoul Servais also reworked the idea of a destructive femme fatale in his film *Harpya* (1979) in which a man innocently rescues a harpy only to find himself overwhelmed by her insatiable appetite. The strange human-headed bird of the film echoes the drawings found in earlier sources such as Ulisse Aldrovandi's *Monstrorum Historia* (Bologna, 1642) in which a woman's head with flowing hair is placed, rather awkwardly, on an eagle-like body.

Fantasy illustration and comic book art have played a significant role in the development of computer games and RPGs, and the exaggerated female attributes of harpies in the work of contemporary fantasy and comic book artists like Frank Frazetta and Boris Vallejo embody the harpy's overtly sexual and predatory aspect.[11] In *World of Warcraft* (2004, Blizzard Entertainment), harpies are winged females with talons for feet. They feature in many other RPGs as well as in anime films, manga art and the fan art and merchandizing that accompany these phenomena. RPGs have become massively popular since their introduction in the 1970s. The beasts that appear, mostly as opponents to the players, are usually based on existing mythical monsters. They are also marketed as collectible figures and other forms of merchandise, and they appear in the fan artwork and additional storylines that players contribute to the virtual communities attached to these games. One of the most interesting features of these monsters is the way their appearance changes as the games develop and the scenarios become more complex. The harpy is a good example of the way they can change in this important and rapidly developing environment. As one of the first beasts introduced to *Dungeons & Dragons*, it appears in the original Monster Manual for *Advanced Dungeons & Dragons*. In early illustrations, it resembles the humanoid creature with wings described by Pliny and Ovid and pictured in Ulisse Aldrovandi's *Monstrorum Historia*.[12] However, in other games, such as *World of Warcraft*, one of the most popular massively multiplayer online RPGs, harpies have become more aggressively female and new types of harpy-like monsters with a range of hybrid features, such as reptilian or insect heads, have appeared. Supplementary handbooks, which, like the medieval bestiaries, explain the various characters' roles, can be purchased to accompany these games.

The fantasy writers Peter S. Beagle and Philip Pullman present a more nuanced picture of the harpy while retaining their classical characteristics. Beagle introduces the harpy, Celaeno, in his fantasy *The Last Unicorn* (1968). The unicorn discovers that she and Celaeno are the only 'real' mythical creatures held captive by a sorceress, unlike the other creatures in this prison-zoo that are ordinary animals under a spell to make them look like mythical creatures. Once freed, Celaeno takes on the character of a winged Fury and kills their tormentor. Harpies figure as guardians of the underworld in Philip Pullman's fantasy trilogy, *His Dark Materials*. In an echo of their classical role as sirens, Lyra (*The Amber Spyglass*, 2000) persuades them to lead the spirits of the dead to a more peaceful afterlife.

In heraldry, the harpy, sometimes referred to as the 'maiden eagle', is a vulture with a woman's head and neck, and it recalls the bird form of the siren as well. This device, carrying weapons and a shield, appears on early images of the arms of the Polish city of Kraków. The figure, known as La Sirena, evokes the classical bird-form of the siren. Her ferocity is protective rather than threatening, and she acts both as a symbol of the city's power and as a protector of its residents. In early depictions, she has a classical form with wings and claws, but over time, she has become more mermaid-like and now sports a fish tail. Like her classical forbears, Kraków's Sirena has evolved into a mermaid.

The griffin and its kin

The harpies, sirens and Furies seem originally to have been winged divine females, and they retained elements of their human characteristics and appearance over time. The griffin or gryphon, however, is a hybrid based completely on animals with the body of a lion and the head and wings of an eagle. The name may derive from Latin *grypho* (to grasp?) or Greek *grypos* (curved). Sometimes the eagle aspect dominates with the entire forepart of this animal resembling a raptor with curved beak, talons, wings and feathers. At other times, it is a leonine-like quadruped with an eagle's head and wings. Its heraldic form, called an *opinicus*, is popular in art and heraldry. Some

FIGURE 3.1 *Sebastian Munster's description of the griffin quotes the classical writer Aelian, one of the oldest authorities on the existence of these mythical beasts.*

griffins have dog-like ears, which may be an influence from the canine aspect of the Persian simurgh, a similar composite of bird and quadruped (Figure 3.1).

Bird-lion hybrids appear in Ancient Mesopotamian and Egyptian art from as early as 3000 BCE. They occur in pairs to reflect the struggle between opposing forces, and act as companions to deities or guardians of sacred places. Paired and flanking entrances, they seem at once to warn and protect, like the leonine quadrupeds with crests and stylized wings, dated back to c. 1700 BCE, who lie recumbent, like peaceful guardians, on either side of the 'throne room' at Knossos in Crete. The griffin was also associated with Apollo. The Greek *Physiologus*, a compendium of bird and animal symbolism, describes a pair of griffins who catch the rays of the morning sun, echoing both the sun-god Apollo and the ancient guardian solar griffins.[13]

In Greek mythology, griffins inhabit a gold-rich country close to Scythia (southern Ukraine) or India. The Hereford *mappa mundi*, which presented a detailed visual representation of the medieval world at the beginning of the fourteenth century, depicted the griffin fighting with a humans figure on the eastern section of the map among other exotic curiosities. Griffins guarding treasure appeared in illustrated accounts of the wonders of the world,[14] and griffins attacking horses were a frequent motif on Scythian gold objects. The battle between griffins and neighbouring equestrians, who attempted to steal the griffins' gold, is one of the oldest traditions associated with these beasts. According to Herodotus, the struggle for gold is the basis for the hostility between the horse and the griffin (*Histories*, Bks 3.116.1; 4.13.1, 27.1; 79.1, 152.4). His account quotes an even older, possibly fictional, source, namely a poem written by Aristeas of Prokonnesos who travelled the world in the seventh century BCE. A modern fantasy novel, *Beyond the North Wind*, by Gillian Bradshaw (1993) reworks the 'lost' tale of Aristeas as a historical fantasy.

The setting provides an unusual background in which the Aristaeus character is a young magician who embarks on an odyssey where modern virtues like compassion and wisdom allow him to save the last tribe of griffins.

Other classical writers included griffin lore. Ctesias, in the *Indica*, a compilation of geographic and travel lore written in the fourth century BCE, locates treasure-guarding griffins in India (*Indica* quoted by Photius, *Myriobiblon* fragment 72). Similarly, Aelian, writing in the second century CE, describes the winged, lion-like Indian griffin guarding his gold hoard in his mountain lair (*On Animals*, Bk 4, 27). Pliny the Elder's *Natural History*, written in the first century CE (Bk 7, 10), synthesized this information and provided a major source for subsequent descriptions, notably the encyclopaedia written by Isidore of Seville in the seventh century. He characterizes the griffin as a feathered quadruped with the body of a lion that is intrinsically hostile to both men and horses (*Etymologies*, Bk 12, 2:17). Much the same description appears in the thirteenth-century account of Bartholomew Anglicus, who adds that the griffin's egg protects against poison (*De Proprietatibus Rerum*, Bk 12). In medieval bestiaries, the griffin is often depicted carrying a large animal, like an ox, in its claws.

Not every classical authority accepted the reality of griffins. Both Pliny and Strabo questioned their existence, while exploration and the rise of natural history writing based on first-hand observation further undermined the belief. In a description of the northern world published in 1518, the Polish writer Matias Michovius found no evidence for the griffin.[15] Ulisse Aldrovandi reinforced this scepticism in 1599 by including griffins in his list of fabulous birds, and Thomas Browne's *Popular Errors* (1646) devoted an entire chapter to disproving their existence (Bk 3, ch. 11). Sceptics explained the griffin as a misunderstanding of some large bird, such as an eagle, although one nineteenth-century antiquary, John Timbs, attributed it to a misunderstanding of the South American tapir.[16] Griffins were not without their defenders (Figure 3.1). In *Arcana Microcosmi* (1652), Alexander Ross, chaplain to Charles I, vigorously defended 'ancient' writings, both classical and scriptural, concerning the griffin against the secular disbelief of scientific upstarts. Griffins' eggs and claws, in reality ostrich eggs and exotic animal horns, appear in the collections of medieval and Renaissance curiosities that were the forerunner of museums.[17] More recently, the classical scholar Adrienne Mayor suggested that dinosaur fossils from Central Asia gave rise to stories about griffins as guardians of gold treasure. She points out that fossils are frequently associated with gold-bearing ores, and that dinosaurs like the *Protoceratops* with its beak-headed profile, which resembles that of a griffin, laid eggs in nests.[18]

In the medieval *Romance of Alexander*, the king creates a flying machine by harnessing griffins to a chair and suspending chunks of meat just out of the griffins' reach, so that they flew upwards lured by the bait. This episode provided an implicit warning against pride, and it featured in manuscript illustrations and on misericord carvings.[19] In a thirteenth-century *chanson de geste*, *Huon of Bordeaux*, a griffin carries Huon to its nest where the mother bird attacks the hero for killing her nestlings. Later, Huon presents the Emperor Charlemagne with a griffin's claw. Such literary references emphasize the wildness and strength of a creature, which can only be defeated by heroic forces. Huon's peril in the griffin's nest shares elements with the adventure of Sinbad who also battles the Roc.[20]

The half-eagle, half-lion type of griffin became popular in Greek art about the eighth century BCE as an adornment in pottery, metalwork and architecture. As a combination of eagle and lion, kings of birds and beasts, respectively, the griffin was a symbol for royalty and courage, while its size and the magic stone egg, which repelled poison, associated it with protection, both literal and figurative. Griffins were carved on Greek and Roman tombs as symbolic guardians of the dead. Herodotus described a bronze vessel in the temple of Hera adorned with griffins' heads, and Strabo, writing in the first century CE, mentions a painting of the goddess Artemis borne aloft by griffins.[21] Neither of these antiquities survives, but the griffins adorn numerous examples of classical art, and they remained a popular literary device. Their significance, however, varied considerably. In Dante Alighieri's *Divine Comedy*, Beatrice flies to paradise on a griffin to lead Dante on the final stage of his journey (*Purgatorio*, Canto 29, 31). The hybrid nature of the griffin in this context suggests the dual nature of Christ's humanity and divinity.[22] By contrast, John Milton's *Paradise Lost* demonstrates how ambiguous the significance of fantastic creatures can be. Milton invokes the legend of the griffin's pursuit of its stolen gold as a metaphor for Satan's relentless pursuit of humanity (Bk 2, 943–50). The heraldic griffin's fierce protective nature is a positive characteristic, and it is usually depicted standing with one leg raised and claws displayed, a *sergeant* posture in heraldic terminology. The merchant guilds of Perugia advertised their reputation for safe trading with a griffin *sergeant* on a bale of cloth. It remains a popular heraldic device and symbol for industry to this day. In the 1960s, the Midland Bank adopted a golden griffin surrounded by gold coins, which echoed the classical griffin as the careful guardian of a precious hoard. The company logo of the Vauxhall Motor Company is still the griffin – here no doubt as a symbol of speed and power, the company website proudly sets out the details of its heritage.[23]

Griffins feature in modern fantasy literature and in role-playing and video games. Although they fight in Aslan's army in *The Chronicles of Narnia* (1939–49) and the young king Arthur and Kay battle a griffin with the help of Robin Hood in T. H. White's *The Once and Future King* (1958), their fierceness tends to dissipate in the context of fantasy and children's literature. Far from showing enmity for humans, these, now gentle, creatures become the means for characters to discover their own identities.[24] Lewis Carroll's *Alice's Adventure in Wonderland* (1865) gently satirized the dual nature of the griffin who speaks half to itself and half to Alice. Friendship between a human and this mythical creature is the subject of Frank Stockton's *The Griffin and the Minor Canon* (1885). The last griffin, old, wise, vain and initially without human emotions, leaves his wilderness home to admire his carved image above the door of the Minor Canon's church. Despite his own kindly nature, the Canon struggles against difficult circumstances and the prejudices of the townspeople. When the frightened populace drive the Canon into the wilderness, the griffin, inspired by his friendship with the good priest, takes his place as schoolmaster and as minister to the poor and the sick. The two characters change places for a time, but they never become identified. Although their attitude towards the Canon changes, the townspeople never really appreciate his simple goodness or the mystery of the griffin. Nor does the griffin ever become a sentimentalized fantasy creature. He loves and admires the Canon, but expresses this as a desire to make him his equinox meal. Stockton's poignant but rather dark fairy tale does not allow the 'otherness' of the griffin to be resolved in the human world and the last griffin slowly fades away, his gaze fixed on his immutable, but passionless, stone image.[25]

Among the antiquities in the British Museum is a Corinthian drinking cup (c. 600 BCE) decorated with three winged mythical creatures: a griffin, a siren and a sphinx. The winged sphinx fits into a discussion on flying creatures despite the fact that the earliest example of this mythical creature, the Great Sphinx at Giza, is a wingless couchant lion with a human head.[26] Sphinx-like creatures with wings, leonine bodies and male heads appear on Mesopotamian seals and amulets.[27] Like griffins and other lion-hybrids, sphinxes, such as the ones that decorate the walls of the palace of King Darius the Great at Susa, guard and protect the entrances of temples and palaces. Female sphinxes are perhaps the most common. By the eighth century BCE, the sphinx was both a votive offering and a grave marker in Greece, suggesting that its function, like other winged female hybrids, was to guard and protect the dead. The citizens of Naxos in the sixth century BCE offered the temple of Delphi a marble sphinx perched on a tall column with stylized curved wings and a characteristic archaic smile. The Greek writer, Aelian, in the second century CE claimed that the sphinx's form expressed her double nature. 'Egyptian artificers in their sculpture, and the vainglorious legends of Thebes attempt to represent the Sphinx, with her two-fold nature, as of two-fold shape, making her awe-inspiring by fusing the body of a maiden with that of a lion' (*On Animals*, Bk. 12, 7). The winged sphinx may have diffused into Asian cultures during the period when Hellenistic influence appears in Buddhist art. Placed high on temple buildings, it serves an apotropaic function, thereby retaining something of its original purpose.[28]

The Theban sphinx who challenges Oedipus to solve a riddle in Sophocles's play *Oedipus Rex* is one of the best-known examples, and the name, sphinx, first appeared in Greek sources. Although the original meaning is not clear, one suggestion links it to an Egyptian term meaning 'living image'. It is one of the monsters listed in Hesiod's *Theogony* (*Theogony* 326 ff.), either as the offspring of the Chimaera and Orphos, a two-headed, serpent-tailed dog, or the half-woman, half-serpent hybrid, Echidna. The sphinx's dwelling is in the mountains of Ethiopia, the most remote and exotic corner of the earth in classical Greek cosmology.[29] Whatever her parentage, the creature, usually a female with wings, is associated with the chthonic deities before the ascendancy of the Olympian gods, and therefore she can both threaten and protect. Like so many mythic narratives, the meaning of the sphinx and her riddle is multifaceted. According to Diodorus of Sicily (*Library of History*, Bk 4, ch. 64. 3–4), the Olympian gods sent the creature to Thebes in revenge for impiety, and she devoured anyone who could not solve the riddle. When Oedipus presented the correct solution, the sphinx committed suicide, like the sirens after their confrontation with Odysseus. Neutralizing the raison d'etre of these mythic creatures seems to render them harmless. Unlike other monstrous beings, such as the sirens, the sea monster known as *ketos* and the Chimaera who confronted various Greek heroes, the sphinx had the power of speech. This enabled her to develop into a more complex and ambiguously shaded figure. She is a hybrid with a cannibal nature, but she is also a wise virginal creature. It is the sphinx who poses the riddle of life, namely what creature walks on four legs in the morning, two in the afternoon and three at night to which the answer is man himself, who, during the course of his life, crawls, walks and hobbles with the aid of a stick.

With the revival of classical learning in the thirteenth century, the ambiguous notion of wisdom associated with the sphinx and its link to the mysteries of Egypt appeared in new contexts. Two thirteenth-century examples, a smiling female and a serious male, guard the entrance to the cloister of San Giovanni Lateran in Rome. The models for these sphinxes were probably Roman copies of Egyptian originals.[30] A fifteenth-century misericord from Limerick Cathedral may depict a winged male sphinx, while the Hereford *mappa mundi* described it very specifically as 'avis est penna, serpens pede, fronte puella' (bird with feathers, serpents' feet and a woman's breast).[31] Towards the end of the Renaissance, the Jesuit scholar, Athanasius Kircher, published his translation of Egyptian hieroglyphs. The frontispiece of his confident, if misplaced, attempt to decipher the wisdom of Egypt, *Oedipus Aegyptiacus*, depicted the triumphant Greek hero confounding the sphinx with his learning.[32] As travel to Egypt and the Middle East increased and ancient texts became more generally available, the sphinx began to reflect European orientalist fantasies, and it soon adorned landscaped gardens, fountains, buildings and all manner of luxury objects.

Often these adornments emphasized the feminine attributes of the sphinx rather than her role as a winged guardian. Shakespeare describes the effects of love as 'subtle as Sphinx' (*Love's Labour's Lost* Act III, sc. iii), and four well-endowed sphinxes support the sixteenth-century tomb at the Chateau d'Anet of the famously beautiful and enigmatic Diane de Poitiers, mistress of King Henri II of France.[33]

In Alciato's *Book of Emblems* (no 88), the sphinx has the face of a young female, feathered wings and a lion's body. The text poses the question: 'What monster is that?' The answer is – 'the Sphinx', which, in a reversal of her classical role, is equated with ignorance rather than wisdom.[34] In other contexts, the sphinx retains her symbolic association with wisdom. Two sphinxes flank the Madonna and her son on Donatello's bronze *Madonna and Child* (1448) in the Basilica di Sant'Antonio, Padua, and a small sphinx accompanies St Bridget of Sweden on a marble relief by Agostino di Muccio (c. 1459), now in the New York Metropolitan Museum of Art. St Bridget had a reputation for prophetic visions as well as piety, and the sphinx may reflect this preternatural wisdom. Over time, the sphinx's wings became less important than her ability to embody the exotic. Jean Cocteau's *The Infernal Machine* (1934) which reinterpreted Sophocles's play, *Oedipus Rex*, incorporates typical Cocteau themes of fate, free will and the nature of identity. The sphinx in Cocteau's play has become a world-weary immortal seeking release from her fate by falling in love with a human. Both Lord Dunsany and Oscar Wilde silence the sphinx's voice. In Lord Dunsany's 'The House of the Sphinx' (1918) and again in 'The Secret of the Sphinx' (1947), the creatures are brooding, but strangely silent. In Oscar Wilde's poem, 'The Sphinx', (1894) the 'exquisite grotesque' is the companion of other fantastic creatures, basilisks, griffins, dragons and hippogriffs, but here too, she remains a silent menace, and the poem's speaker asks the questions.

The opposition of the mysterious feminine quality of the sphinx and the masculine heroic world implicit in the Oedipus story became a metaphor in nineteenth-century art for the artist's struggle against materialism, embodied in the threatening feminine otherness of the sphinx. In Auguste Ingres's depiction of the Oedipus myth (*Oedipus Explaining the Enigma of the Sphinx*, 1808), the sphinx lurks in the shadows. By contrast, *The Caresses of the Sphinx* (1896) by the Belgian symbolist artist Fernand Khnopff shows her as a cheetah with a woman's head, dominant enough to take over the canvas and relegate Oedipus to the edge. Symbolist art embraced the ambiguity of the sphinx as both an enigmatic purveyor of wisdom and a destructive femme fatale. Franz von Stuck painted her as an aggressive attacker in *The Kiss of the Sphinx* (1895) and later dispensed with her animal attributes altogether transforming her as a rapaciously sexual, naked woman in a sphinx pose (*The Sphinx*, 1904). Gustave Moreau (1826–98) also painted the Oedipus myth several times; each painting seemingly emphasizes a different aspect of this complex symbolic creature. In his painting *Oedipus and the Sphinx* (1860), she confronts the hero directly. Indeed, she actually climbs up his body, despite the fact that she has impressive eagle wings, a triumphant embodiment of Alciato's emblematic female. Elsewhere, she is a feathered lioness glorying over the dead who cannot solve her riddle. Contrastingly, Moreau has also painted her falling to her death under the triumphant gaze of Oedipus.[35]

Winged horses and the hippogriff

The swift horses belonging to the hero Achilles were the offspring of Zephyrus, the god of the west wind, and the harpy, Podarge, and there is an obvious link between their parentage and their preternatural speed. Another wind god, Boreas, the North Wind, mysteriously fertilized mares that produced unusually swift horses that could run across a field of grain without bending the tips. On the night before the French defeat at Agincourt in Shakespeare's *Henry V* (Act II, sc. vi), the overconfident dauphin boasts that his horse 'trots the air' like Pegasus, the most famous mythical horse in classical tradition, who even has wings.

The earliest sources, notably Hesiod's seventh-century BCE *Theogony*, suggest that Poseidon fathered both Pegasus and his brother, the golden-youth Chrysaor, and that they were born from the blood of the decapitated Medusa (*Theogony* 270–90). The appearance of the constellation Pegasus in the night sky signals the rains of springtime, and the connection between the winged horse and the life-giving force of water is reinforced elsewhere. The possible meaning of the horse's name, 'springing forth', links the birth of Pegasus with the sources of the Ocean itself. The Muses's well of inspiration, the Hippocrene (horse fountain), on Mount Helicon in Boeotia was created when its hoof struck the mountain. Although the winged horse was eventually absorbed into the myth of Perseus, who killed Medusa, originally, Pegasus was the winged steed who carried Bellerophon during his fight with the Chimaera.[36]

Bellerophon, a demigod and another of Poseidon's offspring, receives a bridle from Athena in a dream. With it, he captures the winged horse as it drinks from the Pierine spring in Corinth. Mounted on Pegasus, he uses a lead-tipped spear to stab the Chimaera, a fire-breathing hybrid monster, whose fiery breath melts the lead-tip, quenching the fire and killing the beast. However, when Bellerophon attempts to ride his flying horse to the Olympian heights, the proud hero falls to earth, while Pegasus continues its flight to become Zeus's lightning-bringer, and a constellation associated with spring rains. Pegasus on his own, helping Bellerophon kill the Chimaera or emerging from the blood of the dead Medusa, appears in Greek, Roman and Christian arts from the seventh century BCE to the fourth century CE. The image of Chimaera and Pegasus continued as conventional art on objects such as coins and medallions for much longer.[37] Quenching unnatural fire and bringing life-giving spring rains are key motifs in the Pegasus story in Greek and Roman traditions, but over time, the significance changed. Some commentators speculate that by the fourth century CE, the depiction of Pegasus and Bellerophon in British mosaics may have become a Christian metaphor for the triumph over sin and the material world.[38]

Once Pegasus was associated with the fountain of the Muses, the flying horse became a symbol for poetic and spiritual inspiration as well as speed and rain-bringing weather. Poets drink from the Muses's fountain with Pegasus flying overhead in an early edition of Pliny. The winged horse appears twice in an illustrated fifteenth-century collection of the works of Christine de Pizan – once as a white horse with scarlet wings flying over the fountain of the Muses, and, in surely one of the earliest artistic depictions of the fusion of the Perseus and Bellerophon narratives, as the steed ridden by Perseus as he rescues Andromeda.[39] Sixteenth- and seventeenth-century commentaries on popular texts like *Ovide moralisé* and Boccaccio's *De Genealogia Deorum*, as well as woodcut illustrations for Ovid's work, influenced the changing role of Pegasus in the legends of Perseus and Bellerophon.[40]

In the eighteenth century, Pegasus provided a way to connect the classical past with the modernity of the Enlightenment world. The magnificent Pegasus Vase, presented by Josiah Wedgwood to the British Museum in 1786, encapsulates ideas of classical inspiration and modern refinement. Wedgwood based the figures of the winged horse drinking at the fountain surrounded by nymphs on engravings of ancient Greek vases, and these decorative images remained among the most popular designs on Wedgwood pottery.[41] The symbolism of Pegasus could also be adapted to political iconography. At the end of the seventeenth century, Louis XIV commissioned two equestrian statues of the winged horse surrounded by trophies of the king's military triumphs to glorify his prowess in war and peace. The statues are now in the Louvre, and there are copies in the Tuileries Garden. However, their original placement near the ornamental 'horse pond' at the royal residence of Chateau Marly outside Paris further emphasized the association of Pegasus with the fountain of the Muses and the continuity of this association from the glorious days of the classical world to the court of King Louis XIV.

For the symbolist artist Odilon Redon (1840–1916), the ascent of the winged horse signified humanity's struggle with the forces of darkness in order to emerge into a higher state of spiritual awareness, for which the role of Pegasus and his contribution to the defeat of the monstrous Chimaera was an apt symbol. The defeat of the monsters that represented ignorance and spiritual darkness embodied the idea of spiritual awakening. Redon incorporated Pegasus into a number of paintings and charcoal sketches, which referenced the classical Muses and the heroes, such as Perseus, Ruggiero from Ariosto's *Orlando* and Bellerophon, all of whom rode winged steeds. Pegasus perches on a mountaintop, tamed by Bellerophon, or ridden by the heroes Ruggiero, Perseus and Bellerophon as they defeat a monster. [42] The various symbolic contexts in which the winged horse appears in Redon's art reflect these important themes in his symbolist philosophy.

The film *Clash of the Titans* (Desmond Davis, 1981) combined the stories of Perseus and Bellerophon with motifs straight out of the *Arabian Nights*. Perseus must capture Pegasus before killing the gorgon Medusa. According to the film, the winged horse is the sole survivor of a herd belonging to Zeus killed by the satyr-like villain who has evil designs on the princess. Perseus rides Pegasus as he rescues the princess and uses the gorgon's head to turn the sea monster to stone. The winged horse continues as a significant theme in contemporary popular culture. An advertisement aired on British Television before the 2015 and 2016 Grand National, which aimed to attract a new audience to horse racing, combined Pegasus and the unicorn. Designed as an animated short film, it is set in a fantasy world of winged unicorns in which a 'dark horse', a rejected foal with a twisted horn and underdeveloped wings, learns to run as fast as the others can fly. He finally leaps into the modern world as the 'outsider' horse who wins the race.[43] The Grand National advertisement echoes a much earlier appearance of herds of winged horses in Disney's reinterpretation of Beethoven's 'Pastoral Symphony' in *Fantasia* (1939) where families of pegasi, unicorns and centaurs cavort as part of a charming classical idyll. In films like Disney's animated *Hercules* (Ron Clements and John Musker, 1997) or Rick Riordan's *Percy Jackson and the Olympians* series (2005–9), the winged horse acts as a companion to a central character. A Pegasus called Skylark is one of the hidden animals protected by the Society for the Protection of Mythical Creatures in Julia Golding's *Companions Quartet* (2006–7). These winged horses of fantasy novels continue to reflect Pegasus's role in the Bellerophon story; moreover, as in much contemporary fantasy fiction, the winged horse has acquired the power of speech, endowing it with the ability to give advice as well as share in the adventures.

The epic poem *Orlando furioso* by Ludovico Ariosto (1516–32) combined the winged horse and the griffin to create a new mythical beast, a hippogriff or hippogriffin that was half griffin and half horse (Figure 3.2). Ariosto's sprawling work drew on the earlier unfinished poetic romance of Matteo Maria Boiardo, *Orlando innamorato* (1495). The character Orlando (Roland) is important in the world of the *chansons de geste*, which concerned the adventures of Charlemagne and his paladins. Although there is a connection to the struggles between Charlemagne's Christian warriors and the invading Saracens, which

FIGURE 3.2 *This illustration from the first English translation of Ludovico Ariosto's* Orlando furioso *by the Elizabethan courtier, Sir John Harrington, depicts the adventures of Ruggiero and the hippogriff.*

informed the original *chanson de geste* plots, these poems add romance features, such as the unrequited love of Orlando for the pagan princess Angelica, as well as magical themes and fantastic creatures of which the hippogriff is one. The wizard Atlantes first tames this creature; later, the heroic knights Ruggiero (Roger) and Astolpho ride the hippogriff whose nature draws on earlier mythical creatures. Like its parent, the griffin, the hippogriff is a wild and spirited creature from the northern edge of the world. The northern home of the hippogriff, the land of the Hyperboreans, is redolent with mythical equine associations, such as the antagonism between the horse-riding Arismaspaens and the mythical griffins. The hippogriff (*ippogrifo*) comes into its own in Ariosto's work, and as a result of the popularity of the Orlando cycle, the word was borrowed into other languages, for example, English, *hippogriffin* and French, *hippogriffe*.[44]

Hybrid beings based on horses, an animal with significant economic and military value, were important in the mythical context as well as the economic one. Usually the forequarters are the equine element. For example, a half-horse and half-fish hybrid, called a *hippocampus*, drew Poseidon's chariot. The hippogriff has forequarters that resemble another fabulous beast, a griffin, while the hindquarters are those of a horse. A phrase from Virgil's *Eclogues*, 'nam iungentur gryphes equis' ('when horses mate with griffins', *Eclogue VIII*, 26–8), provided inspiration for the creation of the literary hippogriff. This classical phrase became a metaphor for the impossible, specifically in the context of ill-fated love. Commentators on Virgil noted that griffins and horses were natural enemies, so it is not surprising that such an unlikely mating would be a notable event. According to tradition, griffins laid marvellous eggs, and Ariosto's hippogriff hatches from an egg produced by a mating between a mare and a griffin. In *Orlando furioso*, the hippogriff symbolizes the contradictory forces of love and desire, and, undoubtedly, the ironic tone of Virgil's metaphor as an image of thwarted love, as well as its impeccable classical heritage, would have appealed to Ariosto and his Renaissance audience.

Although the hippogriff is a creature specific to Ariosto's poem, occasionally the hindquarters of carved griffins appear more equine than leonine. A capital on a Romanesque column from Autun Cathedral (France) shows a figure riding an eagle/horse hybrid that calls to mind Ariosto's description. The winged horse Pegasus is another important influence on Ariosto's hippogriff which fulfils exactly the same role as the winged classical steed when one of the poem's central characters (Ruggiero) rescues a maiden (Angelica) from a sea monster. The earlier unfinished poem, *Orlando innamorato*, by Matteo Boiardo included several magic horses, which also influenced the emergence of Ariosto's hippogriff. The intelligent steed Bayard, whose size could accommodate every rider, was already part of the *chanson de geste* tradition, and Boiardo added a supernatural horse called Rabicano, born, in an echo of the classical myth of Boreas and the mares, of a fiery mare and the wind. The flying mechanical horses featured in a few medieval European romances may reflect the influence of automata from Eastern narratives like the *Arabian Nights*.[45]

Descriptions of the hippogriff's origin and nature draw heavily on griffin lore, and the first English translator called the creature a 'griffeth horse'.[46] Ariosto synthesized classical, medieval and Eastern material about magical–mechanical automata with Pegasus, and with Virgil's metaphor for the marvels and perils of love. The arms of Ariosto's patrons, the d'Este family, contained an eagle, and this too may find an echo in the magic steed in *Orlando furioso*. The result is a creature that plays an important role in late chivalric romance, along with characters from the *chanson de geste* adventures of Charlemagne and his paladins. *Orlando furioso* is a complex tale about restoring the sanity of the hero, Orlando (Roland), who has become mad for love of the Lady Angelica. The wizard Atlantes captures the hippogriff, a symbol of unconquered desire, in an attempt to prevent the marriage between the Saracen knight Ruggiero and a Christian princess. Although Ruggiero mounts the hippogriff and escapes, he must learn how to control both his steed and his unruly human passions. In an episode that parallels the Perseus/Bellerophon story, Ruggiero and the hippogriff rescue Angelica from a sea monster. Later, Ruggiero tethers the fractious creature to a myrtle tree, which is actually a transformed knight, Astolfo. He, in turn, rides the hippogriff to the Earthly Paradise, and eventually to the moon, in search of Orlando's lost wits. Eventually, Astolpho removes the hippogriff's bridle and sets it free.[47]

Sixteenth-century editions of Ariosto's poem, which contains the earliest visual depictions of the hippogriff, show it as a flying horse with an eagle's head, wings and front claws. Gustave Doré created a similar creature for his illustrations for this poem.[48] The episode in which Ruggiero rides the hippogriff to rescue Angelica was a popular subject for artists from Girolamo dei Carpi in the sixteenth century to Auguste Ingres and Odilon Redon in the nineteenth. Thomas Blount described the *Hippogryph* in his seventeenth-century dictionary of foreign words in English usage as a 'feigned beast' part horse, part griffin.[49] At the end of the nineteenth century, the American journalist Ambrose Bierce produced *Devil's Dictionary*, based on his newspaper articles, in which he used the hippogriff to satirize American materialism.[50]

In modern fantasy literature, the hippogriff is popular among writers who favour picaresque adventures or are directly influenced by Ariosto's poem. Merlin becomes involved with a hippogriff in the sprawling political satire, *Merlin l'enchanteur*, written by the nineteenth-century French writer, Paul Quinet.[51] A chapter titled 'How One Came, as was foretold, to the city of Never' is part of the *Book of Wonders* published in 1912 by the Anglo-Irish fantasy writer Lord Dunsany. The central character has a magic halter, which tames any fantastic beast such as 'the hippogriff Pegasus'. Dunsany's piece is more a prose meditation than a tale and contains descriptions of the creatures performing an ethereal aerial ballet.[52] The hippogriff in E. R. Eddison's richly written and somewhat violent tale, *The Worm Ouroboros* (1926), is a direct echo of Ariosto's creature. Lessingham, the narrator, journeys to the planet Mercury in a chariot drawn by a hippogriff, and another character rescues his brother with the aid of a hippogriff hatched from an egg hidden at the bottom of a lake. Ruggiero's quest is echoed in *The Witch-woman: A Trilogy About Her* (1948) by the American fantasy writer James Branch Cabell through a character who rides a hippogriff in his search for the elusive ideal woman. By contrast, the gentle hippogriff Buckbeak belongs to a herd of hippogriffs living in the forest surrounding Hogwarts School in J. K. Rowling's Harry Potter series. Buckbeak, who is the favourite of the giant, Hagrid, is strong, proud and loyal, even when threatened with execution. In a further echo of Ariosto's Ruggiero, it helps Harry's uncle, Sirius Black, escape his enemies (*Harry Potter and The Prisoner of Azkaban*, 1999). The hippogriff has become an integral part of the Harry Potter universe and a themed roller-coaster ride, The Flight of the Hippogriff, was installed in the Wizarding World of Harry Potter at Universal Parks and Resorts in Orlando, Florida, when it opened in 2010.

A hippogriff emerges from a magical bestiary to help young king Lionel defeat a dragon in Edith Nesbit's *The Book of Dragons*, although the creature, described as a white horse with swan's wings, seems more like a misnamed Pegasus.[53] In Neil Gaiman's *Sandman* series (1989–present), a hippogriff, together with the griffin – its mythical parent, is one of Dream's gatekeepers. Like so many other mythical creatures, the hippogriff features in modern role-playing and video games. It was among the earliest fantasy beasts introduced into the *Dungeons & Dragons* universe, and a variant of the hippogriff, with leonine front legs, equine back legs and the head and wings of an eagle, served as a war mount in the *Warhammer* game when it was released in 1984.[54] The hippogriff characters combine elements from classical traditions about griffins, from Ariosto's work, and from fantasy novels, like Eddison's description of raising a hippogriff from an egg, as well as features unique to the gaming universe, like their omnivorous diet.

Myths and traveller's tales

Traditions about extraordinary flying creatures, as stated in the introduction, travelled with the ebb and flow of travellers and civilizations. Establishing the exact origin of a mythical beast can be a difficult task, since the interplay between observations of real animals and legendary traditions about them is not always clear. This final group – halcyon, Roc, simurgh, anzu, Ziz and phoenix – represents winged mythological birds from different traditions, linked up in various ways with cosmic activities such as regeneration, weather or creation. Many are ancient, and, although it is difficult to establish any firm order of precedence, they share a number of related motifs and traditions.

The proverbial phrase 'halcyon days' has come to mean a period of calm in the midst of turmoil. It is associated in classical sources with the story of Alcyone (Halkyone), daughter of the wind god, Aeolus, and her husband, Ceyx, son of the Morning Star. Its theme concerns humans transformed into animals and demonstrates the widely varying functions of mythical beast lore. In the earliest sources, such as *The Catalogue of Women* attributed to Hesiod, the transformation of Alcyone and Ceyx is the consequence of impiety, but in later sources, the halcyon bird represents the important classical virtue of *pietas*, that is, care and devotion to family.[55] Ovid gives the most elaborate account, emphasizing the conjugal love and death-defying devotion of the two protagonists. When Ceyx drowns, his grieving wife throws herself into the sea, but the gods take pity and turn them into halcyon birds (named for Alcyone). During midwinter, when the halcyon makes its nest on the sea, Alcyone's father, Aeolus, calms the winds, so the eggs can hatch safely. Thus the myth is used to explain the term 'halcyon days', although it is not entirely clear whether the tale gave rise to the proverbial expression or was used to explain an already existing piece of weather lore.

In his *Historia Animalium*, Aristotle equates the halcyon with a kingfisher, a bird with multicoloured feathers and distinctive blue-flecked wings that nests in winter and is often observed near ships in harbour (Bk 9, 14–18). Pliny's *Natural History* also links the nesting birds with the weather. Philemon Holland's very free, 1601 translation of Pliny describes them thus: 'They lay and sit about midwinter … and the time while they are broodie, is called the halcyon daies: for during that season the sea is calm and navigable, especially in the coast of Sicilie.'[56] Classical descriptions, rather than direct observation, influenced medieval texts such as the Aberdeen Bestiary in which the halcyon has beautiful blue feathers (fol. 54v). Whatever the source, the halcyon bird is associated with calm seas around the time of the winter solstice, and became, by extension, a proverbial expression for any calm and peaceful period.[57] The change of emphasis to a more positive interpretation of the halcyon tale may have taken place in Ovid's source, a lost work by Nicander of Colophon, a second-century BCE poet and physician from what is now Turkey.[58] Even in the context of weather lore, its meaning can vary. Isidore of Seville's *Etymologies* (Bk 12, 7:25) claims that the bird's name derives from sea foam (*alcyanea*) and that in winter, the sea remains calm for seven days until its eggs hatch. For Shakespeare, however, 'St Martin's summer, halcyon days' (*Henry IV*, Act I, sc. ii) refers to an autumnal period of warm weather, although by this time the term 'halcyon' may have become a more generalized proverbial expression. By the nineteenth century, the halcyon legend had been absorbed into Russian folk traditions in the form of the *alkonost*, a bird that appears on Russian folk icons as a bringer of good fortune. The artist Victor Vesnatsov, whose paintings incorporated folkloric themes, contrasted a white-feathered alkonost with a darker-feathered *sirin* (siren) as 'Sirin and Alkonost, The Birds of Joy and Sorrow' (1896).

Al-rukh (Roc), the giant bird of Arabic tradition, may have originated in travellers' tales about large exotic birds. The rukh first appears in a tenth-century Arab source. Traditionally, it laid huge eggs and was powerful enough to carry off an elephant. Some commentators suggest that it represented a battle between the Indian solar bird, Garuda, and the naga serpent, a mythic struggle between opposing cosmic forces that embodied the air and the earth. Other explanations see it as a traveller's tale, based on reports of flightless birds such as the ostrich (which would account for its unusual feathers) and the large ostrich eggs beloved by early collectors of curiosities. More speculatively, the rukh may be a memory of now-extinct giant bird species that Arab seamen might, or might not, have heard about.[59]

The Arab traveller Ibn Batuta (1304–68) located the rukh's mountain eyrie in China, and it appears carrying an elephant above the China Seas in an early- sixteenth-century geographical drawing of the triumph of Magellan. The rukh became absorbed into the tales of Sinbad the Sailor, which were in turn included in the *Thousand and One Nights*.[60] Sinbad's encounter with the Roc (rukh) is one of the popular episodes in his many voyages. He finds himself marooned on an island inhabited by giant birds that prey on serpents living in a valley filled with diamonds. The canny Sinbad ties himself to a joint of meat, which the Roc carries off to her nest where Sinbad kills the nestlings and steals the treasure (Figure 3.3). The motif of tricking a monstrous bird, by disguising oneself as prey, overlaps with traditions about the griffin, an exceptionally well-attested mythical beast. Bestiaries often show the griffin carrying off an ox, and this ability to carry large prey, its fondness for treasure, the

SINBAD IN THE VALLEY OF DIAMONDS.

myself for joy, when I reflected on the perils that I had gone through ; it appeared as if my present state was but a dream, and I could not believe that I had nothing more to fear.

"The merchants had been for some days in that spot, and as they now appeared to be contented with the diamonds they had collected, we set off all together on the following

FIGURE 3.3 *In John Everett Millais's illustration, Sinbad is about to tie himself to the Roc's enormous talons in order to escape the valley in this nineteenth-century collection of* The Arabian Nights' Entertainments.

remoteness and size of its nests were elements that overlap, and perhaps became assimilated, with the rukh. The Jewish traveller Benjamin of Tudela (c. 1159–73) records a tale about sailors lost in the mysterious seas off China, who escape by hiding in animal skins that are carried away by griffins.[61] The ship-wrecked hero and his men in the medieval German romance, *Herzog Ernst* (c. 1180), use a similar method of escape by sewing themselves into animal skins that the griffins carry away. In the adventures of Hasan of Basra (another predecessor of the Sinbad stories), the giant birds who carry the travellers are vultures.[62] Fra Mauro's world map compiled in 1450 contains textual explanations for many geographical features. Among them is an incident, dated to 1420, about a storm-tossed ship whose starving sailors ate the egg of a Roc, 'as big as a seven-gallon cask'.[63]

The stop-action monsters of Ray Harryhausen included a two-headed female rukh who threatens Sinbad after his crew kills and eats one of her chicks (*The Seventh Voyage of Sinbad*, Nathan H. Juran, 1958), and illustrations of Sinbad carried by the rukh appear in versions of the *Arabian Nights* from the first Western translations to the present day.[64] It is not surprising that such a famous mythical bird should find its way into RPGs. It features in the Monster Manuals, essentially bestiaries for role-playing gamers, that have accompanied *Dungeons & Dragons,* and the episode of Sinbad and the Roc has been adapted as a separate scenario for gaming. [65]

The Ziz of Jewish tradition, whose wings can block out the sun, is mentioned briefly in the Hebrew Bible and its predominance over the birds of the air contrasts with the leviathan who dominates the fishes of the sea. Perhaps the closest parallel to the Ziz is the Anzu, a mythological bird typically depicted as an eagle-headed lion (which links it to the griffin as well). In Sumerian mythology, one of the oldest recorded mythologies, a giant bird steals the Tablets of Destiny only to be killed by a hero such as Marduk or Enlil.[66] The simurgh is a more benevolent creature and more closely bound to its mythological origin. In Persian and Islamic arts, it can resemble a griffin or a phoenix, and sometimes it has a stylized peacock-like tail. In the Persian *Avesta*, the sacred writings of Zoroastrianism, some of which date back to the fifth century BCE, a powerful ancient bird called Saena perches in a healing tree whose branches carry the seeds of all plants. This bird eventually became the simurgh.[67] In the *Shahnameh* (The Book of Kings) written by the Persian poet Ferdowsi at the end of the tenth century CE, the magic bird protected the hero, Prince Zal, and his son, Rustam. When the infant Zal was exposed on a mountain, the simurgh adopted him, raised him and gave him three magic feathers, which later helped Rustam destroy his enemy. The motif of magic feathers for use in time of need occurs in other tales, including the story of the Russian Firebird. Persian miniature illustrations of the *Shahnameh* depict the simurgh as a phoenix-like creature.[68] *The Conference of the Birds*

FIGURE 3.4 *A phoenix rises from the ashes in one of the* 'holsome preceptes, shadowed with pleasant devises' *included by the Elizabethan poet Geffrey Whitney, who compiled this famous emblem book.*

by the twelfth-century Persian poet, Farid al-Din Attar, uses the search for the legendary simurgh to illustrate the principles of Sufi mysticism.[69]

The simurgh with its colourful plumage often resembles the phoenix, which has a particularly rich heritage, and continues to be a symbol for renewal up to the present day (Figure 3.4). The fifth-century BCE historian Herodotus (*History*, Bk 2) claims only to have seen pictures of the phoenix, and questions its credibility. Nevertheless, he records that the phoenix comes from India every five hundred years to the temple at Heliopolis to bury its parent, whose body has been sealed in a ball of myrrh. The account in Ovid (*Metamorphoses*, Bk 15, 391–417) expands this, giving details about how the phoenix builds its own funeral pyre, and how it transports its parent's body for burial. Pliny's *Natural History* (Bk 10, 2) as always provides a synthesis of classical lore. The phoenix is eagle-like, multicoloured and sacred to the Arabian sun god.[70] After the old phoenix immolates itself, the young phoenix emerges as a worm, gathers the corpse of the old bird and buries it at Heliopolis. The text accompanying a drawing of the phoenix on the Hereford *mappa mundi* claims that it is unique (*unica auis in orbe*).[71] The Aberdeen Bestiary says, 'The phoenix can also signify the resurrection of the righteous who, gathering the aromatic plants of virtue, prepare for the renewal of their former energy after death. ... See how the nature of birds offers to ordinary people proof of the resurrection; that what the scripture proclaims, the working of nature confirms' (fol. 55r).[72]

As late as the sixteenth century, the *Physiologus* description of the phoenix was translated into Russian, and this description may have influenced the motif of the Zhar-Ptitsa (Firebird) of Russian folktales. The lifecycle of this mythical bird mentioned in the *Physiologus* was adapted as a folktale creature that sleeps during the day, but lights up the night when it feeds on golden apples with healing properties. In one striking tale, a girl raised in ignorance of light and men finally ventures into real sunlight and falls in love with the picture of a prince.[73] The firebird that sleeps in its cage by day, but comes alive at night, carries her to the prince's castle. The young lovers talk for so long, that the firebird cannot return the princess to her home before daybreak. As the sun rises, the bird sinks and dies. The princess buries it, but takes its wings, which enable her to defeat a witch and rescue the enchanted prince. Another tale about the firebird became the basis for a Stravinsky ballet (*The Firebird*, 1910). The Russian folktale is an example of a popular tale about a quest undertaken with the aid of a supernatural helper. It is similar to the tale of the Golden Bird in the Brothers Grimm collection, in which a young prince (or youngest son) finds a feather from the firebird (or golden bird) and is sent to capture the bird itself, which he does with the aid of a magic companion who eventually helps him win a princess. A more classical meaning for the phoenix as a symbol of elusive perfection underpins Shakespeare's poem 'The Phoenix and the Turtle' (1601). However, Shakespeare adopts a slightly different meaning for this mythical bird in his play *Henry VIII* when Cranmer addresses the infant Elizabeth as 'the maiden phoenix'. This metaphor for the queen is reflected in a portrait attributed to Nicholas Hilliard, in which Elizabeth wears a jewel in the shape of a phoenix, signifying that she can ensure that Britain 'Shall star-like rise, as great in fame as she was, And so stand fix'd: peace, plenty, love, truth' (*Henry VIII*, Act V, sc v).

The symbolic meanings of the phoenix revolve around its association with fire, renewal and uniqueness, and they persist throughout its long history. It provides an evocative title for films such as *The Flight of the Phoenix* (Robert Aldrich, 1965) about the survivors of an aeroplane crash; the name for the famous Venetian opera house, renamed *La Fenice* after it was rebuilt following a fire; and the titles of numerous businesses which use the name to reassure customers. These same qualities of light, goodness, renewal and uniqueness are invoked in the name of the secret society that opposes the evil forces of Voldemort in *Harry Potter and the Order of the Phoenix* (2003), the fifth book in J. K. Rowling's fantasy series. E. Nesbit's children's fantasy, *The Phoenix and the Carpet* (1904), follows the adventures of five children and their super-natural companion, a phoenix. The children discover a mysterious egg in their new nursery carpet. When they throw the egg into the fire, a phoenix appears. Nesbit's phoenix is more a wonderful talking pet, whose existence needs to be kept secret from the adult world, than the mythical creature of earlier sources, but there are plenty of daring adventures before the children have to bid farewell to their magical companion.

Another mythological bird, the Chinese *fenghuang*, which shares some characteristics with the phoenix, is also identified with the colourful, and very real, Argus pheasant. Originally, it was the female aspect of the male and female pairing of yin and yang. It became associated with the imperial household, and later embodied the grace of the empress that complemented the power of the emperor's symbol, the dragon.[74] As such, it retains overtones of balanced opposites, and, in contemporary Asian cultures such as China and Japan, it often symbolizes the union of husband and wife at weddings. Japanese popular culture has become a global phenomenon through manga comics, anime films and RPGs. The video game *Pokémon*, created by Satoshi Tajiri for Nintendo in 1996, spawned an entire media franchise. The game strategy involves 'catching' and 'taming' a wide range of 'pocket monster' characters. Among them is a phoenix-like rainbow bird. The main character in *Hi no tori* (Bird of Fire), a cycle of twelve manga books written by Osamu Tezuka between 1954 and 1989, resembles the Chinese fenghuang, although Tezuka also drew inspiration from Soviet animation films of the Russian firebird with its magic feathers. Reincarnation is an underlying theme of the Japanese books, which in a Buddhist setting is a natural progression of life, but in these books, which combine elements of fantasy and science fiction, the blood of the phoenix/ firebird promises immortality and is therefore a mixed blessing.

Lizards with wings

The fifth-century BCE Greek historian Herodotus describes the bones of creatures that seem halfway between mythical bird-like beings and flying dragons and are, for the most part, venomous and malevolent. He tells us:

> There is a place in Arabia not far from the town of Bouto (Buto) where I went to learn about the Winged Serpents (*ophies pteretoi*). When I arrived there, I saw innumerable bones and backbones of serpents: many heaps of backbones, great and small, and even smaller. This place, where the backbones lay scattered, is where a narrow mountain pass opens into a great plain, which adjoins the plain of Aigyptos (Egypt). Winged serpents are said to fly from Arabia at the beginning of spring, making for Egypt; but the ibis birds encounter the invaders in this pass and kill them. (*Histories*, 2. 75. 1–4)

Adrienne Mayor suggests that this provides evidence for assemblages of fossil bones in classical sources, but, as is so often the case, these passages are less clear than they first appear. Herodotus was seeking proof that winged lizards were an actual living species. He notes that the ibis, an incontestably real bird, attacked them, and this suggests to some commentators that Herodotus's winged lizards were actually locusts.[75] Whatever lies behind the observation of these 'bones', they certainly fall into the category of winged and venomous creatures with reptilian characteristics.

The *cockatrice*, with its serpentine body and tail, cockerel's head, legs and wings, is such a creature, and it draws on a number of real and fictional animals. Its unnatural birth, hatched from a cock's egg incubated by a serpent or a toad, is one indication of its monstrous heritage. The glance of this snake-like hybrid is lethal to everything except the weasel. The cockatrice, in bestiaries, and elsewhere, was identified with another bird/reptile hybrid that hatched from an egg, namely the basilisk, and aspects of this creature were further confused with descriptions of the Nile crocodile. The heraldic cockatrice is a hybrid monster with the head, wings and feet of a cock and a serpent's tail that frequently ends in a second serpentine head. This links it to yet another snake-like creature, the *amphisbaena*, which has a snake's head at each end of its body. The cockatrice in alchemical literature shared features with the salamander, which could survive in fire, as well as the reptilian winged dragon, and with the mysterious *ouroboros*, a serpent-like creature who constantly renews itself by swallowing its own tail.[76] The cockatrice became a symbol for the transmutation of metals during the alchemical process, although in the context of traveller's tales and bestiary literature, it was a fearsome venomous opponent.[77]

The monstrous cockatrice has a complex heritage that combines beliefs about snakes and crocodiles as well as some of their natural enemies like the weasel and the ichneumon (*Herpestes ichneumon*, the Egyptian mongoose). The early histories of both cockatrice and basilisk begin with the Greek physician and poet Nicander (second century BCE) whose poem on the nature of venomous animals, *Theriaca*, describes a small, hissing, extremely poisonous snake, which he identifies with the basilisk.[78] It has crown-like markings on its head, it moves with its forepart upright, and its venom is powerful enough to travel up a spear shaft and kill both man and horse. An Egyptian hieroglyph depicting a cobra with its hood raised and ready to strike was associated with royal power in Egypt, and beliefs about the hooded cobra, the spitting viper and other North African snakes, may contribute elements to this creature. Such imagery informed early descriptions of the basilisk and the cockatrice and, no doubt, influenced illustrations in medieval bestiaries and elsewhere. For example, a cockatrice confronts a basilisk in the spaces between Arthurian scenes in a medieval embroidery.[79] In medieval zoology, its only enemy was the weasel, and some bestiary illustrations show this little creature attacking a cockatrice.[80] Pliny the Elder's *Natural History* (Bk 8, 33) claims that a glance from this animal is lethal and its breath destroys vegetation. This description was repeated and expanded by subsequent authors such as Isidore of Seville who described the basilisk in his seventh-century work, *Etymologies* (Bk 12, ch. 4:6–9), as the king (*regulus*) of snakes because of its extremely poisonous nature. Several centuries later, Alexander Neckham (c. 1180) included another tradition, namely that the basilisk hatched from a cock's egg incubated by a toad, and fifteenth- and sixteenth-century sources record instances of the destruction of these so-called cockerel eggs.[81] This unnatural birth from the seemingly infertile cock's egg added an element of unnatural monstrosity to the already dangerous basilisk and cockatrice.

The Vulgate translation of the Psalms lists the asp (*aspidem*), basilisk (*basiliscum*), lion (*leonem*) and dragon (*draconem*) as symbols of evil, which will be trampled by the forces of good (Ps. 91 (90) 13). Medieval iconography shows Christ trampling these evil symbols, which are usually reduced to a lion and a serpent, or just a serpent. In a few examples, all four creatures appear, and the basilisk usually takes the form of a cockerel with a snake's tail.[82] The poison emitted by the basilisk could pollute the air, destroy vegetation and cause birds to fall from the sky, qualities often attributed to dragons. The ninth-century pope Leo IV miraculously destroyed a basilisk who was causing a plague, a type of miracle commonly ascribed to dragon-slaying saints.[83] A pamphlet from 1669 recorded the destruction of a cockatrice at Saffron Walden, together with a flying serpent in Essex, as 'strange newes'. The destruction of two such poisonous menaces was enough of a curiosity to be reprinted in the nineteenth century and to influence a modern gothic novel.[84] An incident, which seemingly took place in Warsaw in 1587, involved the deaths of two little girls and their nursemaid who wandered into a cellar inhabited by a basilisk. A condemned prisoner dressed in mirror-encrusted clothing dragged the creature, which apparently had all the physical characteristics of a basilisk, into the light.[85] The Alexander legend, popular throughout Europe and the Middle East, recounts a similar incident about a basilisk being killed with mirrors.[86]

Although the crocodile has no wings, it contributed several details to the creation of the cockatrice. According to Pliny (Bk 8, 24 (35), 88), the Egyptian ichneumon was able to enter the mouth of a sleeping crocodile and kill it by tearing its stomach open. In some medieval bestiaries, clearly influenced by this description, a water-dwelling *hydrus* is ripped apart by a small, rodent-like animal, which emerges through its stomach. The cockatrice drew elements from all these descriptions and emerged as a separate animal in twelfth-century French sources. *Li Livres dou Trésor* (c. 1263), a compendium of knowledge by the Italian humanist Brunetto Latini (1220–94), uses the term *cocatris* in the context of Pliny's remarks about the crocodile and its enemies, which may be the first usage or, at the very least, one which influenced later sources. The cockatrice appears in English somewhat later. John of Trevisa in his fourteenth-century English translation of Bartholomew Anglicus's work, *On the Properties of Things*, equated cockatrice with Latin basiliscus *(De Proprietatibus Rerum*, Bk 18), while the Wycliffe Bible (1382) used 'kokatrice' to translate basiliscus. Writing in the seventeenth century, Sir Thomas Browne attempted to resolve this complex mixture of creatures in his study of *Vulgar Errors* (*Pseudodoxia Epidemica*, Bk 3, vii). He accepted the existence of a real serpent, which he calls the basilisk, and which he attempted to distinguish from the mythical cockatrice.

It is not surprising that the basilisk, as the deadly king of snakes, became identified with the serpent in the Garden of Eden. Sometimes St George's opponent resembles a basilisk rather than a dragon, which illustrates once again the degree of overlap in mythical beast traditions. The heraldic basilisk embodied very different qualities. Its potency, upright posture and crown-like markings suggested kingly power or the immortality of fame.[87] English alchemical works such as George Ripley's *The Compound of Alchymie* (1477) and Thomas Vaughan's *Lumen de lumine* (1651) equate the cockatrice and the basilisk. The alchemical cockatrice also acquired something like the salamander's resistance to fire, and the tail-devouring ouroboros that could renew itself. George Herbert's poem 'Sinne's round' (1633) applies the alchemical meaning of cockatrice as a symbol of renewal to the dialectic of sin and penitence. Alchemical writing stressed the nature, rather than the appearance, of the cockatrice, and it became a symbol of alchemical transformation and transmutation.[88] In an elegy titled 'The Perfume', the metaphysical poet John Donne (1573–1631) characterizes the actions of a suspicious father towards his daughter's lover, 'As though he came to kill a cockatrice' (Elegy IV: 'The Perfume' l. 8). In *Romeo and Juliet* (1595) (Act III, sc. iv), and in one of Edmund Spenser's love sonnets, 'Amoretti' (49, 1599), the cockatrice embodies the power of a love-inducing glance, metaphorically described as 'deadly'. The villainous Richard III in William Shakespeare's play has the dubious distinction of being compared twice to a basilisk and once to a cockatrice. He first hints at his talent for dissembling in *Henry VI, part III*: 'I'll slay most gazers than a basilisk' (Act III, sc. ii), and later the widowed Anne responds to the soon-to-be King Richard's compliment on her eyes with the memorable phrase 'would they were basilisks to strike thee dead' (*Richard III*, Act I, sc. ii). Later, his own mother bemoans the fact that her 'accursed womb' has 'hatched' a cockatrice (Act IV, sc. i).

Edward Topsell in *The History of Serpents* (1608) cites an 'old wives' tale' about a man wearing crystal armour who destroyed many cockatrices by forcing them to see their own death-inducing reflection.[89] This particular 'old wives' tale' is commemorated in a local museum in the village of Wherwell in Hampshire (England) that houses a weathervane from the village church in the shape of a cockatrice. This antiquity supports a local legend about one of these poisonous creatures that hatched from a duck egg and caused terror among the inhabitants until a brave man lowered a mirror into its lair and killed it.[90] In *The Book of the Dun Cow* (1978), Walter Wangerin Jr makes use of the complex monster lore connecting serpents, basilisks and the cockatrice. In the *Dun Cow* fantasy books, the cockatrice is the evil reflection of the good cockerel, Chanticleer, who attempts to invade Chanticleer's kingdom at the head of an army of basilisks. A cockatrice is one of the many perils encountered by the young hero in John Masefield's fantasy novel, *A Box of Delights* (1935), but a short story, 'Kind Little Edmund or the Caves and the Cockatrice' from Edith Nesbit's *The Book of Dragons* (1900), presents a rare positive view of the cockatrice. A restless young boy who wants 'to know the true things they don't know in school' rescues a dying cockatrice, and the wise beast advises him on how to defeat a dragon.

The lore surrounding both the cockatrice and the basilisk evokes human revulsion to reptilian coldness, poison, parasitic invasion and slimy death, while changing attitudes to these monsters reveal the ways in which we continue to conceptualize and externalize this revulsion. Horror films and fantasy fiction continue to embody widespread fear of reptiles, parasitic invasion of the body and painful death by poison. The basilisk, which threatens Harry and his young wizard friends in J. K. Rowling's *Harry Potter and the Chamber of Secrets* (1998, film 2002), is more serpentine in appearance. Its glance petrifies (literally), but rarely kills. The ghost of Moaning Myrtle is its most noteworthy casualty, but other characters only suffer temporary paralysis upon seeing its reflection. The dystopian future depicted in Margaret Atwood's *Oryx and Crake* (2005) is full of bio-engineered animals, many with poisonous and reptilian traits, science-fiction cousins to the traditional basilisk and cockatrice. Since the basilisk is poisonous in so many ways, it is hardly surprising that it appears so often in RPGs, and its hybrid characteristics are infinitely variable as it acquires new gaming values. The illustrations on the 'basilisk' cards produced for the trading card game *Magic the Gathering* launched in 1993 keep the basic reptilian nature of this mythical beast, but add dragon, snake or even dinosaur characteristics.[91] The modern monster that seems to encapsulate the mixed heritage of the cockatrice best is the ever-changing creature of the *Alien* films. With its reptile-like appearance, parasitic larvae, corrosive body fluid, preternatural speed and seemingly unstoppable nature, it echoes qualities of the cockatrice found in earlier sources and reinvigorates it as modern science fiction.[92]

Another creature that appears with wings often, but not always, is the boa. Although comparatively rare in bestiaries, it appears as a winged lizard attacking an ox, a wingless red dragon-like creature or a huge snake wrapped around a tree.[93] According to Pliny (*Natural History*, Bk 8, 14), the boa is an enormous snake found in Italy that can swallow a child whole. It feeds on cattle and oxen by sucking their milk, hence its name, which Isidore of Seville derives from *boves*, Latin for oxen (*Etymologies*, Bk 12, ch. 4:28), because it kills cattle by sucking them dry. According to St Jerome, the hermit saint Hilarion destroyed a monstrous boa which plagued the citizens of Epidaurus in Dalmatia.[94] This type of tale, in which a local hero destroys a local menace, overlaps with dragon lore, which is discussed in the next chapter. Sometimes, the so-called dragon is more like the invading serpents popular in saints' legends and early natural history sources. Like the sphinx, not all these creatures are winged, but they are associated with disease, symbolized by their pestiferous breath, and by purging the disease, the saint/hero makes the area safe for habitation (and Christianity).[95]

Although dragons are undoubtedly the first reptilian beasts that spring to mind in connection with Wales, there is at least one poisonous snake found in the country, namely the adder (*Vipera berus*). Like the deadly varieties that have contributed to the creation of the basilisk and the cockatrice, the Welsh adder (*gwiber* i.e. viper), with added wings, figures in Welsh legends that contain elements found in local dragon lore elsewhere. The gwiber in these tales is hostile, appears suddenly and decimates livestock, and occasionally, like the boa, its monstrosity is associated with suckling milk. A young hero contrived a plan to destroy one, which depended as much on cleverness as on strength, but the lingering poison in the dead beast, another common dragon-lore motif, caused the hero's death. Glasynys, the bardic name of Owen Wynn Jones (1828–70), was a cleric and a folklorist who added a distinctly gothic gloss to anecdotes about the gwiber in his collection of tales, *Cymru Fu*.[96] A man from Gwibernant (Viper's stream) in Penmachno not only died from the viper's bite, he also suffered a dramatic triple-death similar to an incident attached to the wizard Merlin. The poison from the viper's bite caused him to fall from a cliff and drown in the river below.[97] When a magician predicted that the heir to a great estate would die from a viper's sting, his well-wishers lured the viper into a pit and killed it. When the heir returned, however, he kicked the corpse contemptuously and died, as predicted, of the poison. A similar incident was localized in the Vale of Conway: A man dreamed of being bitten by a viper and later died when he kicked the dead creature's corpse. In other examples, a young smith received a reward for destroying a basilisk-like viper which inhabited Llyn Cynwch near Dolgellau, and a viper living near Llanidloes turned the water of the Severn green. This one fed on oxen, a characteristic it shared with the boa as described in medieval bestiaries. Eventually, it fell asleep after gorging on oxen and a fisherman killed it.[98] There are tales about winged gwibers that are tricked into battering themselves to death on a booby-trapped pillar covered in red cloth. A standing stone near Llanrhaeadr-ym-Mochnant in Powys, called Post Coch (red pillar) or Post-y-Wiber (viper's pillar), commemorates such an event. The pillar supposedly stood 'in the line of flight' between its two lairs. An existing local monument on this spot may have provided a setting for this much-travelled legend.[99] A similar variant was attached to the famous Hereford-shire dragon that terrorized Mordiford, and who, in one version, beats itself to death.[100] The Welsh folklore writer Marie Trevelyan, who lived in Llantwit Major in South Wales, described a race of winged serpents with beautiful colouring that lived near waterfalls and had their own 'king' and 'queen'. She collected a number of anecdotes about local people who killed these creatures, because they attacked poultry and were 'worse than foxes'.[101] Trevelyan's folk anecdotes provide a fitting coda to the varied traditions about basilisks, cockatrices and their winged cousins. Her fellow Welsh folklorist, Glasynys, recalls a similar event about a flying serpent dated back to 1812, but he identifies the creature as an escaped cock pheasant.[102]

Conclusion

This chapter has focused on a variety of non-human winged creatures, but this does not exhaust the possibilities of things with wings, a feature that emphasizes both their power and their often-transcendent nature. Angels are winged, and the Greeks conceived of messenger gods like Hermes and Iris as winged so that they could go anywhere and swiftly deliver their messages to mortals and immortals alike. Personifications of abstract concepts such as Love (Eros), Victory (Nike), Sleep (Hypnos) and Death (Thanatos) appear as winged humans. Sirens, who were originally human-headed birds whose song promised the dangerous acquisition of secret or prophetic knowledge, are among the many winged creatures with human heads. The *lamassu*, a human-headed bull (or lion) with wings, was a guardian spirit in Mesopotamian mythology and pairs of them were often placed at gates, a position also occupied by winged sphinxes or griffins. Al-Buraq, a mythological steed that transported the prophet Mohammad on his Night Journey, appears in Persian manuscripts with wings and a human head. An equestrian figure, often called the rider-god, was popular in an area now occupied by Turkey and the Balkans. It appears on graves as a man riding a horse and slaying a monster, from which it was adapted into Roman tradition and beyond. Although the horse is not winged, the monster recalls stories of Bellerophon and the Chimaera, Perseus mounted on Pegasus to rescue Andromeda from the sea monster, and even the tale of St George and the dragon. Perhaps it is not too far a stretch to mention briefly the Tulpar, the winged horse in Turkic mythology. Because of its association with the Tatars, whose hunting practices centred on horse riding and falconry, the winged Tulpar may be a fusion of these two animals.

In the floating mountains of the planet Pandora live winged hybrids, which combine features of prehistoric pterodactyls and the ability to form psychic bonds with their riders. They are part of the fauna in one of the most success-ful science-fiction adventure films of recent years. *Avatar* (James Cameron, 2009) combines the well-nigh universal theme of heroic journey with the modern twists of self-discovery and an added ecological, anti-imperial mes-sage. The theme of a disillusioned warrior drawn into, and eventually saved by, an alien culture echoes Edgar Rice Burroughs's early- twentieth-century *John Carter Warlord of Barsoom* series, as does the exceptionally well-realized alien environment. Internet fan sites and explanatory handbooks characteristic of the self-supporting popular 'folk' cultures that such films produce are a fur-ther reflection of the popularity of the film and the enduring fascination with fantastic creatures.[103]

Alien worlds work by providing variations on the familiar and by creating a sense of strangeness mediated by a comforting sense of familiarity. The fauna of Pandora embodies this to an exceptional degree. Among the many spe-cies created for the film, two fit particularly well into this discussion of mythi-cal winged beasts. The inhabitants of Pandora, the Na'vi, form a bond with pterodactyl-like creatures known as *Ikran* (or mountain banshee), while an even larger and more spectacular flying creature called *Toruk* (or *Last Shadow*) can only be ridden by the greatest hero, namely the earth-warrior, once he identifies himself with his new and imperilled culture. The creatures with their distinctly prehistoric features reflect the current interest in linking fabulous creatures with real prehistoric animals, while their ability to communicate with humans plays into ecological fantasies about the connectedness of all life.

The bird-like sirens eventually became mermaids, while griffins and the sphinx retained their appearance over long periods. The traditions associated with them, however, underwent fundamental changes. A general trend over time has provided rational explanations for the origin and behaviour of many of these creatures, although it would be a mistake to assume that literal belief is outdated or that they were ever wholeheartedly accepted as real at any period. However, changing attitudes have allowed for greater symbolic and metaphorical interpretations of their function and meaning. For example, the symbolist artist Gustav Moreau made significant use of several fantastic beasts – Pegasus, sphinx and hippogriff – to express the dangers and rewards of artistic and spiritual achievement. Fantasy writing for adults and for chil-dren, which became popular in the nineteenth century and has seen a revival in the twentieth and twenty-first centuries, uses these figures extensively, often giving them voices and active anthropomorphized personalities.

The serra or sawfish combines elements of a winged dragon and a sea monster. It appears in medieval bestiaries where it is sometimes called a harpy. According to the moral analysis of this creature as given in the bestiary texts, the serra is likened to someone with good intentions who fails to live up to them.[104] It is difficult to decide what actual creature, if any, lies behind this beast, and the variety of medieval images suggests that medieval artists and authors had no clear idea either. Some creatures will always defy categorization, and the serra has elements that might be likened to flying fishes or the manta ray. However, its size, serrated crest or dorsal fin and aggressive nature do not conform to any particular species. This concludes the discussion of fantastic flying beasts, drawing as it does on the winged and watery capacities of the sirens and harpies, and the idea of a winged sea dragon and the desire to integrate these creatures into the world of human morality and experience.

4

The age-old scourge: Dragons and monstrous serpents

Like to a lonely dragon, that his fen
Makes fear'd and talk'd of more than seen

CORIOLANUS ACT IV, SC. II

In the Anglo-Saxon *Beowulf* poem, the mound-dwelling fiery dragon who will bring about the hero's death is called the 'age-old scourge'. Its traditional and literary descendants from Fafnir to Smaug and the dragons that stalk the game world of *Dungeons & Dragons* are just as fierce. However, for the elegant ladies in Terry Pratchett's *Discworld*, small dragons of the species *Draco vulgaris* are a kind of dainty pet that make useful hand muffs and foot warmers in winter. Anne McCaffrey's fantasy series *The Dragonriders of Pern* also has miniature dragons, rather like hunting falcons, that interact with humans and complement the impressive psychic powers of the huge dragon steeds ridden by the warriors. Other companion dragons like Toothless in *How to Train your Dragon* (Cressida Cowell, 2011) and *Puff the Magic Dragon* (Leonard Lipton and Peter Yarrow, 1963) populate fantasy literature and song. The friendly behaviour of these 'reallio, trulio, little pet dragons', to paraphrase Ogden Nash's words from 'The Tale of Custard the Dragon' (1936), is very different from the traditional Western image of the dragon as a fierce, fire-breathing menace. Ultimately, however, from frightening to cute, dragons draw on a particular, and for the most part familiar, set of traditions and are among the best known of all fantastic creatures. (Figure 4.1) Dragons have a long history stretching back to ancient Mesopotamia, Egypt and India. They flourish throughout China, Japan and East Asia as well as Europe, and their

De draconibus Indiæ & Aethiopiæ.

Raco maximus est ferpentum, habet que dentes acutos & ferratos:um ta me maiorem habet in cauda quam dentibus, nec habet tā tum de ueneno ficut alij fer pentes. Siquem cauda ligauerit, occidit, nec elephas tutus est corporis sui magnitudi ne. Nam circa semitas delitescens per quas elephanti gradiuntur, crura cauda sua alli gat & innodat, suffocatosque perimit. Gignitur in India & Aethiopia. Vnde Plinius. Generat Aethiopia dracones Indicis pares, uicenum cubitorum. Solent autē quatuorde cim aut quindecim mutuo se cōplecti & erectis capitib. uelificare per mare & flumina ad pabula

Dracones uice nis cubitorum.

FIGURE 4.1 *Sebastian Munster describes the nature and habitat of dragons living in the remotest corners of the world.*

watery cousins, the sea serpents, have an even wider range. Whether they are symbols of chaos that must be brought under control, a sign of evil and sin that must be destroyed, powerful bringers of precipitation and portents or companions in the world of fantasy, dragons are creatures of power.

J. R. R. Tolkien's Middle-earth novels have influenced the perception of dragons as winged, fire-breathing, reptilian quadrupeds, but, as so often with fantastic creatures, they come in many forms. Some are wingless, legless or multi-headed, while a popular heraldic beast, the wyvern, has two legs, wings and a serpentine tail. The names reveal something of their heritage. Wyvern derives ultimately from the Latin word for viper (*vipera*); dragon is related to Greek *drakon* (a large serpent); and the Germanic word *wyrm* is cognate with Latin *vermis* (worm). Norse and Germanic dragon names frequently include the element 'worm', while terms for Slavic dragons incorporate *smej*, for 'snake', reflecting the serpentine characteristics of many dragons. They are prominent in Indo-European cultural traditions. The *nagas*, the serpent deities of Hindu and Buddhist traditions, are their important relatives. Nagas are associated with the powerful cobra, but also appear in hybrid human form with serpentine bodies. They are tutelary deities inhabiting water or caves and are bringers of rain with its fertilizing and destructive powers. As Buddhism spread, nagas absorbed many local traditions, which influenced the very different characteristics of the dragon in China and Japan. The watery and serpentine associations of the nagas also have affinities to traditions connected with mermaids and sirens, a reflection of the inherent complexities of mythical beasts.

The exact point at which these snake-like beings become dragons is not always clear. Although depictions of snakes are not found among the cave paintings of prehistoric Europe, various snake-like representations have been found at prehistoric sites in the Americas, Asia, Africa and Australia. The Bab-ylonian goddess Tiamat, who is both a creator goddess and an embodiment of chaos, appears as a huge horned serpent, often with dragon-like attrib-utes of claws and wings. A serpent tempts Eve in the Garden of Eden, and dragons feature in the biblical Apocalypse, although they are not prominent elsewhere in Christian depictions of Creation. They are, however, an essen-tial feature of Chinese and Asian models of the cosmos as embodiments of weather and landscape. Serpent creators are important in South American tribal myths, and the feathered serpent is a prominent cosmic figure in pre-Columbian cultures. Although there are exceptions, Indo-European and Ori-ental dragons combine characteristics drawn from several animals, while the creatures of South American and African cultures usually retain serpentine features.

Dragons and their enemies

In the Bible, Yahweh, speaking through Ezekiel, compares the wicked pharaoh variously to a sea monster, a serpent or a whale, depending on the translation, who will be caught in a net and cast upon the land to be devoured like carrion (Ezek. 32.2-4). In the Septuagint, he is compared to a 'serpent', while the Vulgate opts for the dragon's sea-going cousin, 'draconi qui est in mari'. Bishop Morgan's Welsh translation of 1588 introduces a sea monster, which produces a wonderfully alliterative phrase 'morfil yn y moroedd', and the 1611 King James Bible uses the phrase 'as a whale in the seas'; elsewhere the pharaoh is even compared to a crocodile.[1] The Greek Septuagint and the Latin Vulgate use the terms drakon and *drako* for the beasts in The Book of Revelation (the Apocalypse), and many English translations follow this. A 'great red dragon' attacks the woman clothed in the sun (Rev. 12), the whore of Babylon rides a 'scarlet-coloured beast' (Rev. 17-18) and 'the dragon, that old serpent' is cast into the abyss (Rev. 20). This and other dragon-like creatures in the Bible function as symbols for chaos and evil, and reflect the influence of earlier Mesopotamian mythic struggles in which a hero or creator god defeats a dragon-like creature associated with water and binds it in some fashion.[2] No doubt, biblical accounts also influenced the prevalence of dragons, and their negative qualities, in Western ecclesiastical writing and beyond that, in folklore, art and literature.

Copies of the Apocalypse (The Book of Revelation) were lavishly illustrated with the dragon in all its varying guises. Dragons appear in at least seven different forms in a fifteenth-century French Apocalypse (Pierpont Morgan Library MS M. 133), often with an explanatory inscription as to their identity and meaning. A many-headed example is called 'Dragon' (fol. 36v). Elsewhere it is winged with a protruding tongue inscribed *le deable* (fol. 38v), or with horns (fol. 39v). One version has a human face, rather like a two-legged manti-core (fol. 40v). Another with the inscription 'leniemy' (the enemy) is wingless with four legs (fol. 41v). There are numerous flying and multi-headed dragons (fol. 42v, fol. 63v, 66v), while the gaping jaws of Hellmouth take the form of a sea dragon (fol. 76v). The satanic dragon extends well beyond a purely bibli-cal context. Christ acts as dragon-slayer in the poem 'On the Resurrection of Christ' ('Surrexit Dominus de sepulchro') by the fifteenth-century Scottish poet William Dunbar, in which he overcomes 'the dragon blak', 'the deadly dragon Lucifer' and 'the crewall serpent with the mortall stang'.[3] On his search for the Holy Grail, Perceval has a religious vision in which the 'New Law' is a woman riding a lion, the symbol of Christ, followed by the 'Old Law', a woman mounted on a dragon.[4]

The Archangel Michael who leads the forces of good against Satan dur-ing the war in heaven in The Book of Revelation (ch. 12:7–9) has evolved into a popular warrior saint who defends his devotees against a multitude of physical and spiritual threats. The saint's cult spread into Western Europe about the fourth century CE. About the same time, images of the god Horus on horseback spearing his divine opponent, Seti, in the form of a crocodile began to appear. Horus does not adopt this position in Egyptian art, and this may indicate a fusion of Egyptian and Greco-Roman artistic forms.[5] Often, Michael appears as a winged warrior with sword, spear and shield in the act of killing a serpent or dragon. Sometimes he thrusts his spear or sword directly into the dragon's mouth, other times it enters the body crossways.[6] Other warrior saints, like George, adopt a similar stance. There are, however, interesting variations in the iconography of St Michael. For example, he con-ducts an air battle with a fierce winged dragon above Mont-Saint-Michel, one of his most important cult sites,[7] and elsewhere, he stands on a horned dragon holding a naked praying soul in each hand, thus combining his role in defeating Satan with that of a psychopomp who leads good souls safely to heaven.[8] In one of the earliest depictions of the archangel, the famous Saxon tympanum at Southwell Minster in Nottinghamshire, both saint and dragon are winged. Michael's dragon is evil personified, but there are sur-prisingly few dragon-slaying episodes among the miracles attributed to him. One exception occurs in a fifteenth-century collection of sermons in which Michael defeats a cave-dwelling dragon with poisonous breath. The putrefy-ing corpse of the defeated dragon is tossed into the sea.[9] This dragon is as much a personified plague as a symbol of Satan, and these motifs appear in other dragon-slaying tales.

The theme of the dragon-slayer is one of the most common human-versus-beast encounters in ancient and classical myths, heroic epics, medieval saints' legends and local folktales. Combats between heroic deities and monsters with snake-like characteristics figure prominently in Indo-European creation myths. Apollo defeats the Python and takes control of the Delphic sanctuary, and Marduk triumphs over Tiamat. Their actions embody a fundamental theme, namely that by overcoming these fearful and destructive dragon-like creatures, the heroic warrior (or deity) proves himself worthy to rule and assumes to himself some of the power of the defeated enemy.[10] The importance of god-warriors like Marduk is reinforced by images on Mesopotamian seals, coins and temple walls in which a heroic or crowned figure stands over a defeated serpentine monster.[11] The Greek and Mesopotamian myths may be part of a cosmogonic story that subsumes the defeated monster into an ordered world. Other dragons hunted by dragon-slayers represent the forces of evil overcome by virtue, or there are local monsters that embody disease and whose petrified bodies become features in the landscape. Despite the many variations, a common theme underpins many dragon-slayer tales. The hero both conquers and identifies with his enemy, and his success brings a great reward, be it a kingdom, a wife, treasure or some talisman.

Greco-Roman tradition is particularly rich in dragons. Heracles, a notable dragon-slayer, destroyed the serpent-headed Hydra, killed the dragon who guarded the apples in the Garden of Hesperides and slew another dragon while in the service of Omphale. He rescued the princess Hesione by disguising himself in her clothes, entering the mouth of a sea monster and cutting his way out.[12] The sea monster that Perseus defeats rises from the sea in numerous paintings, sculptures and frescoes, and in Lord Leighton's interpretation, painted in 1891, now hanging in the Walker Gallery, Liverpool, it is a winged, serpent-tailed dragon that breathes fire. Cadmus, the founder of Thebes, kills a serpent guarding a sacred spring. Ovid describes the creature as golden with flashing eyes, huge and full of venom (*Metamorphoses*, Bk 3, 50–137; Bk 4, 563–603). After he despatches it, Cadmus sows its teeth from which spring armed men. Eventually the gods transform Cadmus himself into a serpent, and his loving wife, Harmonia, pleads to be granted the same fate.

Jason also sows dragons' teeth that produce a deadly crop of armed men. He kills the dragon who guards the Golden Fleece, although he relies on Medea and her sleeping potion to accomplish the task. Homer, and other classical writers, noted that Bellerophon destroyed the part-serpent hybrid, known as the Chimaera. A twelfth-century commentator on Homer adds that the hero killed the Chimaera with a spear whose lead tip melted inside the fire-breathing monster causing it to suffocate. A number of elements of this story, such as the false accusation of adultery; the sealed letter that calls for the bearer's death; the monster that decimates the country; the lead-tipped spear; and the eventual reward of rulership and a bride, are features of other dragon-slayer tales.[13]

Latin chronicles compiled in Poland recorded the origins of the city of Kraków. Bishops Vincent Kadłubek and Stefan Mierzwa in the thirteenth century and Jan Długosz in the fifteenth century recorded traditions about a ruler named Krak (Graccus). A dragon who demanded a ransom of cattle ravaged his land until Krak, or his son, fed the greedy monster cattle-hides stuffed with sulphur, which caused it to immolate itself. Mierzwa compares the actions of these Polish heroes to the biblical Daniel. According to the Vulgate translation, which the chronicle writers would have known, Daniel promised 'interficiem draconem absque gladio et fuste' or, as the King James Bible (1611) renders it, promised to kill the dragon 'without sword or staff' and accomplished this task by feeding it lumps of combustible material. Długosz further localizes the incident in a cave at the foot of Mount Pawel. Eventually, this famous Polish dragon acquired the multiple heads typical of Slavic dragons, and the hero became a poor tailor who tricked the dragon and married the princess. An illustration in Sebastian Munster's *Cosmographia Universalis* (1544) commemorates the story, the supposed bones of the dragon are still preserved in Kraków cathedral, and the cave site remains a popular tourist attraction, complete with a fire-spouting dragon statue. [14]

In the *Shahnameh,* the tenth-century epic by the Iranian poet Ferdowsi, two famous Persian heroes, Esfandiyar and Rostam, fight dragons. Esfandiyar, a princely follower of Zoroaster, undertakes a series of tasks, one of which involves a dragon. Esfandiyar sheaths his chariot in spiked armour plates and drives into the dragon's mouth, shredding the creature from within. The action echoes encounters with the basilisk and the cockatrice and, although this fight takes place on land, there are other tales about a hero who enters the mouth of a sea monster and later cuts himself out.[15] During a quest to free his companions, Rostam encounters a serpentine dragon that emerges from a forest while the hero is sleeping. Fortunately, Rostam's horse warns him of the dragon's approach. Motifs such as the animal companion and the spiked armour echo other more localized dragon tales. For example, a memorial to a knight with a small lion at his feet adorns a medieval monument in the church at Nunnington, Yorkshire. According to a local tradition, this knight was a dragon-slayer who clothed himself in spiked armour and defeated a dragon with the help of his faithful hound. Unfortunately, the dog carried some of the poison back to his master, and they both perished.[16]

The earliest versions of the *Yamata no Orochi* legends are recorded in two ancient Japanese texts, the *Kojiki* (seventh century CE) and the *Nihongi* (eighth century CE).[17] After the storm-god Susanoo's expulsion from heaven, he meets an old couple, whose names suggest links with agricultural deities. They must sacrifice their daughter to the dragon-like *Yamata no Orochi* with its eight heads, eight tails and red eyes, or in the more elaborate description of the *Nihongi*, eight heads and tails, red eyes, plus a body large enough to cover eight hills. In return for the girl's hand in marriage, Susanoo baits a trap with sake, which the greedy monster drinks. He then cuts off its heads, dismembers it and seizes a magic sword-talisman embedded in the sea monster's tail. The tale resembles the dragon-slayer myth of Perseus, Andromeda and the sea serpent. Both Greek and Japanese heroes marry beautiful women threatened by dragons, but the function of the dragon differs in these tales. The Greco-Roman monster is sent by the gods as a punishment; Perseus's victory, on the other hand, demonstrates his suitability to be king. Susanoo is the Shinto god of the sea and storms, and there are overtones of agricultural mythology as reflected in the names of other characters and the sea-monster *Yamata no Orochi*'s association with water.

Another man against dragon narrative, which is less straightforward than it first appears, is the Norse account of how the god Thor baited a hook with an ox-head to catch Jörmungandr, the Midgard serpent, one of Loki's monstrous offspring.[18] The fishing line snaps, or is cut, and the serpent escapes. When they confront one another again at Ragnarok, Thor kills Jörmungandr, but dies from its poison. The confrontation between god and sea monster is recorded in Snorri Sturluson's *Prose Edda*, the eddic poem 'Hymiskviða', and on a number of stone monuments where the monster appears as a giant serpent with a dragon-like head.[19] Although this has elements of a cosmic creation myth in which chaos gives way to order, at least until the end of time, the motif in which the hero kills the dragon, but dies from its poison occurs in local dragon tales, and suggests that the encounter is more complex than just a cosmic myth.[20]

Warrior saints are obvious candidates as dragon-slayers, given the link so often made in a Christian context between serpents and sin. St George's story fuses the theme of a Christian saint who defends goodness against evil, and a secular hero who defeats a dragon, then rescues and marries the endangered woman. George does not seem to have originated as a dragon-slaying saint. This part of his legend enters European tradition in the thirteenth century in the famous medieval collection *The Golden Legend* (*Legenda Aurea*) in which a dragon causes death and destruction near the city of Selene in Syria unless a human victim is sacrificed to placate the rapacious beast. George arrives just in time to save a princess who binds the dragon with her belt and leads it to the city to be killed. The motif of a Christian saint overcoming a satanic dragon underlies this version of the legend, but George's dragon does not put up much of a fight nor in this version does the dragon-slayer gain a wife.[21] St George was venerated as a saint of healing and protection throughout the Middle East, the eastern Mediterranean and North Africa before his cult arrived in England. As a defender against disease, St George is associated with wells and healing sites, and he protects crops from pestilence and bad weather. As he became more popular in Britain, the story became more localized. The church at Brinsop in Hereford, which is dedicated to him, has a beautiful medieval tympanum showing the saint spearing a monster. The dragon, according to local tradition, supposedly lived in a well near the church, and the saint fought it in a local field. The Dragon's Mound near the Uffington White Horse, Oxfordshire, is another site where traditions about a battle between George and a dragon have been localized.[22]

Prior to the Reformation, the dragon's defeat was the occasion for converting a populace, rather than marriage with a princess, but after the Reformation in England, George's cult was associated with authority and nationhood, and the romantic element became more prominent. He features in a printed romance tale by Richard Johnson (1573–1659) called *The Seven Champions of Christendom*. In this charming 'heroic' tale, six saints, Denys of France, James of Spain, Anthony of Italy, Andrew of Scotland, Patrick of Ireland and David of Wales, help St George rescue a princess. The saints become knightly heroes and companions on a grand boy's own adventure, and their usual functions as national saints are set aside in favour of the English St George.[23] As a warrior saint, he served as an appropriate patron for knightly societies and royal authority, such as the Order of the Garter founded in 1348. He is the saintly protector of countries, such as England and Georgia, and of cities like Kiev. He is the patron of cathedrals, churches and public buildings, and appears on flags and insignias.[24] In all these contexts, the dragon embodies 'otherness' in the form of illness, bad weather, evil or the enemy of a town or city. As is obvious from this range of functions, the symbolism of George and his dragon is very malleable, and this has produced some interesting contemporary interpretations. In an illustration by the English artist Briton Rivière, St George lies spent and exhausted on the ground near the body of the dead dragon. This image with its implied acknowledgement of struggle appeared in a booklet extolling the courage of the Belgian people after the German invasion at the beginning of the First World War.[25] On a war memorial outside a church in Groningen, another weary and pensive George gazes at a dragon carved onto the plinth on which he stands.[26] A monument outside the United Nations in New York strikes a more hopeful note. The dragon, composed of pieces of Soviet and American ballistic missiles, confronts St George in a gesture to the dangers of the nuclear age.[27]

Another Eastern warrior saint who influenced the development of George's cult, St Theodore, was important among Coptic Christians. He is one of the patrons of Venice, and a representation of Theodore subduing a large crocodile surmounts a pillar in St Mark's Square. Despite the popularity of warrior saints like George, Michael and Theodore, saintly dragon-slayers, both male and female, do not necessarily engage in outright combat with the dragon.

As a symbol of sin and the errors of paganism, the dragon has obvious echoes of the serpent in the Garden of Eden and the Apocalypse dragon in the bottomless pit. Its expulsion, confinement or destruction by a saint may signal the triumph of Christianity, but it can also function as a foundation legend of a city or a territory. This symbolism informs one of the miracles of Sylvester, a pope as well as a saint, who sealed a dragon, whose pestilential breath was killing the people of Rome, in its own lair.[28] In the life of St Marcellus written by Bishop Venatius Fortunatus in the sixth century, the serpent/dragon is poisonous rather than fire-breathing. Its connection with Roman ruins has overtones of gladiatorial games, and its subjugation provides a foundation legend for cities like Metz, a link, reinforced in the twelfth century, when a pageant dragon was introduced in connection with the Rogation Day festivities that continue to the present day.[29]

Narratives about dragon-slayer saints are surprisingly local, and, for the most part, follow recognizable patterns.[30] St Samson of Dol, an important saint in Brittany, Cornwall and Wales, subdues several dragons by force of personality rather than combat.[31] For example, he ties his belt around the dragon's neck, a dragon-taming action performed by the princess rescued by St George and other saintly figures. Dragons with pestilential breath often haunt marshy areas on which cities are founded. A local Umbrian warrior saint and converted Roman soldier, Crescentino, overcomes a dragon in battle. This event is commemorated in an eighteenth-century painting in the cathedral dedicated to him at Cittá di Castello, the centre of his cult where 'bones' of the dead dragon were once preserved,[32] and an eighteenth-century statue of Crescentino trampling a dragon stands among the saints on the Colonnade of St Peter's Basilica, Rome. Another pestilential dragon, who roamed the area near the river Nera in Umbria, was slain by a hermit, St Felice, and a relief in the church of San Felice di Narco near the Umbrian town of Castel San Felice shows him in the act of hacking a serpentine creature. Tales of local dragons who bring danger and pestilence to a region are also attached to secular heroes. The folklorist Mary Lovett Cameron collected an example from the Maremma district of Tuscany, which was formerly very marshy, at the beginning of the last century. The hero was an unspecified ducal member of the powerful Sforza family who established a stronghold at nearby Santafiore. The temporal setting is vague – according to the narrator, before any of the audience was born. The dragon, who lived in a cave high on a mountain, terrified the population and decimated their livestock. The beast was no match for the brave and cunning Duke Sforza who killed the dragon after luring it out of its cave by attaching a red flag to the end of his lance. Afterwards, he gave its jawbone to the friars of La Trinità.[33]

Isidore makes a distinction between serpents (*anguis*) who creep and *dracones* who can be lured from their dens into the air (Bk 12, 4). Elsewhere, such distinctions between dragons and serpents are not always clear, as the life of the Apostle Philip illustrates. According to the *Legenda Aurea*, the saint refused to worship at the temple of Mars in Scythia, which was inhabited by a dragon. Philip banished the dragon to the wilderness and restored life to victims overcome by its poisonous breath.[34] A thirteenth-century mosaic in St Mark's Church in Venice shows the dragon with wings, a serpentine body and a typical, vaguely equine head, a clear symbol of pagan error. Earlier sources have a more elaborate account, although the message of triumphant Christianity remains. Philip and his companions undergo a series of adventures in the manner of other tales of heroic travelling companions. They overcome serpents in the wilderness and dragons that guard the gates of a city, and eventually arrive in a place whose inhabitants worship the *Echidna* (literally 'she-viper', originally a primordial half-woman, half-serpent monster). Philip banishes the Echidna, her dragon and serpent offspring and her pagan priests to a bottomless pit.[35] In the fifteenth-century painting by Fra Filippo Lippi in Florence's Strozzi chapel, the Echidna, a snarling, but rather small, reptilian creature with something of the basilisk about it, emerges from a hole and cringes before the wrath of the saint.

A dragon called the *Graouilly* parades through the city of Metz each year, and the history of its association illustrates the ease with which fantastic creatures adapt to different contexts. St Clement of Metz, whose life is set in the eighth century, confronted a huge snake-like Graouilly whose breath polluted the atmosphere, and, with other poisonous snakes, inhabited the local Roman amphitheatre. This dragon, with its serpentine form and its association with Roman ruins, symbolized the corruptions of paganism, and after the citizens converted to Christianity, the saint drove the creature into the wilderness.[36] St Clement's *Graouilly* has become a focus for communal activities, both religious and secular, in Metz. A banner and later an effigy of the dragon, which would be 'fed' and 'beaten' by the populace, were carried in the Rogation Day procession and are mentioned by Rabelais (*Gargantua and Pantagruel*, (trans Urquhart) the Fourth Book, ch. 59). The dragon effigy remained in the cathedral throughout the year, and today, it continues to unite the city, attracting tourists and adorning the arms of Metz's football club. Although pageant dragons do not seem to have been a part of the medieval cult of St Petroc, the patron saint of Cornwall, the saint does tame a serpent/dragon. According to the life of St Petroc, an evil lord kept a pit full of snakes. After his death, they ate one another until only one huge dragon-like specimen remained. St Petroc tamed it by putting his belt around its neck, a technique often adopted by both male and female saints.[37] The dragon in these narratives, whether secular or religious, is a polyvalent symbol that can signify pagan error, personify plague and nature, tamed by the process of urbanization, or provide a rallying point for civic pride.

Treasure hoards and Germanic dragons

Dragons are plentiful in Germanic, Norse and Anglo-Saxon traditions, where the words *worm/orme* and *dreki* refer to creatures that range from serpentine to reptilian. These beasts are often associated with the earth and with guarding treasure. They come into conflict with a national, local or semi-divine hero, and finally, we meet some who regularly breathe fire and fly. Dragons are associated with mounds in Anglo-Saxon and Germanic traditions, and the addition of treasure and death is a feature of many accounts.[38] The fight between the ageing Beowulf and the firedrake epitomizes the qualities of both dragon and dragon-slayer. At the end of the poem, a huge, fire-breathing monster with snake-like coils and the ability to fly has taken possession of a hoard of gold buried in the barrow of a pagan lord. After an intruder steals a piece of its treasure, the firedrake wreaks terrible revenge on Beowulf's people, by burning their homes to the ground. Beowulf challenges the dragon, who surrounds the hero with a ring of fire and fatally wounds him. Only one companion comes to Beowulf's aid. Together they eviscerate the beast, although the dragon's poison kills Beowulf, and eventually, its carcase is tossed into the sea (*Beowulf*, fitt 31–43). This is undoubtedly one of the most famous dragon fights in Western literature, not least because of its influence on J. R. R. Tolkien.[39] This complex and layered episode is far from a simple pagan survival; it reflects analogues in hagiographical romance and other heroic tales.[40] Beowulf's sacrifice to keep his people safe echoes cosmic dragon legends, but a number of elements, the cave dwelling, the destruction of the carcase to prevent pollution and the hero who conquers the dragon but dies from its poison, echo more local dragon tales.

The *Beowulf* poem contains a reference to another Germanic hero, Sigemund, who kills a dragon and appropriates his hoard.[41] However, the most elaborate account of dragon slaying is associated with Sigemund's son, Sigurd (Sigurðr), the bane of Fafnir the dragon, whose story appears in several medieval sources, the *Völsunga Saga*, *Þiðrekssaga*, *Fáfnismál*, Snorri Sturluson's *Prose Edda* and a variety of church and runestone carvings.[42] The dragon, Fafnir, killed his father and cheated his brother in order to possess a great treasure. He was once human, but some sources suggest that Fafnir became a dragon by wearing his father's magic Helm of Dread. His brother, Regin, encourages his apprentice and foster-son, Sigurd, to kill Fafnir. The young hero digs a pit and, as the dragon passes above him, plunges his sword into its body. Later, while cooking the dragon's heart for Regin, he puts his burnt thumb in his mouth and acquires the power to understand the birds who warn him about Regin's murderous plans. In an alternative version, recorded in the Old Norse *Þiðrekssaga*, Regin becomes a fire dragon (*linnormr*) because of his devotion to sorcery. His brother Mimir tries to rid himself of his apprentice,

Sigurd, by sending him off to the forest to be killed by his dragon/brother. Sigurd, however, kills Regin, burns himself while cooking the dragon's flesh and learns from the birds that Mimir is his enemy.[43] As Siegfried in the *Nibelungenlied*, this dragon-slaying hero acquires invulnerability by bathing in the dragon's blood, except for one vulnerable spot, which eventually brings about his death.[44]

Arthur's dragons: Under the tower, in the sky and in his dream

In the margin of a Book of Hours produced in Paris at the end of the fifteenth century, possibly for the use of Lady Margaret Beaufort, is a red, fire-breathing dragon, one of the emblems of the Tudor king, Henry VII.[45] It is all too easy to over-interpret marginalia in manuscripts, but it is certainly tempting to link this with Geoffrey of Monmouth's story of the red and white dragons and the rise of the Tudor dynasty.

In laying the foundation of the Arthurian legend, Geoffrey of Monmouth frames the life of his famous, and fictional, king with three dragon adventures. The first is the incident of the two buried dragons that cause Vortigern's tower to fall. The king digs up the chests containing the dragons on the advice of the child wizard, Merlinus Ambrosius. The fight between these red and white beasts is richly symbolic. It signals Vortigern's failure in allowing the Saxons' entry into Britain, the sagacity of Merlin the prophet and the eventual triumph of the Britons over their enemies at some point beyond the conclusion of Geoffrey's history (Bk 6, ch. 19). After a long prophetic section concluding with the promise that eventually the 'Saxon worm' (the White dragon) will be defeated, Geoffrey warns the king that Aurelianus and Uther, the 'sons of Constantine', are about to return (Bk 7). The second dragon appears when Uther observes a comet in the form of a golden dragon, and Merlin interprets its significance. The comet signals the death of Uther's brother Aurelianus, Uther's future as king, the even more glorious reign of Uther's son, Arthur, and the role of his daughter and her descendants as British rulers. To commemorate the occasion, Uther commissions two golden dragons, 'cunningly wrought', one for the church at Winchester and one to carry into battle, and at this point, he takes the name 'pendragon' a title that signifies his role as leader (Bk 8, ch. 1–2, 15–17). Geoffrey says, not quite accurately, that it means 'dragon's head' and that Uther received this soubriquet because of Merlin's prediction that he would become king. The fiery comet/dragon and Uther's name change became a standard feature of the many versions of Geoffrey's story, which were incorporated into the developing Arthurian legend.

The third instance of dragons in connection with Arthur is his ominous prophetic dream before his departure to engage the emperor of Rome. Arthur inherits his father's dragon standard and, like him, wears a helmet surmounted by a golden dragon. Geoffrey's account of Arthur's life is essentially one of conquest leading to a 'pax arthuriana' when the noblest men of the world visit Arthur's court, until the jealous Roman emperor challenges the British king's authority. Arthur musters his troops, but before he departs for Rome, he has a disturbing dream in which a bear is defeated by a dragon coming 'from the west with fiery eyes'. His courtiers assure him that he is the dragon and the bear is just some dreadful imaginary creature, perhaps a giant (Bk 10, ch. 2). Geoffrey, however, gives his readers a hint that not all is well. Arthur remains disturbed despite the assurances of his followers, and ironically, Arthur's name is often interpreted as bear (Lat. *artus*, W. *arth*). When the king defeats the giant of Mont St Michel, the courtier's interpretation appears to be correct, and as he marches towards Rome, Arthur raises the dragon standard to provide a place of sanctuary for the wounded (Bk 10, ch. 6). During Arthur's battle with the Emperor Lucius, the wounded Cei retreats to the safety of this golden dragon standard. Eventually, however, the real implications of the dream become clear. Arthur learns that Mordred has usurped his kingdom, and he rushes home to fight a final battle, after which the wounded Arthur departs to Avalon. The implication of the dragon dream is never fully explained, unlike the fight between the red and the white dragons or the appearance of the golden dragon comet. Merlin prophesies correctly about the first two, but he is absent when Arthur has his dream, and the courtiers, lacking Merlin's prophetic sagacity, interpret the dream incorrectly.

These three dragon events, linked by a master storyteller, contextualize a typical heroic biography, namely the rise and fall of a hero whose passing holds hope for the future. Perhaps because the incident of the red dragon is so famous, and has parallels elsewhere, speculations about the possible origins of this episode have overshadowed the function of the dragon episodes in Geoffrey's overall plan. Illustrations in medieval Arthurian romance manuscripts show Merlin or Arthur carrying Uther's dragon standard,[46] and the fight between the red and white dragons was a subject for medieval illustrators. In a manuscript now in the British Library, a young Ambrosius addresses Vortigern with the two dragons in their watery chests beneath their feet, and later the dragons conduct an aerial fight next to Vortigern's tower (Cotton Claudius B VII, f. 224). In the St Albans chronicle, a splendidly royal Vortigern observes the battle between the two dragons (London, Lambeth Palace, LPL, MS 6, f.43r). In an account from an earlier work, the *Historia Brittonum*, a fatherless boy, Ambrosius, whom Geoffrey renames Merlin, appears before King Vortigern, ostensibly to be sacrificed so the tower can stand. Instead, he convinces the king to retrieve two chests containing the little creatures who grow into two dragons (*Historia Brittonum*, Part III, 40, 41, 42). This account was a major influence on Geoffrey. Another version of the dragon story, without the Arthurian characters, appears in the tale of 'Lludd a Llefelys' from the *Mabinogion*, a collection of medieval Welsh tales, in which the dragon is one of the three plagues, which 'can be seen as variants on the theme of the historical invaders who threatened the sovereignty of the Island of Britain'.[47]

The dragon on the Welsh flag, designed by the Welsh artist and folklorist, T. H. Thomas, was only adopted officially in the 1950s. The heraldic Welsh dragon is a fierce protector, a role it has in other heraldic contexts, rather than the symbol of chaos or sin, but its immediate cultural significance lies in its ability to provide an identifier for Wales as a nation. Welsh traditions locate King Arthur's court at the old Roman fortress town of Caerleon, an important Roman military and trade centre. Not surprisingly, discussions of the origin of the red dragon focus on possible Roman and Celtic connections between the Roman draco standard and the Welsh flag. *Draig* is used in Welsh poetry as a metaphor for a warrior. It has been suggested that the draco standard came to be identified with the fierceness of British warriors as *dreigiau*, and that this tradition survived until Geoffrey came to write his history.[48] On the surface, this argument makes some sense, but there is no indication that *draig* was especially favoured as a title over other warrior metaphors. Attempts to identify Geoffrey's sources, and the reasons he chose them, highlight the interesting, but complex, attempts to discover whether Arthur was, or was not, a real king. If Arthur was not a historical person, which seems likely, then discussions about whether the Roman 'draco' banner might have been transferred to an early British lord called Arthur are moot. Nevertheless, forging links with the classical world was important, and both early Britons and Anglo-Saxons may have imitated the imperial constructs of Rome without the need for a 'real' hero. The Anglo-Saxon title 'Bretwalda' can be translated 'ruler of Britain', which might imply a quasi-roman claim to territorial rule in a non-Arthurian context. The banners and standards of Edwin of Deira, as described by Bede, could reflect Roman emblems of authority, either through images on coins or perhaps because Bede himself was familiar with the Vegetius writings on the art of war,[49] and a red 'dragon of Wessex' banner is embroidered on the Bayeux tapestry. The question of why such traditions became absorbed into Arthurian lore remains interesting. If Arthur was a legendary figure undergoing historicization, then forging a fictional continuity with Rome makes sense and gives an insight into Geoffrey's motivation without the need for complicated quasi-historical speculations.

The episode of the dragon fight, in the wider context of folk narrative, shares significant features with migratory legends, because they become attached to widely distributed sites. Conflicts between rival dragons are not unknown.[50] Vortigern's falling tower has elements comparable to legends associated with the location of sacred buildings in which anything built during the day falls down at night. Often the location and stability of the building depends on someone with the appropriate power of being able to exorcize a troublesome spirit. This person, usually a minister or cunning man, reads down the spirit, tricks it into some container or forces it to perform some difficult task.[51] Vortigern's tower has much in common with this migratory legend. However, in the Arthurian versions, the red dragon is not a troublesome spirit, but rather one that will bring salvation, and Merlin's power lies in his ability to interpret the meaning of the dragons' actions rather than overcome them.

A carving in the Breton church of St-Jacques at Perros-Guirec may show the Breton saint, Euflamm, rescuing Arthur from a dragon. However, in the life of this Breton saint, Arthur, wielding a club and a lion-skin covered shield, destroys a monster who dwells in a cave. Since there are few details about the monster's appearance, it is difficult to tell whether this is an actual dragon. Its closest relative may be the *afanc*, which attacks Owein in the Welsh Arthurian romance *Iarlles y Ffynnwn*, which also has human (spear throwing) and dragon-like characteristics.[52] The detail of Arthur unusually carrying a club suggests a comparison with Heracles who kills dragon-like serpents.[53] Other Arthurian heroes, Lancelot, Owain/Yvain and Tristan, all have close encounters with dragons. Lancelot kills a dragon that emerges from a tomb (*Lancelot en prose* BnF Fr 112(3) f. 23r), and Owain acquires a helpful, perhaps too helpful, lion companion after saving the poor beast from a serpent.[54] These episodes were a popular subject for illustration. As the hero of a later ballad 'Kemp Owyne' (Child 34), Owain rescues a lady who has been transformed into a serpentine dragon. The dragon story in the Tristan saga is, in many ways, a classic dragon-slayer tale, one that includes a seemingly impossible task, killing a dragon in order to gain a wife, and a posthumous poisoning.[55] Jealous courtiers send the young hero to Ireland to win Isolde as a bride for his uncle Mark, hoping that he will be killed. The Irish king has promised his daughter in marriage to anyone who can rid the kingdom of a ravaging dragon. Tristan kills it and cuts out its tongue, but the poisonous venom temporarily overcomes him. Meanwhile, a cowardly courtier removes the dragon's head and claims the princess, but Tristan produces the beast's tongue and proves that he is the real dragon-slayer.[56] As so often with such a popular plot structure, there are interesting variations. Tristan wins a bride for someone else and does not die from the poison, although these events initiate a complex tragic love story. The number of surviving medieval examples reflects the popularity of Tristan's dragon adventure. These include a tile from Chertsey Abbey in Surrey, a series of fourteenth-century murals in Runkelstein Castle near Bolzano in the South Tyrol and several elaborate, and very rare, medieval embroideries.[57]

Dragon lore

A number of factors, not least of which is the degree of overlap with other fantastic creatures, complicate the task of tracing developments within dragon lore. For example, narratives about the sea monsters that threaten Andromeda and Hesione resemble tales in which St George rescues a princess from a dragon. The picture is further complicated by the fact that dragon narratives are contextualized in different genres: hagiographic legends, like those of George or Martha; classical narratives, like the adventures of Perseus or Jason; widely translated romances, like the story of Tristan; and literary tales, such as the rescue of Angelica in Ariosto's Renaissance poem.

For all their power, dragons are very susceptible to human heroes. A story first recorded at the beginning of the eighteenth century opens with the common motif of a poisonous cattle-killer. A reward is offered, and a brave young peasant wins land and glory by destroying the serpent. This tale is also linked to an Anglo-Saxon carving of a stylized beast in St Mary's Priory Church, Deerhurst, near Gloucester, which traditionally is said to represent the defeated serpent.[58] In *De Nugis Curialium*, a collection of anecdotes and tales compiled by the twelfth-century courtier Walter Map, a hermit takes pity on a seemingly insignificant little snake and gives it a dish of milk. The creature returns daily and eventually surrounds the hermit's cell with its enormous bulk, until a visiting saint, similar to a wandering dragon-slayer, kills it.[59] The story of the Lambton Worm begins in a similar way. The heir to a great estate throws a strange little creature that he has caught on an illicit Sunday fishing expedition into a well where it grows into a menacing dragon. Eventually, he dons a suit of armour studded with knives and destroys the beast. However, a witch revealed the secret of killing the dragon and demanded something in return. That something turns out to be his father, and when he refuses to keep this terrible bargain, he brings down a curse on the family.[60]

The Roman writer Apuleius (124–170 CE) wrote a series of picaresque adventures known as *The Metamorphoses or the Golden Ass*. It contains an unusual and very graphic example of a shape-shifter dragon who appears in the guise of a kindly old man and then lures his victims, usually young men, to some remote place where he devours them.[61] Dragons are often credited with the deaths of humans and animals, and the motif of a young virgin sacrifice is common, but this example is caught in the act of devouring its young victim. Two Renaissance painters, Luca Signorelli and Vittore Carpaccio, add a similarly macabre touch to the St George legend by depicting the attacking dragon among the decomposing remains of its previous victims. Sometimes, however, the dragon scores a posthumous victory. Tristan succumbs temporarily to the dragon's poison, and one of the most famous dragon-slayers, Beowulf,

FIGURE 4.2 *Charles Owen's* An Essay Towards a Natural History of Serpents *(1742) distinguishes the snaky basilisk from the more reptilian cockatrice, but both are crowned as 'regulus', kings of their species.*

dies from poison. Thor kills the monstrous serpent, Jörmungandr, when the two confront one another at Ragnarok, but the god subsequently dies from its poison. Sir Peter Loschky meets a similar tragic end, and a dragon-like Welsh viper occasionally claims its slayers.[62] The basilisk and the cockatrice, near relatives of the dragon by virtue of their reptilian features and ability to fly, are also poisonous.[63] (Figure 4.2)

Traditionally, dragons are not friendly beasts, which makes it even more interesting that dragon companions and comedic encounters have become such a prominent feature of modern fantasy writing. A handful of dragon tales seem to incorporate elements of an elaborately exaggerated narrative genre known as the tall tale in which a narrator exploits an implausible situation for comic effect. The dragon-slayers in tall tales about large and seemingly intimidating animals who meet rather comical ends are more like trickster heroes, than noble knights-errant. In the Sussex legend of the Knucker of Lyminster, the dragon dies of indigestion after it eats a badly cooked pudding or a poisoned pie.[64] The fierce Somerset dragon known as the Gurt (i.e. great) Worm of Shervage Wood was despatched by a woodcutter who mistook it for a log and then chopped it to pieces.[65] The account of the Dragon of Wantley, first published as a mock-heroic ballad in 1685, and included in Bishop Thomas Percy's *Reliques of Ancient Poetry* in 1765, is a satirical account of a hero wearing studded armour, one More of More-Hall, who kills the cave-dwelling dragon by kicking the creature in its only vulnerable spot, its backside.[66] The studded armour, cave-dwelling dragon and vulnerable spot are features common to many local dragon tales. (Figure 4.3) However, the undignified, slightly risqué death of the Wantley dragon sets a more satirical tone, which Owen Wister, best known as the writer of an iconic Western novel, rewrote as a success-ful children's book.[67] The American folk hero, Davy Crocket, fought alligators, the next best thing in a country where dragons are scarce, and many of his adventures resemble the humorously exaggerated tall-tale genre. A popular almanac of 1837 shows not Crockett but his wife beating up an 'alligator' that resembles many dragon-like cousins in similar popular publications.[68]

Land-dragons frequently retain an association with water, favouring marshes and wells as dwellings. Sometimes the dragon is killed while slaking its thirst after a killing spree.[69] Robert Chambers, in his impressive nineteenth-century

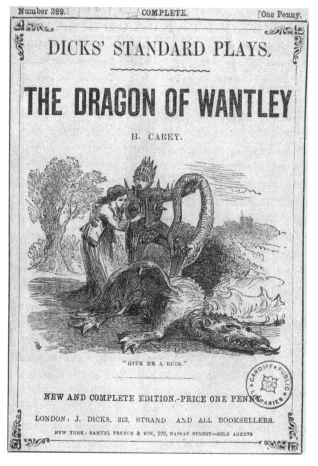

FIGURE 4.3 *A knight in studded armour saves a damsel from the Dragon of Wantley, in an eighteenth-century stage version of the tale.*

collection of antiquarian lore, describes a dragon living near a well in Scotland who killed nine maidens. Eventually, a young man called Martin despatched it at a site known locally as Martinstane. The tale is a common legend type, here associated with a carved Pictish monument, the Balluderon cross slab stone in Angus, Scotland. The, now damaged, stone was once covered with typical pictographs, which include horsemen, a serpent and a strange hybrid beast possibly a stylized dolphin, which might have inspired the idea of the dragon and its slayer.[70]

A dragon's habitat provides a clear hint to its character. The Hereford *mappa mundi* locates a fiery mountain inhabited by dragons on the island of Taprobane (modern Sri Lanka), a very remote part of the world at the beginning of the fourteenth century when the map was drawn. A fifteenth-century map made by a Venetian cartographer locates a nest of sea monsters at the bottom of the world below the southern tip of Africa. This 'nidus abimalion' (nest of creatures of the abyss) places winged dragons among more conventional mermaids.[71] On another Venetian nautical chart from a century earlier, a flying dragon carries off a victim, while a kraken attacks the ship sailing near the mythical Atlantic island of Braçil.[72] The location and its purpose is more than just decorative; it indicates the dangers of navigation and the elasticity of boundaries, and demonstrates how often different creatures are bracketed together.

It is not surprising that as creatures with serpentine attributes, dragons inhabit caves, deserts and remote mountains, locations that reinforce their connection with boundaries, both geographic and metaphoric. Fire-breathing dragons were often the enemies of Germanic heroes, but the *Historia Monachorum in Aegypto* (fourth century CE), an account of the lives of Egyptian hermits, contains fiery and fierce dragons. Egypt was an area that Greek and Roman writers considered the natural home of strange and dangerous creatures. Illustrated copies of this text depict various hermit saints taming winged, fire-breathing dragons,[73] and the Egyptian location reinforces their liminal nature in terms of geographical remoteness. However, serpent dragons overcome by early Christian saints were specifically located in Roman ruins, a motif that underscores the triumph of Christian wisdom over pagan ignorance and, through the transformation of inhospitable areas into thriving cities, an indication of society's power over nature and disease.

Dragon ladies and lady dragons

In a legend localized at Ben Vair in Scotland, a mother dragon who takes revenge for the death of her young is tricked into beating herself to death against a rock, subsequently known as Leac-na-Beithreach (Dragon's rock).[74] Female dragons are less common than their male counterparts, but specific creatures with dragon-like attributes such as the snake-tailed Chimaera and the Hydra, a multi-headed swamp beast slain by Heracles, were female. Another of Heracles's adventures concerns the Scythian Drakaina, a half female and half serpent, who refused to restore his stolen horses until the hero had intercourse with her. This particular account, as told by Herodotus, may derive from a Scythian origin myth transferred to the Greek hero (*Histories* Bk 4, ch. 9), and the later Christian legend of St Philip overcoming the Echidna may also resonate with this incident.

Although women are often potential victims in dragon tales, they can connect with dragons in a variety of ways. For example, Athena, although not a slayer herself, supports several Greek heroes in their battles with dragons. Dragon-like winged serpents drew Medea's chariot. She drugged the sleepless dragon of Colchis that guarded the Golden Fleece, and one source even described her comforting her erstwhile pet, before its death.[75] An early-sixteenth-century stained-glass depiction of St George may add a lascivious aspect to the feminized dragon as a direct contrast to the saint's chastity, a quality much emphasized in medieval accounts.[76] The child-snatcher Lamia was initially a woman who became a snake-like monster out of grief for her lost children. Later traditions, many associated with the Libyan Desert, depict lamias as part women, part snake, who lure and devour young men.[77] In his *Life of Apollonius of Tyana*, Philostratus recounts how a young philosophy student fell in love with an apparently beautiful woman whom Apollonius exposed as a shape-shifting Lamia (Bk 4, ch. 25). Her serpentine rapaciousness concealed in a seductive shell remained a feature of many romantic nineteenth-century realizations of Lamia's story.[78]

In the Alexander Romance, various dragons, some studded with emeralds, others with two heads or horns are among the exotic creatures defeated by the conquering king. An alternative birth tale also links Alexander to a mythical dragon. The Egyptian pharaoh and magician, Nectanebus, a shape-shifter who takes the form of a dragon, prophesies to Alexander's mother, Olympias, that her son will be the offspring of a god. One night, according to the Middle English version in John Gower's *Confessio Amantis*, he enters her chamber, 'Thurgh the deceipte of his magique … of a dragon tok the forme' (Gower, Bk 6, lines 2060–3). Illustrations of a dragon-like creature entering Olympias's bed appear in numerous copies of the Alexander Romance. However, an early Syrian mosaic shows Olympias with a serpent rather than a dragon and demonstrates the comparative ease with which characteristics flowed between snakes and dragons.[79] Plutarch's *Life of Alexander* (Part 1, sect. 2) rationalizes the tale by suggesting that Olympias was a follower of a mystery cult, whose rites involved tame serpents.[80] Something of this link between females, snakes and ancient mystery rites is reflected in Bram Stoker's novel, *The Lair of the White Worm* (1911). The melodramatic plot revolves around a femme fatale who lives on the site of an ancient temple to Diana and who can shape-shift into a gigantic, rapacious, squeamishly unpleasant white serpent that terrorizes the neighbours.

The dynamic tensions between gender and dragon forms are nowhere better illustrated than in the popular Chinese tale 'Madam White Snake'.[81] The earliest versions, which in some ways resemble the Western Mélusine legends, date back to seventh-century China. The central female character is a succubus-like demon who, like Mélusine, has an affinity for water, and a double form of a beautiful woman and serpent-like beast. She is literally a dragon lady who lures a young man to a beautiful palace (actually a graveyard) and begins to drain him of life, until a monk rescues him. However, as the tale developed, the central character changed from a demon into a supernatural being seeking immortality, a motif it shares with tales like 'The Little Mermaid' and some Mélusine tales. In these versions, the White Snake falls in love with a young scholar and becomes a faithful spouse. They have a son, but a monk who disapproves of the marriage between the disparate realms of human and supernatural threatens their happiness. The centrepiece of the story is a great flood, which becomes a battle between the White Snake and the monk and is only resolved when the son reaches maturity, after which the family is reunited or the White Snake finally becomes an immortal. This immensely popular tale has been adapted many times and across a wide range of genres. It is the basis for a popular traditional Chinese opera, a joint Chinese/American opera venture (2010), two Chinese language martial arts films (1939 and 2001) and an early Japanese anime film, *Panda and the White Serpent* (1958).

The links between women and dragons are not always so sexually charged. (Figure 4.4) An important episode in the *Shahnameh* centres on the motif of a tiny creature that becomes a huge menace. A poor young spinster finds a little worm in an apple which later grows into a huge dragon. Her family becomes rich and powerful and challenges the power of the semi-mythical hero Ardashir. Eventually, the hero kills the worm by feeding it melted lead, a time-honoured method of despatching dragon-like creatures.[82]

The martyred St Perpetua left an account of a vision in which she sets her foot on the head of a serpent coiled around a ladder to heaven. The references to Eve's sin and the Virgin Mary's triumph over the serpent (Gen. 3.15) are clear in illustrations of *The Passion of Sts Perpetua and Felicity* in which the serpent takes on a more dragon-like appearance.[83] Female saints who defeat dragons are more like dragon-tamers than dragon-slayers, and two of them, St Martha and St Margaret of Antioch, appear in the most famous collection of medieval saints' lives, *Legenda Aurea*.[84] A demonic dragon, which she subsequently destroys, swallows St Margaret of Antioch, but St Martha's dragon dwells in

FIGURE 4.4 *Tennyson describes the moment when the Arthurian knight Geraint hears Enid singing. In this illustration, a dragon curls protectively around her, perhaps an indication of the trials she will endure.*

a cave and lives on a diet of sheep. However, its breath poisons the atmosphere, blasting crops and killing people. As a result, the land has become unfit for human habitation and the inhabitants have fled. Many dragon-slayer tales, whether the protagonist is male or female, result in the conversion of a pagan populace. The implication is that a non-Christian world is by definition desolated and polluted. Saints and secular heroes take pity on the remaining populace and agree to destroy the dragon. Sometimes dragon-slayers engage directly with the beast, killing it with a weapon; other times they induce it to eat explosive material disguised as food and immolate itself. Martha however simply dowses the monster with holy water, whereupon it becomes docile and allows her to lead it, bound only with her belt, into the town. An annual festival in Provence celebrates this event, in which an effigy of Martha's dragon, La Tarasque, now a tame mascot, is paraded through the town of Tarascon.[85]

In the *Legenda Aurea* version of the St George story, the freed princess also leads the tame dragon. Books of Hours frequently illustrated these dramatic miracles, and they were as much a part of the experience as the texts and prayers assembled in these books for personal devotion. The Hours of Henry

VIII contains a splendid example in which Martha, holding a vessel of holy water, leads the tame dragon from the cave, a pair of human legs still protruding from its mouth (Pierpont Morgan Library MS H.8, fol. 191v). Sainthood is not a requisite for a lady dragon-slayer. A dragon-slaying female who is associated with the exotic world of Siberia appears in a nineteenth-century collection of tales drawn from various central Asian cultures and retold for Western audiences. In the printed version, she is a princess, called Altyn-Aryg, who rescues her people from inside the body of a serpentine monster by striking its heart with her sword.[86]

In the British ballads recorded by Francis James Child, women fulfil both positive and negative roles in connection with men in dragon form.[87] In 'Alison Gross' (Child Ballad 35), a wicked witch transforms a reluctant lover into a dragon. Despite his transformation, his sister performs the task of combing his hair, and, eventually, a benevolent fairy queen restores him to his human shape. A wicked stepmother transforms a young man into a dragon in 'The Laily Worm and the Makrel of the Sea' (Child Ballad 36). Here too the sister combs the dragon's hair, forcing the stepmother to restore his shape. In other tales, a malevolent supernatural opponent changes a woman into a dragon. The island of Kos was the traditional home of the Greek physician Hippocrates (Ypocras), and legends about him began to develop in the Hellenistic period. A biography of Hippocrates, written by the Greek physician, Soranus, in the second century CE, mentions a son called Draco and a daughter. By the fourteenth century, sources such the *Travels of Sir John Mandeville* (*Mandeville's Travels*, ch. 4) claimed that the goddess Diana had transformed the daughter into a dragon until some brave knight agreed to kiss her. There is no explanation for Diana's action, although in other traditions about her, she punishes her erring followers by turning them into beasts. In the tale recounted in *Mandeville's Travels*, a knight tries to rescue the transformed girl, but dies when his terrified horse leaps off a cliff. In another version, Ypocras's daughter can take human form inside an old castle that she inhabits, but her potential rescuer is terrified when confronted with the maiden in dragon form. The fate of the woman in the nineteenth-century English ballad 'Kemp Owyne' (Child Ballad 34) and the tale 'The Laidly Worm of Spindleston Heugh' is much happier, since a knight who is not frightened by her surface transformation frees the dragon-lady[88] (Figure 4.5).

The term 'dragon lady' has been applied to exotic, seductive, domineering Asian women. Its exact origin is unclear, although foreign femme fatales from nineteenth-century sources contain hints of this figure. The name was attached to the villainess in the comic strip 'Terry and the Pirates' which appeared in American newspapers in the 1930s and 1940s. This 'Dragon Lady' was a pirate leader constantly opposing the heroic all-American adventurer Terry Lee. The illustrations of this character drew heavily on the idea of a femme fatale, and

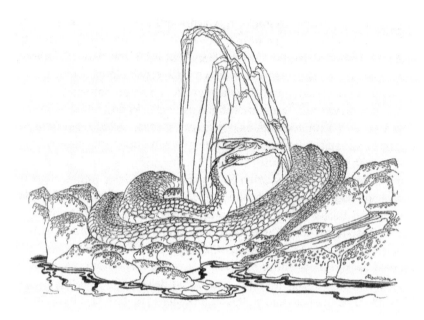

FIGURE 4.5 *A princess transformed into a dragon curves sinuously around the rocky outcrop of 'Spindleston Heugh' as she waits for her rescuer from a Victorian retelling of 'The Laidly Worm of Spindleston Heugh'.*

she was usually sexily dressed, as for an evening out. The Chinese American actor Anna May Wong epitomized the idea of the 'dragon lady' in the film *Limehouse Blues* (Alexander Hall, 1934), in which her costume enhanced her exotic persona as Oriental femme fatale. The black satin, Hollywood version of the form-fitting cheongsam dress popularized in the 1920s, had an elaborate sequined dragon whose sinuous body twisted down the front of the dress and across the train, fusing the concepts of dangerous woman and sinuous dragon.[89] If the orientalist-fantasy dragon lady was a product of 1930s popular culture, a very different dragon lady had appeared in the 1909 'National Pageant of Wales' held in Cardiff. This huge outdoor extravaganza presented Welsh history as an inspiring pageant in which aristocrats and dignitaries took the roles of famous Welsh figures. The Marchioness of Bute, wife of Wales's richest industrialist, played the part of 'Dame Wales' dressed in an elaborate white gown emblazoned with a red dragon. The original 'Dame Wales' character, symbolizing the communal voice of Welsh women, created in the 1890s by a newspaper cartoonist, was a plump, middle-aged lady wearing Welsh national costume, but this was no doubt unsuitable for the dignified Marchioness and the high-minded principles of a National Pageant.[90] Fantasy novels and films have also enlisted 'dragon ladies', exploiting the idea of a strong woman coupled with the immense power of this mythical beast. Daenerys Targaryen in *Game of Thrones*, the television adaptations of George R. R. Martin's books, is the survivor of a murdered clan whose power is linked to dragons, and Anne MacCaffrey's first Dragonrider novel, *Dragonflight* (1968), has a similar theme of a lone surviving woman named Lessa, whose psychic bond with a dragon helps save her alien world.

Dragons in art

Artistic realizations of dragons portray them as serpents, aquatic sea monsters and reptiles with and without wings. Some are purely decorative, while others have an allegorical significance or embody narrative themes. There are even a few oddities such as the centipede-like creature chasing its hapless victim on a Viking stone from Gotland, now in the National Historical Museum, Stockholm. More typical are the dragon motifs on the fifteenth-century misericords in Carlisle Cathedral. One shows St Michael defeating a satanic dragon, while a lion, symbol of Christ, confronts a dragon on another misericord to remind the onlooker of the perils of sin. Elsewhere a serpentine dragon kills an elephant, a popular medieval version of classical traditions about the boa and other dangerous serpents.[91] Other misericords contain beautiful winged dragons, two legged wyverns or serpent-like monsters whose function seems more decorative than didactic. Legends about local marauding dragons may be the subject of a misericord in Norwich Cathedral in which a knight kills a wyvern that has carried off a sheep.

Not surprisingly, St George's fight with the dragon is popular. A misericord in Holy Trinity Church, Stratford-on-Avon, depicts the saint killing a dragon while the princess looks on. In St Botolph's Church, Boston, Lincolnshire, the saint skewers a winged dragon who bears more than a passing resemblance to a gryphon. In a European context, there is a tendency for dragons to become more reptilian over time, and St George's opponent reflects the changing shape of the Western dragon. In Orthodox Christian icons, George's dragon often has serpentine or crocodile-like features, although winged and reptilian forms do occur. Paulo Uccello painted the subject twice. In the version now in the Musée Jacquemart-André (c. 1460), the creature has leather wings, but is somewhat awkwardly bi-pedal. In the National Gallery of London version, painted ten years later, the creature, still with leather wings and two legs, stands menacingly between George and the princess. A fifteenth-century German aquamanile depicts the saint gracefully attempting to dislodge a small winged dragon that has attached itself to his horse's leg, while in Carpaccio's painting for the Scuola San Giorgio degli Schiavoni in Venice (1502), George faces a four-legged dragon whose composition – a lion's body with the front legs of an eagle – recalls descriptions of the Chimaera. One of the most strik-ing and surely one of the largest realizations of St George's legend is a larger than life-size wooden set piece in Storkyrkan, Stockholm, created at the end of the fifteenth century. It served a triple purpose of religious, political and funer-ary monument (at least for a time) for the victorious Swedish commander who commissioned it. St George embodies all the virtues of a chivalrous knight. Riding a horse whose *chafron* recalls the power of the unicorn, he defends a princess, who also represents Christendom, from a hermaphroditic dragon bristling with antler spikes that lies on its back among its offspring who feed on the body parts of former victims.[92]

There are comparatively few fiery dragons associated with the warrior saints, George, Michael or Theodore. Fire-breathing dragons, like Beowulf's opponent and the ones who die from eating combustible material, are a sur-prising exclusive group. One miniature in the De Grey Hours (c. 1400), now in the National Library of Wales, has a small winged reptilian dragon whose mouth emits fiery tongues, although this may represent the pestilential breath characteristic of dragons who oppose saints. Dragons fighting various crea-tures, especially lions and elephants, appear in ecclesiastical settings and as marginalia in manuscripts. A coiled serpentine dragon biting its own tail forms a boss at the intersection of the roof vaulting in the chancel in Iffley Church, Oxfordshire. As it bites its tail like the ouroboros, it may be a symbol of eter-nity, and its serpentine form may further reflect the serpent's ability to renew itself by sloughing its skin. A central hole in this carving could have supported a pyx, a vessel that contained the Eucharist, and this suggests a more positive significance for a dragon entrusted with carrying a sacred vessel. Occasion-ally, there is even a bit of whimsy, as in a dragon with a foliated tail who plays a musical instrument in the margin of a fifteenth-century French Book of Hours (Pierpont Morgan Library MS M.358, fol. 32r). Leonardo da Vinci rendered the traditional fight between a dragon and a lion with a fierce dragon having a tail, lion's legs and wolf-like head, which was a popular Renaissance interpretation. However, he included a small dragon with cat-like characteristics among draw-ings of real cats in one of his notebooks, now in the Royal Collection.[93]

The plethora of dragons in public and ecclesiastical art is balanced by dragon imagery on more personal items. Dragonheads were popular as the figureheads of Viking boats, and a flying dragon motif adorns a spectacular helmet from Sutton Hoo.[94] Dragons are an obvious choice of motif for war-riors and continued to serve the ideals of chivalry. A parade saddle, tenta-tively dated back to the fifteenth century now in the New York Metropolitan Museum of Art, is covered with bone plates decorated with chivalric imagery that includes St George slaying a dragon and a unicorn hunt. This image of St George, if the dating is correct, may refer to the Order of the Dragon founded in 1408 by Sigismund, king of Hungary and Holy Roman emperor.[95] Personal dragon items often possess an endearing and very personal quirkiness. When Sir Samuel Hellier created a fantasy garden for his estate, Woodhouse (now Wodehouse near Wombourne, Staffordshire), he placed a weather vane in the shape of a gilded dragon on the steeple of a local church, which presented 'a delightful object when seen from the wood'.[96] In the 1880s, Antoni Gaudí created a wonderful symbolic fantasy of buildings, the Güell Pavilions, for his wealthy industrialist patron and fellow Catalan nationalist Eusebi Güell. The inspiration for the buildings was a poem, L'Atlàntida, written in 1877 for Güell's brother-in-law by the Catalan poet and patriot Jacint Verdaguer. The centrepiece of Gaudí's design was an iron gate in the form of the dragon Ladon, guardian of the Garden of the Hesperides, defeated by Heracles. The architecture creates a link between mythic and real geography since, according to some sources, the mythological garden was located in Spain near the Pillars of Heracles, the entrance to the Atlantic Ocean.

Literary dragons

The symbolic use of the dragon has an extensive pedigree in medieval bestiaries and in legends about dragon-slaying saints. In later sources, however, fantastic beasts such as these acquired new meanings as they became the focus for poetic and allegorical elaborations in works such as emblem books. The most famous of these works, Andrea Alciato's *Emblematum Liber* (first edition 1531), links the story of Cadmus slaying the dragon (*viperos*) and sowing its teeth with the creation of the alphabet (Emblem 184). In Edmund Spenser's allegorical poem *The Faerie Queene* (1590), the Redcrosse knight defeats a dragon who threatens Una's country (Bk 1, canto 11–12). Spenser created a complex Elizabethan allegory in which the Redcrosse knight embodies the idea of a Christian warrior whose quest for holiness takes on the trappings of a dragon-slayer legend. The basic dragon-slayer format of a hero who rescues the beautiful maiden remained, and the Redcrosse knight kills the dragon by entering its mouth in an action reminiscent of heroes swallowed by whales and sea monsters. The knight fights the dragon for three days (the period between Christ's death and resurrection), and the dragon's fire represents the purifying fires of Purgatory. Spenser's detailed allegory is striking and complex, and critics, among them C. S. Lewis in his *Allegory of Love* (1936), continue to discuss the full implications of its significance. Lewis also used the dragon as a didactic metaphor in his own fiction. The continually grumbling Eustace learns some valuable life lessons once he is transformed into a dragon in *The Voyage of the Dawn Treader*. Lewis also placed the dragon in an allegorical setting in one of his earliest fantasy works, *The Pilgrim's Regress* (1933), which traced a quotation about snakes becoming dragons, a motif comparable to the insignificant creatures that grow into huge dragons, through citations by European humanists to an original Greek proverb.[97]

What we now recognize as the increasingly elaborate dragons of fantastic fiction begin to emerge in the nineteenth century. Tenniel's illustration for Lewis Carroll's 'Jabberwocky' (1871) shares many of the hybrid characteristics of the dragon in Paolo Uccello's Renaissance painting of St George. Its jaws, claws, scales and antipathy to humans evoke the dragons of the Germanic sagas in works by Richard Wagner, Andrew Lang and William Morris. However, Jabberwocky is a bizarre beast in which the hybrid characteristics of the dragon are made even more fantastical, a trend which has become prominent in fantasy writing, video games and in films such as J. K. Rowling's *Fantastic Beasts and Where to Find Them* (David Yates, 2016). Variations on a creature, which is already hybridized, feature prominently in computer games and RPGs. They owe much to the antediluvian or alien reptiles depicted in Frank Frazetta's illustrations for editions of Edgar Rice Burroughs' *Tarzan* and *Warlords of Barzoom* series and Robert E. Howard's *Conan the Barbarian*, which in turn influenced the original versions of *Dungeons & Dragons*.[98]

The position of the dragon in RPGs deserves special mention. As the co-term in the original and still popular *Dungeons & Dragons*, it embodies the perils, whether from dragons or other antagonists, encountered by players wending their way through the labyrinthine 'dungeons' that characterized the original game and informed its many descendants. As a form of interactive storytelling in which the player gains access to a game world through a board, pack of cards or computer screen, these games are well suited to the symbolic possibilities of fantastic creatures.[99] The interactive nature of RPGs, whether played on a board, as a card game or on computer, allows players to fight dragons or acquire dragon characteristics. The ability of these creatures to morph into ever more fantastic forms provides a useful mechanism for increasing the complexity of quest-format games as dragons, and other characters, become increasingly more varied in 'Monster Manuels' and websites.

'Dragon' has become almost a shorthand for games set in heroic alternate worlds, and numerous games, too numerous to list, include 'dragon' in the title, from the biblical-inspired *Dragonraid* (1984) to the novels, gaming modules and related licensed products of the Dragonlance saga.[100] The alternate universe, Krynn, is the setting for *Dragonlance* in which its creators claim, 'Men rode dragons into a tremendous war.' There are classes of dragons, both good and evil, named dragons that act as steeds for significant actors, dragon/human hybrids called *draconians*, plus objects like dragon orbs and dragon lances that give power to the players.[101] The dragons in this shared universe define the parameters for a rich alternate world with an almost infinite capacity for player participation.

Critics use the term 'high fantasy' to characterize works set in imaginary worlds, as opposed to those in which magic intrudes into the real one. When creatures like dragons appear in 'high fantasy', they must conform to the rules for that world. In Anne McCaffrey's *Dragonriders* (1968) fantasy, Christopher Paolini's *Eragon* (2003) and George R. R. Martin's *A Song of Ice and Fire* series (1996), dragons hatch from eggs and bond, to varying degrees, with humans. In the worlds created by J. R. R. Tolkien and Ursula Le Guin, dragons are creatures of power with special knowledge. In Tolkien's heroic world, the dragon Smaug guards his treasure and opposes the peoples of Middle-earth, but Ursula le Guin sets her *Earth Sea* novels (1962–2001) in a non-industrial society comparable to the European Iron Age. In *Earthsea*, dragons are powerful rather than moral in a setting in which good magic maintains a balance, while evil magic is disruptive. The main character, Ged, is a wizard and a dragon lord, not someone who kills dragons, but someone who can communicate with them. One of the most original uses of the dragon in these 'high fantasy' works is E.R. Eddison's tail-swallowing ouroboros, which gives the novel its title, *The Worm Ouroboros* (1922). As a medieval and Renaissance symbol, the ouroboros was associated with eternity and with fame that supersedes death. Here the serpent has elements of the world-encircling Jörmungandr and perfectly embodies Eddison's unusual cyclical world, which fuses medieval, Renaissance and heroic Norse elements with the writer's own eclectic imagination. The classical flying horse Pegasus influenced the hippogriff mount with which Ariosto provided his heroes, but it took some time for this splendid marriage of winged creature and heroic action to evolve into the idea of a winged dragon with a human rider.

Not all fantasy dragons followed this particular route. A sympathetic dragon, in reality something of an aesthete, emerges with the appearance of Kenneth Grahame's *The Reluctant Dragon* (1898) which was animated by Walt Disney Studios in 1941. The tale centres on a young boy, an example of wise and unspoilt youth so important in children's fantasy fiction, who mediates between an elderly knight and the dragon. This gentle reworking of the St George legend is set in the Berkshire Downs where, according to tradition, the saint fought a dragon at a site known as Dragon's Mound near the Uffington White Horse. Dragons in Edith Nesbit's collection of short stories, *The Book of Dragons* (1901) although conventional in appearance with wings, serpents' tails, claws and fiery breath, provide opportunities for children to act bravely and wisely. In a short story she wrote much later, 'The Last of the Dragons' (1925), the dragon protagonist actually asks to be changed into an aeroplane.

Theatrical dragons

Theatre, public celebrations marking commemorations of dragon-slaying saints like St George, the popular Chinese dragon dances and more recently film and the virtual world of computer games provide opportunities, old and new, to 'interact' with dragons.

Among the delightful marginal illustrations in the fourteenth-century Luttrell Psalter (British Library, Additional MS 42130) are some with grotesque faces and bulbous bodies ending in fantastic twists and curlicues. One is even set on two wheels with a gaping mouth and a twisted tail.[102] Although the faces are not particularly dragon-like, the bulbous shapes and curled tails recall the kind of pageant figure used in saints' day celebrations. A more recognizably dragon-like pageant figure, whose curled tail provides a convenient steering handle and who belches fire, appears in an engraving of 'The St George's Day Fair' (1559–60) by Peter Breughel the Elder. Pageant dragons were associated with saints' feasts and with springtime Rogation celebrations that reaffirmed the boundaries of towns and parishes. The Reformation and the general secularizing tendency of modern life affected these celebrations, although a surprising number have survived or been revived. In Norwich, the medieval Guild of St George incorporated a pageant dragon known as Snap. As with many of these saints' day celebrations, the festival became more secular after the Reformation. The dragon survived, although no longer connected to the saint. Examples of Snap, which consists of a hollow body large enough for someone to stand inside and operate its head, are on display in the Norwich Museum.[103] These pageant dragons have an element of deliberate caricature; frequently the bodies are somewhat bulbous to accommodate an internal operator, the curled tail allows attendants to manoeuver the dragon, and sometimes fireworks simulate fiery dragon's breath. The city of Mons in Belgium celebrates the feast of St George as a public festival. In Mons, the dragon's tail (composed of horsehair) is especially important as its hairs are supposed to bring good luck.[104] In Provence, the festival of St Martha and her Tarasque has been a tourist attraction, as well as a local festival, since the nineteenth century.[105] In certain areas of Japan, straw serpents, created as an offering or as a representative of a god in serpent form, are associated with local festivals. Some resemble large serpents, woven from or stuffed with straw, others have more dragon-like features, like the street puppets associated with the Chinese dragon dance.[106]

Although their purpose now relates more to civic identity than to religious observance, one factor that links these dragon celebrations is that they actively engage participants. Street celebrations create temporary spaces for carnivalesque activity and the celebration of shared identity, rather than awe and religious fervour. Breughel's sixteenth-century drawing of St George's Day included a number of leisure activities that emphasized the play aspect of the dragon fight, which became stronger as the celebrations became more secular. Although various forms of the Chinese dragon dance (*wu long*) date back to the Han dynasty (180–230 CE), this custom has become especially popular with immigrant Chinese communities. The 'dragon' is often a very elaborate street puppet operated by troops of dancers that perform at festivals, such as the Chinese New Year. As these dancing Chinese dragons have become an increasingly prominent element in contemporary street theatre, dragons with both Western and Oriental features have become increasingly common.

Dragons have a great symbolic value in royal and civic events, especially as expressions of political and technological power. A huge Welsh *draig coch* (red dragon) led the civic procession to mark the opening of the Commonwealth Games in Cardiff, 1958, a national symbol hosting an international event.[107] During the meeting between Henry VIII and the French king, Francis I, on the Field of the Cloth of Gold (1520), a flying dragon appeared to amaze the crowds.[108] In his treatise *Pyrotechnia*, the mathematician and ordinance expert John Babington gave instructions for creating fire-breathing dragons for public spectacles, including one of the most dramatic motifs in dragon narrative, namely a fire-breathing dragon emerging from a cave.[109] Methods for producing artificial flying dragons also appeared in John Bates's *The Mysteryes of Nature and Art* (1634) where even the author acknowledged that 'the flying Dragon is somewhat troublesome to compose'.[110] In the mid-fifteenth century, St Botolph's Church in Billingsgate, London, owned a moving model of St George. A winding crank operated machinery that caused dragon and saint to move towards one another.[111] Protestant reformers regarded such machinery as evidence of 'idolatrous' corruption, and many were destroyed. Today, however, passers-by can watch St George chase a dragon on the mechanical clock that adorns the 1920s Tudor revival building that houses Liberty's shop in London.

The techniques for creating pageant dragons and automata continued essentially unchanged as stage and film effects well into the twentieth century. George Méliès's film of *Baron Munchausen's Dream* (1911) included a typical pageant dragon with curled tail and wings animated by an actor inside the dragon's body. A more elaborate design, which needed complex stage machinery to bring it to life, was produced for his *Le Palais de mille et un nuit* (1905). The complex dragon prop and the stylized nature of the cinematography greatly aided the impact of the fight between Siegfried and Fafnir in Fritz Lang's 1924 film of *Die Nibelungen* (Figure 4.6). Dragon automata also invoke a playful use of fantastic creatures. Overtones of terror, complex poetic allegory or reminders of sin and temptation are conspicuously absent from dragon-themed fairground rides. The segmented serpentine dragon body adapts easily to accommodate multiple 'riders', and roller-coaster rides simulate dragon 'flight'. An early example, namely the famous Dragon Coaster that opened in

FIGURE 4.6 *Siegfried confronts the magnificent and complex stage dragon that was created for Fritz Lang's 1924 film version of* Die Nibelungen. *Courtesy of Collection Christophel / Alamy Stock Photo*

1929 in Playland Amusement Park in Rye, New York, offered an exciting, and then relatively new, experience, while 'Dragon World' in Singapore aimed to combine local culture and heritage with the commercial demands of tourism.[112] Whatever the intentions, theme parks create areas of play, which have a greater degree of permanence than the temporary spaces of annual festivals, but still encourage carnivalesque activity.

Early cinematic dragons were notable more for the ingenuity of the special effects than their relevance to the plot. Their deliberate, often ironic, artifice echoes the pageant and ritual dragons of street performance and folk theatre. Costumed actors aided by off-camera marionette operators brought these early dragons to life. George Méliès introduced them into at least two films, and neither time were they essential to the plot. Méliès's design for the dragon in *Le Palais de mille et un nuit* was realized as a mechanical, fire-breathing monster for Martin Scorsese's film *Hugo* (2011). It showed the dragon as it might have appeared in the original film, but in the context of Scorsese's set with all the operators in view. Most film dragons conform to a common stereotype influenced by medieval images of winged, lizard-like, fire-breathing monsters, but there are a few exceptions. A three-headed dragon of the Slavic type, Zmey Gorynych, appeared in Alexandr Ptusko's film of the Slavic epic, *Ilya Muromets* (1956), and its English language version *The Sword and the Dragon* (1960). Godzilla's opponent, the three-headed King Ghidorah (*Gojira/ Godzilla,* Ishiro Honda, 1954), drew on the many-headed classical Hydra as well as the *Yamata no Orochi* of Japanese tradition. The film version drastically reduced the number of heads from eight to three, presumably because of the limits of special effects technology at the time, but retained the wings and lethal breath of more conventional cinematic dragons. It still needed a costumed actor and a team of puppeteers to bring the monster to life.

Fantasy writing and illustrations have influenced film and television productions. Tolkien himself drew the original Smaug for *The Hobbit* (1937). Numerous illustrations and, more recently, animation and CGI have reinterpreted Tolkien's creation, and the relative ease with which CGI can create realistic images has no doubt encouraged the prevalence of cinematic dragons. In recent films, models continue to supplement the CGI effects used to create the dragons in *Dragonheart* (Rob Cohen, 1976), *Dragonslayer* (Matthew Robbins, 1981) and *Reign of Fire* (Rob Bowman, 2002). RPGs and the increasing sophistication of virtual reality in video games have also affected the development of contemporary dragon lore. *Dungeons & Dragons,* the first role-playing game to attain wide popularity in the 1970s, has been a major influence on subsequent computer and video games, and the enormous industry that they have spawned. Dragons display a wide range of functions, characteristics and colours in these games and provide an arena for interactive storytelling.[113] Frequently they are an enemy that needs to be obliterated in numbers, and this has spilled over into films such as *Reign of Fire.* This film harks back to a format made popular in earlier creature features in which human activity disturbs some deeply buried monster, in this case a lost species of dragon. Unlike the single monsters of earlier creature features, these dragons are a threatening apocalyptic menace that come in droves like H.G. Wells's Martian invaders or the zombies of George Romero's films

Serpent creators

A mythic feathered serpent was a prominent supernatural entity in Mesoamerican religion. Known as Quetzalcoatl to the Aztecs, it also functioned in Mayan cultures and may date back even earlier. Its hybrid avian and serpentine characteristics suggest duality in contrast to European dragons where the mix of species usually indicates monstrosity. The role this figure played varied in different cultural contexts, but it was consistently associated with creation and the power of rain or its lack to bring fertility or drought. Aboriginal Australian myths associated a serpent with creating and shaping the landscape, especially important water sources, and with the origins of particular tribes. Rock drawings of serpents, often coloured and in bowed 'rainbow' shapes, date back at least 6,000 years. Anthropologists coined the term 'rainbow serpent', although there is no indication that it represents either a universal aboriginal myth or chief deity. It has many local and tribal names, can be male or female, and is the subject of a range of myths about how it became attached to features in the landscape.[114] Another serpent creator, the Amazonian figure Serek-A, whose story has elements resembling European Mélusine legends, takes the form of an anaconda.[115] The divine serpent *orishas* of West African religion, such as Ayida-Weddo, Oshunmare and Damballah, also act as serpentine shape-shifters in the context of syncretic beliefs systems such as *candomblé* and *voudon*. They shape the land and bring both fertilizing and destructive rain, qualities they share with dragons and serpent creators. Among the Nez Perce, an indigenous people inhabiting the Columbia River Plateau in the United States, the trickster-creator Coyote was said to enter the mouth of a serpentine monster. Like other heroes who escape from inside a whale, Coyote builds a fire and, together with the animals trapped inside, cuts himself free. Landscape features in the Kamiah Valley in Idaho are associated with the snake's heart and liver turned to stone.[116] These close links with the land and with cosmic forces are also features of Oriental dragons.

Oriental dragons

Images of dragons existed in prehistoric China, and by the time of the Han dynasty (1206 BCE to 220 CE), the Chinese dragon had assumed a more or less definite meaning and form. Characteristic features of Chinese dragons include scaly bodies, horns, whiskers, ears, clawed feet and round eyes. Chinese dragons were typically a compilation of nine creatures, nine being an auspicious number, in contrast with the monstrous dragon hybrids in European lore. Oriental dragons controlled the weather, especially the rain essential to agriculture, and were a sign of good fortune. Dragon imagery continued to develop during later Chinese dynasties as part of complex symbolic systems, and they came to symbolize the cardinal directions, as well as specific features of the landscape and the protective role of the emperor. A red dragon chasing a red globe is associated with Chinese New Year, a time when the constellation Draco approaches the point of the setting sun, although the globe also represents the moon, which rises before New Year. A similar image of a dragon chasing a pearl carries overtones of the Buddhist idea of the 'pearl of perfection' and of the moon as a symbol of balance and harmony which underpins the Daoist traditions of China. Nine dragons in a dramatic mountainous landscape painted by Chen Rong (c. 1244) appear on a hand scroll now in the Boston Museum of Fine Arts. The *Nine Dragons* scroll illustrates the Daoist principles of nature as a dynamic force, and the dragons represent the nine sons of the dragon king, the ruler of the oceans.[117] Because of their generally positive nature, guardian dragons appear on ridgepoles, gates, the corners of roofs, doorways and other architectural features. According to tradition, the dragon-horse (a creature whose attributes combined the forces of earth, water and heaven) emerged from the Yellow River to present the legendary emperor Fu Xi with the I Ch'ing. Against this background, it is hardly surprising that the dragon has come to embody China as a whole.[118]

Ryujin is the common term for the Japanese dragon, specifically as god of sea, who lives in an underwater dragon palace with his beautiful daughters, and who, in the manner of many sea deities, controls storms.[119] Among the adventures of the legendary Japanese prince, Yamato Takeru, as recounted by the Anglo-Japanese writer Yei Theodora Osaki, is in a contest with a monstrous serpent who lives on a mountain. The prince kills the serpent with his bare hands, then falls ill due to the snake's poison, but is cured by bathing in a sacred spring.[120] The samurai hero, Fujiwara no Hidesato, meets the dragon king on a bridge and undertakes to rid him of a monstrous centipede.[121] Other characters in these Japanese tales visit the palace of Ryujin, the sea-dragon king, whose function is similar to the Otherworld beings of Western fairy tales. Even taking into account that these tales are adapted for Western audiences, many motifs overlap, such as the dead monster who poisons its killer. In another tale, popular in Japan and in reconfigurations for Western audiences, a childless couple find a small serpent-like creature whom they raise as their child. The serpent grows and eventually goes in search of a bride.[122] The Japanese tale is a variant of a widespread wonder tale, 'The Serpent's bride' (ATU 433B), and it incorporates the motif of small creatures who grow large. However, other serpents who start out small like the Lambton Worm and the creature in Walter Map's tale are not as benevolent as this one.

The fiction of Ryūnosuke Akutagawa (1892–1927), best known as the writer of *Rashōmon*, introduced contemporary perspectives into material drawn from traditional Japanese dragon lore. Based on a thirteenth-century story, 'Dragon, The Old Potter's Tale' provides a contemporary critique of religion. A young monk falsely claims that a dragon will ascend to heaven from a pond on a certain day. He repents his deception, but despite his attempts to dissuade the gathered crowd, people believe that they have witnessed the ascension of a dragon so firmly that the monk himself becomes convinced.[123] Asian dragon lore has had an impact on the crossover fiction of modern fantasy, anime and film. R. A. MacAvoy's *Tea with the Black Dragon* (1983) combines a contemporary setting in San Francisco, a thriller plot involving a missing person and fantasy elements drawn from Asian dragon lore. The fantasy revolves around a gentleman who may be a transformed Asian dragon, called very appropriately, Mayland Long (*long* being a Mandarin word for dragon), who helps a mother search for her missing daughter. A novel series, *Sohryuden: Legend of the Dragon Kings* (1987), by the Japanese novelist Yoshiki Tanaka concerns four dragon kings ruling the four quarters of the world who have been reborn as modern humans to fight against the forces of technology. The novels have been adapted as anime films, but the most popular of recent films involving a dragon is Hayao Miyazaki's *Spirited Away* (2001). This is the story of a girl Chihiro, who must negotiate the perils of the spirit world in order to save her parents and, as part of her quest of discovery, also helps a young boy, Haku – in reality the dragon spirit of the Kohaku River who has forgotten his name and identity because he stole a cursed talisman. Chihiro lovingly nurses the wounded Haku and breaks the curse, which enables Haku to remember his true identity and to regain his dragon shape.

Real dragons: Did they exist?

In the sixth century, Gregory of Tours linked an outbreak of disease with the death of a number of serpents, one of them a large serpentine proto-dragon of a type so often overcome by saints.

> In the ninth month of the previous year the river Tiber so flooded the city of Rome that ancient temples were destroyed and the storehouses of the church were overturned and several thousand measures of wheat in them were lost. A multitude of snakes, among them a great serpent like a big log, passed down into the sea by the channel of this river, but these creatures were smothered among the rough and salty waves of the sea and cast up on the shore. Immediately after came the plague. [124]

Much later, the testimony of reputable witnesses provided validation for the existence of local dragon-like beasts. In a seventeenth-century pamphlet entitled 'The flying Serpent or Strange newes out of Essex', a 'gentleman' observed a flying serpent near Henham in Essex in May 1668. A similar pamphlet described a venomous serpent in St Leonard's Forest near Horsham in Sussex. [125] These were not dragon-slayer tales originally, but notices of anomalies and portents. Eventually, the St Leonard's story acquired a dragon-slayer when it became the site for a fight between St Leonard and a dragon, probably because of the proximity of a local chapel in this area of Sussex dedicated to this popular medieval saint. [126] An unusual feature of this account is that the saint's blood, shed during the fight, produced the lilies of the valley, which grow in abundance here.

The seventeenth century proved something of a watershed for dragon tales, as this was the period that reassessed and eventually questioned the existence of dragons and many other mythical animals. However, the Anglican clergyman Edward Topsell published *The History of Four-Footed Beasts and Serpents* in 1658, ten years before the appearance of the Essex serpent. His work drew heavily on earlier descriptions. After describing various types of dragon and imparting valuable information on the medicinal uses of dragon fat, he declared, 'This which I have written, may be sufficient to satisfie any reasonable man, that there are winged Serpents and Dragons in the world.'[127] Belief in dragons died slowly. A nineteenth-century vicar at Mordiford near Hereford supposedly found two local women drowning newts in the church stoup thinking they were the offspring of the famous Mordiford dragon that lived in the woods.[128]

One would think that biology and science would cause flying, fire-breathing, treasure-hoarding dragons to retire into the world of myth and legend. On the contrary, discussions about their reality, especially their possible links with prehistoric fossils, have proved surprisingly tenacious. The huge range of serpentine, winged and leonine-like reptiles of medieval and Renaissance art do not look much like dinosaurs, but there is one prehistoric discovery that did become the foundation for a dragon tale. It concerns the founding of the Austrian town of Klagenfurt and the killing of a *lindwurm* who inhabited the marshes. A large skull unearthed when the swamps around the growing town were drained was rumoured to belong to the dragon. At the end of the sixteenth century, it served as the model for the head of the dragon on the town fountain. It is, however, the skull of an Ice Age rhinoceros, which is now preserved in the town's natural history museum.

The transition from legend to relic, to prehistoric exhibit reflects changing attitudes to the dragon at least in the European West. However, the dragon and the dinosaur have recently become speculative cousins, rather than stages in the emergence of rational science. The classicist Adrienne Mayor has suggested that discoveries of the fossil bones of the Cretaceous dinosaur, Protoceratops, influenced beliefs about griffins, and, more generally, that fossil bones shaped ideas about dragons.[129] Although the beautifully restored dinosaur skeletons in museums may resemble the reptilian dragon, fossil dinosaur bones are seldom found in fully articulated form. Ancient bones, some from dinosaurs, even more from extinct mammals, undoubtedly contributed to ideas about huge creatures, but whether these ancient bones gave rise to, or merely reinforced, belief in dragons is difficult to determine. The depiction of dragons in European art from the seventh to the fifteenth centuries evolved from serpent to winged, fiery reptiles. Some critics have challenged Mayor's assumption that the human imagination needs a specific stimulus to create such ideas,[130] and many finds of large bones were identified with giants rather than dragons.[131] Nevertheless, Mayor's work has linked our fascination with dinosaurs and our fascination with dragons in a way that reinvigorated interest in the science of palaeontology for a new generation, and this re-enchanted nature has brought the real and imaginative worlds closer together. For example, the Makara is a fantastic beast ridden by Ganga, the eponymous goddess of the Ganges River, or by the sea god, Varuna. As with so many fierce creatures, carvings protect the entrances to temples and palaces. Its form varies from an animal with a snout-like head and fish-like tail to one with scaly skin and feet like a crocodile, or even with a feathered tail like a peacock. The once common Ganges river dolphin (*Platanista gangetica*) may have influenced its appearance in much the same way that manatees and seals are linked to sightings of mermaids and sea serpents. However, a fossil discovery in Pakistan in the early 1990s provided cryptozoologists with a far-older speculative possibility. This semi-aquatic cetacean, *Ambulocetus*, with a long snout, tail and stubby legs ending in webbed feet inhabited the coastal waters of what is now Pakistan.[132] It provides a link between land-dwelling amphibians and whales. Despite its resemblance to some depictions of the Makara, the suggestion that memories of an ancient animal that existed before humans somehow influenced ideas about the fictional one seems a bit far-fetched.

The 'link' between dinosaurs and dragons is somewhat problematic as the reptilian dragon shape is far from universal, but it is hardly new. Nineteenth-century folklorists suggested something similar, however, as Jacqueline Simpson points out, 'Whether they can be regarded as its actual origin is more doubtful. The human mind seems to have a passion for constructing monsters onto which to project its feelings of awe, terror or aggression and does not always require confirmatory evidence from the external world in order to believe in the reality of its own creations.'[133] This has not hindered speculation, both serious and fantastic, about our need for myths. In his popular book, *The Dragons of Eden* (1977), Carl Sagan suggested that the struggle for survival and fear of predators, especially reptiles, might have influenced cultural beliefs and myths about dragons and snakes.[134] Another author, Peter Dickenson, presented an ingenious, if not entirely serious, solution to the problem of dragon flight in *The Flight of the Dragons* (1979) speculating that dragon bones were especially light and filled with gas.[135] The film *Reign of Fire* offered a pseudo-biological explanation for the fire-making ability of menacing dragons in the film. The *Dragonology* books also play with the idea of 'real' dragons. Supposedly written by a nineteenth-century 'expert' on dragons, these charming interactive books invite its readers to 'learn' about dragons with tactile samples, secret pockets containing letters and spells and a dedicated website.[136] A fictional docudrama, *The Last Dragon* (Channel 4, 2004), adopted the premise that a real species underlies the ubiquity of dragons in world mythology and presents a 'discovery' in the Carpathian Mountains of the last dragon killed in the fifteenth century defending her young.[137]

Dragons did not disappear completely from zoological taxonomy. In the eighteenth century, the pioneering taxonomist Carl Linnaeus gave the name *Draco volans* (flying dragon) to a small gliding lizard. Related species range from the Philippines to Indonesia, and they retain the generic name (Draco) of this ancient monster. A small marine fish found along the coasts of Australia, *Phycodurus eques*, whose common name is Glauert's sea dragon (or the leafy sea dragon), is a delicate looking creature that has become a focus for marine conservation. By a strange coincidence, its leafy camouflage bears a curious resemblance to third-century BCE mosaics of the Ketos or sea monster from the ancient city of Caulonia in Magna Grecia (now modern Reggio Calabria). Perhaps the most impressive 'real' dragon, if only because of its size, is a large monitor lizard, *Varanus komodoensis*, commonly called the Komodo dragon that is native to the remote Komodo Island in Indonesia. It was first documented by Dutch colonial officials, and in the 1920s, a wealthy American adventurer mounted an expedition to investigate this strange creature. William Douglas Burden was in his twenties when he financed an expedition under the auspices of The American Museum of Natural History. His adventures echoed the glamour of nineteenth-century lost world novels and the search for mysterious fauna like a 'real' unicorn. His book, published by the evocatively named Boone and Crockett Club, is subtitled, 'An Expedition to the Lost World of the Dutch East Indies'. Interestingly, Burden described his first sight of this 'dragon lizard' from the perspective of a dinosaur hunter rather than a dragon-slayer: 'The sun slanted down the hill so that a black shadow preceded the black beast as he came. It was a perfectly marvellous sight – a primeval monster in a primeval setting . ... Had he only stood up on his hind legs ... the dinosaurian picture would have been complete.'[138] He later noted, more prosaically, that the lizards seemed larger when seen alive, but never measured more than about eight or nine feet when dead.

Discoveries of prehistoric creatures at the beginning of the nineteenth century provoked a range of reactions. When evidence emerged of their carnivorous eating habits, they were condemned as Satan's creatures dominating an antediluvian world, and many illustrations of the period bear a striking resemblance to the monsters depicted on early maps.[139] Eventually, and not without arguments on all sides, the concept of an 'age of reptiles' emerged and was accepted. It allowed large, carnivorous, prehistoric reptiles to be accommodated into a system of scientific classification, and many of the species identified at the time, and for many years afterwards, incorporated the element 'saurus' (lizard) in their names. Whatever one's reservations about the dinosaur-as-dragon hypothesis, it has sparked new interest in science, and modern dinosaur names often nod in the direction of dragons. A newspaper recently announced, 'Dragons really did roam Wales', heralding the discovery in Wales of a new Jurassic dinosaur, which has been named, *Dracoraptor* (dragon thief). A newly discovered dinosaur in China also includes the word for dragon,[140] and the incorporation of the element 'dragon' into scientific names is a reflection of the continued importance of the dragon in both countries.

Dragons are also the source of precious and profitable products. Isidore of Seville mentions gem-like 'dracontites', which can only be obtained from the brains of sleeping dragons and are associated with one of the most precious of medieval gems, the pearl (Bk 16, ch. 14.7). However, the most famous dragon products are associated with their blood and bones. After Heracles killed Ladon, the dragon guardian of the Garden of the Hesperides, his carcase became the constellation Draco, and his blood coagulated into red droplets valued for their magical and medicinal properties. The Romans identified dragon's blood with cinnabar according to a first-century *Periplus Maris Eryth-raei* (Section 30), which described the maritime trade routes of the Roman world. However, like unicorn horn, dragon's blood came from a number of plants, and its name is indicative of its colour and value rather than a specific fixed source.[141] Even today, substances identified as dragon bones and teeth feature in Chinese medicine. Some derive, no doubt, from the country's rich sources of palaeontological fossils, but in reality, they come from a variety of sources.[142] In his extensive collection of medicinal lore, Edward Lovett noted that factory-girls bought something called 'dragon's blood' from London chemists to use as a love philtre.[143] Pliny's exotic explanation for its origin claims that it formed during the death throes of a dragon and its natural enemy the elephant (Bk 8, ch. 11).[144] The name of the plant genus from which this substance is derived is *Dracaena*, the Greek word for a female dragon. Many of these succulent plants and shrubs yield a resin substance often with a red colour, which continue to be marketed as 'dragon's blood'.

Conclusion

Although the phrase 'here be dragons' does not actually appear on any map, it has come to signify a generalized idea of exoticism. The sixteenth-century Hunt-Lenox Globe comes closest with the words 'hc sunt dracones' inscribed on the Asian coast, although it is not clear whether this refers to dragons or to an anthropophagous tribe mentioned by Marco Polo.[145] In fact, dragons, far from being exotic, appear in quite localized European legends about saints and heroes. They also inhabit the widest range of environments. They fly in air, swim in water and live in caves, wells, mounds, deserts and mountains. Their form varies from simple, albeit evil, serpents to huge winged, clawed, fire-breathing reptiles. Dragons can control the weather or appear as comets that predict future events. They can embody disease, on the one hand, while their bones and blood provide medicinal cures.

As with other fantastic creatures, dragons provide metaphors for human behaviour, such as the elaborate moral lessons in medieval bestiaries and Renaissance books of emblems. The range of suggested meanings reflects the ease with which such figures can be linked to modern notions of archetypes or the romanticism of universal mythic significance, now part of contemporary spirituality. As exotic animals in foreign lands, dragons can carry moral messages, provide metaphors for alchemical and other occult processes, embody the weather, bring luck and present new ways of engaging with prehistoric beasts.

Some dragon narratives have a cosmic background in which gods and culture heroes create, or at least organize, the world by defeating dragon-like serpents: Apollo, the sun god, takes control of the Delphic oracle after killing the divine Python that lives in a cave; the Bible confines the devil-dragon to a bottomless pit; Mesopotamian heroes defeat serpentine monsters; the Egyptian god Ra battles nightly with the underworld serpent; and the storm god Susanoo overcomes the serpentine sea dragon. As widespread as this primordial myth seems to be, it is by no means universal, and the creator serpents of South American and African creation narratives fulfil roles that are more positive. Guile as well as strength is required to defeat dragons as evidenced by heroes, both mythic and local, who make the dragon in effect swallow its own medicine. As actors in cosmic myths, dragons help create a world where order dominates over chaos, yet many of them are associated with local landscape features, the origins of families and local monuments. Despite the similarity of many of the themes, dragon narratives vary. On the one hand, when a hermit performs a kindly act of giving milk to a little creature, it grows into a threatening local dragon. However, a similar tale concerns an elderly Japanese couple who adopt a little snake-like creature who eventually wins a bride in a 'happily ever after' variant of this theme. Dragon-slayers too, saints, gods, heroic warriors or local lads, confront dragons in various ways. The heir to Lambton attempts to conceal his Sunday fishing by throwing the strange creature into a well where it becomes the Lambton Worm, yet countrywomen from Hereford supposedly drowned newts in the church font to prevent them from turning into dragons.

Newly popular genres like fantasy and gaming help us navigate through existing representations of reality, and dragons have become important actors in these contemporary contexts. The Babylonian goddess Tiamat, a cosmic dragon-like creature in the foundation myths of the Near East, has become a character in the modern *Dungeons & Dragons* fantasy game, and dragons of all types feature in role-playing and computer games.[146] Modern fantasy literature has turned dragons into wise companions, while cuddly plush dragon toys and dragons fashioned in a range of materials turn these symbols of fear or power into companions and collectible commodities.

Conclusion

Opinionis enim commenta delet dies, naturae iudicia confirmat
CICERO *DE NATURA DEORUM*, BOOK II, CH. 2

Writing in the first century BCE, the Roman senator and rhetorician Cicero confidently stated 'Who believes that the Hippocentaur or the Chimaera ever existed? Where can you find an old wife senseless enough to be afraid of the monsters of the lower world that were once believed in? The years obliterate the inventions of the imagination, but confirm the judgements of nature'. Two thousand years later, far from being obliterated as Cicero suggests, interest in creatures of fantasy is as strong as ever. Why has this interest continued for so long? The question is easier to ask than to resolve, but this book has attempted to shed light on the popularity and importance of at least some fantastic creatures.

One reason for the continued popularity is, no doubt, our delight in the imaginative, yet beyond this, fantastic beasts provide ways to engage with the world around us. By their very nature, these fantastic hybrids that combine features from actual and imagined animals create boundaries between the real and the unreal. However, they also provide an interface, which allows access to the very special worlds they inhabit, spatial in the context of geographical writing, supernatural in the context of folklore, fantastic in the context of literature, and interactive in the context of gaming. The myths surrounding these creatures are mutable, changing and developing over time, but they continue to shape our perception of reality and impose meaning on the ways we interpret the world.

Annette Kellerman in her mermaid incarnation was both an erotic fantasy and an expression of growing female power. By contrast, the plight of the little mermaid in Andersen's tale and in the Disney film, for all Ariel's' feistiness, is resolved into more conventional gender roles. The creatures depicted on early maps reflected a mental cosmos, as well as the world as it was understood at the time. Exploration dispelled some of the myths about older fantastic beasts, but changes produced new creatures, transforming certain sea mammals into something more than feared monsters or economic commodities. Living cryptids are still being sought and ecological discourse has conferred 'mythical' status on creatures like the dolphin and the whale. The mythologized whale has been everything from an embodiment of evil to the rallying banner of ecological consciousness. While the discovery of species of giant cephalopods has dispelled the myth of the ship-eating kraken, it still leaves a tantalizing possibility for cryptozoologists to prove that other fantastic beasts are not mythical after all. The unicorn, a fierce embodiment of geographical and cultural otherness in early classical accounts evolved into a complex medieval religious and cultural symbol. Later it became a modern mystical embodiment of eternal truth, which is further expanded today in digital and video games whose virtual environments become increasingly real.

Hybrid beasts have developed into the even more fantastical creatures of science fiction, familiar from films such as *Avatar* with its beautiful fauna and dystopian novels such as Margaret Atwood's *Oryx and Crake*, or from parallel worlds of fantasy literature like that of J.K. Rowling whose work features both mythical and fantastical creatures. Although crypto-beasts and 'phantom' cats have replaced tales of marauding dragons and brave dragon-slayers, fantasy fiction has given them a new existence, while spectacular CGI effects in computer games and 3D films have given them new life. While no single attitude to these creatures is consistent through time or across different cultures, narratives that embody interactions between humans and fantastic nature show some remarkable cross-cultural similarities. If complementary principles of separation and continuity provide an underlying framework for cultural constructions of the relationship of human to the non-human, then the notion of fantastic creatures, which are an amalgam of human and non-human, benevolent and monstrous, foreign and familiar, can be useful in understanding ideas about self and otherness.

This study has offered ways of 'reading' the varying functions of a range of fantastic creatures. One constant feature underpinning this polyvalence and ambiguity is the ability of these creatures to change and adapt. Horses with horns or wings do not exist nor do humans who are half fish and half horse, or lions that can fly like eagles or reptiles that breathe fire. These are creatures of fantasy in the sense that that they are impossible in nature, while the classical Pegasus, the Inuit sea-woman Sedna, the whale-riders of the Pacific are 'fantastic' in the sense that they are the subject of cultural myths that convey important information about how particular cultures relate to the world. On the other hand, whales, dolphins and the giant squid are very real, but their mythologized nature is the result of culturally imposed meanings that vary over time and space. Literary works, both ancient and modern, have adopted and adapted these creatures, and modern fantasy literature, video games and RPGs provide a fruitful source for the generation of new hybrids. Fantastic creatures from all cultures are alive and well and living in fantasy literature and cyber space. If the great ages of exploration are over, we can now explore virtual worlds. The Otherworld is now part of the World Wide Web, and it is possible to create these worlds ourselves through fantasy literature, computer games and films. The classical world introduced many strange and exotic creatures that we still enjoy today and Cicero's assertion, as I hope this book has shown, could not have been more wrong. Fantastic beasts, 'these inventions of the imagination', will continue to exist and to evolve.

Notes

Introduction

1   *De Vitae Patrum, Life of St Paul the Hermit* by St Jerome, Book 1a, ch. vi. 1628 edition. http://www.vitae-patrum.org.uk/page5.html (accessed 5 January 2014).

2   Eric Csapo, *Theories of Mythology*. Oxford: Oxford University Press, 2005, xi–xii, 6–7, 9.

3   Alan Dundes, ed., *Sacred Narrative: Readings in the Theory of Myth*. Berkeley: University of California Press, 1984, 1.

4   For a concise introduction to the subject, see Robert A. Segal, *Myth: A Very Short Introduction*. Oxford: Oxford University Press, 2015.

5   William Bascom, 'The Forms of Folklore: Prose Narratives', *Journal of American Folklore* 78 (1965), 3–20.

6   Lauri Honko, 'The Problem of Defining Myth', 49 in Dundes, 1984; Robert Segal, *Theorizing About Myth*. Amherst: University of Massachusetts Press, 1999, provides a comprehensive overview of approaches to myth.

7   Lise Gotfredsen, *The Unicorn*, translated by Anne Brown. London: Harvill, 1999.

8   Odell Shepard, *The Lore of the Unicorn: Myths and Legends*. London: Allen & Unwin, 1930.

9   An extensive index of images in medieval bestiary manuscripts can be found at http://bestiary.ca/beasts/beastgallery140.htm and Aberdeen Bestiary. https://www.abdn.ac.uk/bestiary/translat/54v.hti; Richard Barber, *Bestiary*. Woodbridge: The Boydell Press, 1999; Willene B. Clark and Meradith T. McMunn, eds, *Beasts and Birds of the Middle Ages: The Bestiary and its Legacy*. Philadelphia: University of Pennsylvania Press, 1989.

10 Harriet Ritvo, *The Platypus and the Mermaid and Other Figments of Classifying Imagination*. Cambridge, MA: Harvard University Press, 1997.

11 Michael Newton, *Hidden Animals: A Field Guide to Batsquatch, Chupacabra, and Other Elusive Creatures*. Santa Barbara, CA: ABC-CLIO and Greenwood Press, 2009.

12 Elizabeth M. DeLoughrey and George B. Handley, eds, *Postcolonial Ecologies: Literatures of the Environment*. Oxford: Oxford University Press, 2011.

13 Robert Bartlett, *The Natural and the Supernatural in the Middle Ages*. Cambridge: Cambridge University Press, 2008, 7–12; Peter G. Platt,

Wonders, Marvels, and Monsters in Early Modern Culture. Newark: University of Delaware Press; London: Associated University Presses, 1999.

14 Mary Douglas, *Purity and Danger: Analysis of the Concepts of Pollution and Taboo.* London and New York: Ark Paperbacks, 1966, 73, 114–28.

15 Jeffrey Jerome Cohen, *Monster Theory: Reading Culture.* Minneapolis, MN: University of Minnesota Press, 1996; Bettina Bildhauer and Robert Mills, eds, *The Monstrous Middle Ages.* Cardiff: University of Wales Press, 2003.

16 Balaji Mundkur, 'Human Animality, the Mental Imagery of Fear and Religiosity', in Tim Ingold, ed., *What Is an Animal?* London and New York: Routledge, 1994, 162–78.

17 Ingold, ed., *What Is an Animal?*, xxii, 10–13, 84–5.

18 See Christopher Partridge, *The Re-enchantment of the West: Alternative Spiritualties, Sacralization, Popular Culture and Occulture*, vol. 1. Edinburgh: T & T Clark, 2005, for an overview of these issues.

19 See Appendix pp. 204–213.

20 Jenny Strauss Clay, 'The Generation of Monsters in Hesiod', *Classical Philology* 88:2 (April 1993), 105–16.

21 Michael J. Curley, trans., *Physiologus: A Medieval Book of Nature Lore.* Chicago: University of Chicago Press, 2009; Kay, Sarah, 'The English Bestiary, the Continental Physiologus, and the Intersections between Them', *Medium Ævum* 85:1 (2016), 118–42.

22 Clark and McMunn, eds, *Beasts and Birds of the Middle Ages.*

23 Chet Van Duzer, *Sea Monsters on Medieval and Renaissance Maps.* London: The British Library, 2014, 16–19.

24 Gisli Palsson, 'The Idea of Fish: Land and Sea in the Icelandic World-View', in Roy Willis, ed., *Signifying Animals: Human Meaning in the Natural World.* London: Routledge, 1994, 119–33.

25 Van Duzer, *Sea monsters*, 42.

26 Ibid., 82–6.

27 Juliette Wood, 'Another Island Close at Hand: The Irish Imramma and the Travelogue', in Hilda Ellis Davidson, ed., *Boundaries & Thresholds: Papers from a Colloquium of the Katharine Briggs Club.* Woodchester, Stroud: Thimble Press, 1993, 55.

28 John Elsner, 'Hagiographic Geography: Travel and Allegory in the Life of Apollonius of Tyana', *The Journal of Hellenic Studies* 117 (1997), 28–33.

29 C. J. S. Thompson, *The Mystery and Lore of Monsters.* With accounts of some giants, dwarfs and prodigies, etc. London: Williams & Norgate, 1930.

30 Richard Ellis, *The Search for the Giant Squid.* New York: Lyons Press, 1998; Peter Dendle, 'Cryptozoology in the Medieval and Modern Worlds', *Folklore* 117:2 (August 2006), 190–206.

31 Barry Atkins, *More Than a Game: the Computer Game as Fictional Form.* Manchester and New York: Manchester University Press, 1993, 22–3, 39–47.

32 For a summary of the history and development of fantasy RPGs, see Lawrence Schick, *Heroic Worlds: A History and Guide to*

Role-Playing Games. Buffalo, NY: Prometheus Books, c1991, 10–34; Gary Alan Fine, *Shared Fantasy: Role-Playing Games as Social Worlds*. Chicago and London: University of Chicago Press, 1983, 246–8.

33 Andrew Burn and Diane Carr, 'Defining Game Genres', in Diane Carr et al., eds, *Computer Games: Text, Narrative and Play*. Cambridge: Polity, 2007, 18–29; Atkins, *More Than a Game*, 42–3; Janet H. Murray, *Hamlet on the Holodeck: The Future of Narrative in Cyberspace*. New York and London: Free Press, 2017.

34 Schick, *Heroic Worlds*, 105–6; Gary Gygax, *Monster Manual: An Alphabetical Compendium of All of the Monsters Found in Advanced Dungeons & Dragons* (1st edn). Renton WA: Wizards of the coast, 1979.

35 In-depth studies, both old and new, on individual mythical beasts are a testament to the continued interest in the subject. Two excellent studies on mermaids appeared too late to be included, Sophia Kingshill, *Mermaids*. Little Toller Monograph. Toller Fratrum, Dorset: Little Toller Books, 2015 and Philip Hayward, *Making a Splash: Mermaids (and Mer-men) in 20th and 21st Century Audiovisual Media*. Bloomington: Indiana University Press, 2017.

Chapter 1

1 Brave Little Tailor ATU1640; *Der Wegkützer* (c. 1557) by Martinus Montanus, Oliver Loo, *The Original 1812 Grimm Fairy Tales: A New Translation of the 1812 First Edition Kinder – und Hausmärchen / Children's and Household Tales, Collected Through the Brothers Grimm* Volume I, Self-published 2014, 72–4.

2 Gotfredsen, *The Unicorn*, 19–20, 24; John Cherry, ed., *Mythical Beasts*. London: British Museum Press, 1995, 45–6; Chris Lavers, *The Natural History of Unicorns*. London: Granta, 2009, 3–6.

3 Gotfredsen, *The Unicorn*, 20–1; Shepard, *The Lore of the Unicorn*, 26–39; Jorge Luis Borges, with Margarita Guerrero, *The Book of Imaginary Beings*. London: Vintage, 2002, 146–7.

4 Gotfredsen, *The Unicorn*, 22; Lavers, *The Natural History of Unicorns*, 31–2, 36–8.

5 Ibid., 22–4; Ibid., 40–2.

6 Gotfredsen, *The Unicorn*, 23.

7 Lavers, *The Natural History of Unicorns*, 56–67; A. H. Godbey, 'The unicorn in the Old Testament', *The American Journal of Semitic Languages and Literatures* 56 (1939), 256–96.

8 'Search for the unicorn', Metropolitan Museum of Art Exhibition, 2013. http://www.metmuseum.org/exhibitions/listings/2013/search-for-the-unicorn (accessed 1 May 2016); Natan Slifkin, *Sacred Monsters: Mysterious and Mythical Creatures of Scripture*. Talmud and Midrash. Israel: Zoo Torah, 2007, 44.

9 Slifkin, *Sacred Monsters*, 55–64.

10 Israel Aharoni, 'On Some Animals Mentioned in the Bible', *Osiris* 5 (1938), 461–78.

11 Asko Parpola, 'The Harappan Unicorn in Eurasian and South Asian Perspectives', in Toshiki Osada and Hirishi Endo, eds, *Linguistics, Archaeology and the Human Past.* Japan: Kyoto Research Institute for Humanity and Nature, 2011, 140–2.

12 Gotfredsen, *The Unicorn*, 31–3; Shepard, *The Lore of the Unicorn*, 282 n.36.

13 Gotfredsen, *The Unicorn*, 34–5.

14 Berne *Physiologus*, Burgerbibliotek Berne, MS cod. 318 fol. 16v; Brussels *Physiologus*, Biblioteque Royale Albert I, Brussels, MS Bruxelles, K.B.R. 100066-77, fol. 147r.

15 Theodore-Psalter, British Library Additional MS 19352, fol. 124.

16 For example, The Floreffe Bible, British Library Additional MS 17738, fol. 168, Khudov Psalter, State Museum Moscow GIM 86795.

17 There is an extensive index of images in medieval bestiary manuscripts at http://bestiary.ca/beasts/beastgallery140.htm. T. H. White, *The Book of Beasts Being a Translation of a Latin Bestiary of the 12th century*. London: Jonathan Cape, 1954, 20–1, 230–1; Janetta Rebold Benton, *Medieval Menagerie: Animals in the Art of the Middle Ages*. New York: Abbeville Press, 1992, 74–5. In the elaborately illustrated Worksop Bestiary presented to the Augustinian Priory in that English town in 1187, the unicorn is tinted a beautiful blue, with a green horn.

18 Pierpont Morgan Library MS M.1031, fol. 14r; 'And there shall come forth a rod out of the root of Jesse'.

19 Karen Stone, ed., *Middle English Marian Lyrics*. Kalamazoo, MI: Medieval Institute Publications, 1997. Poem 88 'Marye, mayde mylde and fre' Lines 63–5. http://d.lib.rochester.edu/teams/text/saupe-middle-english-marian-lyrics-poems-in-celebration-of-mary (accessed 5 May 2016).

20 Pierpont Morgan Library MS M.69, fol. 17v, 33r.

21 Christa Grossinger, 'The Unicorn in English Misericords', in *Medieval Art: Recent Perspectives: A Memorial Tribute to C.R. Dodwell*. Manchester and New York: Manchester University Press, 1998, 145; Cherry, *Mythical Beasts*, 51–3, Shepard, *The Lore of the Unicorn*, 45–56.

22 Guillaume le Clerc, *Bestiaire Divin*, translated by C. Hippeau, 1852, Slatkine Reprints Geneva, 1970, 236–7, lines 1350–1400.

23 Examples can be found in Erfurt Cathedral, the Marienkirche in Gelnhausen, Germany (c. 1500), Gyrstinge (now in the National Museum Copenhagen), and Limborg (c. 1617); Gotfredsen, *The Unicorn*, 64–6, 74; Cherry, *Mythical Beasts*, 51.

24 In an example from St Mary's Nantwich, a hunter stands behind a seated female figure holding a book with a unicorn in her lap, Cherry, *Mythical Beasts*, 53.

25 Grossinger, 'The Unicorn in English Misericords', 143–9, 153.

26 *Master Richard's Bestiary of Love*, translated by Jeanette Beer. Berkeley: University of California Press, 1986, 15–16; Gotfredsen, *The Unicorn*, 82.

27 Bruges Book of Hours c. 1520, Pierpont Morgan Library, MS M.307, fol. 145v.

28 Cherry, *Mythical Beasts*, 54.

29 *Le Roman de la dame à la lycorne et du biau chevalier au lyon: Text Image Rubril. French Studies* 51:7 (January 1997), 1–18; Friedrich Gennrich, ed., *Le Roman de la dame à la lycorne et du biau chevalier au lyon*. Dresden, 1908; *The Knight of the Parrot* (Le chevalier du papegau), translated by Thomas E. Vesce. New York: Garland, 1986.

30 Adolfo Salvatore Cavallo, *The Unicorn Tapestries at the Metropolitan Museum of Art*. New York: Harry Abrams, 1998, 100.

31 Alain Erlande-Brandenburg, *La dame a la licorne*. Paris: Réunion des musées nationaux, 1989.

32 Gotfredsen, *The Unicorn*, 175–7.

33 Cavallo, *The Unicorn Tapestries*, 13–17, 19–75; 'Search for the Unicorn' Metropolitan Museum of Art Exhibition, 2013 (accessed 8 January 2016). http://www.metmuseum.org/exhibitions/listings/2013/search-for-the-unicorn.

34 Shepard cites a claim by Edward Webbe, *His Travels*. London, 1590, 91.

35 Anna Contadini, *A World of Beasts: A Thirteenth-Century Illustrated Arabic Book on Animals (the Kitāb Na't al-Ḥayawān) in the Ibn Bakhtīshū Tradition*. Leiden: Brill, 2011, 26, quoting Father Luis de Urreta, *Historia Ecclesiastica Politica*, Natural, y Moral, de los Grandes y Remotes Reynos de la Etiopia, Monarchia del Emperador, llamado Preste Juan de las India. Valencia, 1610, ch. 25, 245.

36 Contadini, *A World of Beasts*, 22, 27.

37 Parpola, 'The Harappan Unicorn', 133–4.

38 A marginal illustration in a fifteenth-century French Book of Hours depicts a wild man with unicorn horn in the centre of his forehead. Pierpont Morgan Library MS M.167 fol. 40v.

39 Gotfredsen, *The Unicorn*, 10–14.

40 Simon Pearse Brodbeck, 'Putrika Interpretation of the Mahabharata', in *Samskrtavimarsah*. New Series World Sanskrit Conference, Special Rahtriya Sanskrit New Delhi: Santhan Deemed University, 2012, 142–57; Simon Pearse Brodbeck, *The Mahabharata Patriline: Gender, Culture and the Royal Hereditary*. Farnham: Ashgate, 2009, 82–3, 99–100, 130.

41 Alan Dundes, 'Structuralism and Folklore', *Studia Fennica* 20 (1976), 149–94.

42 J. A. B. van Buitenen, ed. and trans., *The Mahabharata*. Chicago: University of Chicago Press, 1975, 191.

43 Cherry, *Mythical Beasts*, 57, 68.

44 Other examples by Francesco Pesellino (Isabella Gardner Museum, Boston) and Francesco di Giorgio Martini (Getty Museum, California).

45 Morretti, *St Justyna* (Uffizi Gallery, Florence), Raphael, *Lady with Unicorn* (Galleria Borghese, Rome), Domenichino Zampieri, *Virgin with Unicorn* (Palazzo Farnese, Rome), and (possibly?) Giorgione, *Allegory of Chastity* (Rijkmuseum, Amsterdam).

46 Cherry, *Mythical Beasts*, 66; Metropolitan Museum of Art Accession no. 20.53.3.

47 Oliver Evans, 'Selections from the Bestiary of Leonardo Da Vinci', *The Journal of American Folklore* 64 (1951), 395.

48 Cherry, *Mythical Beasts*, 68–9; Cavallo, *The Unicorn Tapestries*, 47; Gotfredsen, *The Unicorn*, 80–1. http://www.harvardartmuseums.org/collection (accessed 1 May 2016).

49 Gotfredsen, *The Unicorn*, 162–3.

50 Slifkin, *Sacred Monsters*, 45; David Ruderman, 'Unicorns, Great Beasts and the Marvellous Nature of Things in Nature in the Thought of Abraham Ben Hananiah Yagel', in Isaac Twersky and Bernard Septimus, eds, *Jewish Thought in the 17th Century*. Cambridge, MA: Harvard University Press, 1987, 343–64.

51 The Medieval Bestiary. http://bestiary.ca/beasts/beast140.htm (accessed 21 April 2017).

52 Parpola, 'The Harappan Unicorn', 152–9.

53 Württembergische Landesbibliotek, Stuttgart cod. Bibl. 20 23, fol. 27.

54 Steve Roud, *Folk Song Index* no. 2017. http://library.efdss.org (accessed 23 July 2014); Iona and Peter Opie, *Oxford Dictionary of Nursery Rhymes*. Oxford: Oxford University Press, 1951, 269.

55 *Hortus deliciarum (Garden of delights)* by Herrad of Landsberg, edited and translated by Aristide D. Caratzas, New Rochelle, NY: Caratzas Brothers, 1977.

56 Grossinger, 'The Unicorn in English Misericords', 143; Gotfredsen, *The Unicorn*, 51, 52; The Utrecht Psalter, British Library Additional MS 10024, fol.4v.

57 Cherry, *Mythical Beasts*, 66.

58 Rachel Bromwich, ed., *Trioedd ynys Prydein: The Welsh Triads* (4th edn). Cardiff: University of Wales Press, 2014, lxxxii–lxxxiii, 115, 121.

59 Cherry, *Mythical Beasts*, 64–5; Daniel W. Mosser, Ernest W. Sullivan II, with Len Hatfield and David H. Radcliffe. *The Thomas L. Gravell Watermark Archive*. 1996-www.gravell.org (accessed 23 July 2014).

60 Cherry, *Mythical Beasts*, 60–2.

61 Lauren Catelan, *Histoire de la nature, chasse, vertus, proprietes, et usage de la Lycorne*. Montpellier, 1624, 11; Natalis Comes, *De Venatione*. Venice 1551, 4,1, 298.

62 *Itinerarium Joannis de Hese presbyteri ad Hierusalem* (1389) quoted by Contadini, *A World of Beasts*, 26–7, 33 n.46.

63 Grossinger, 'The Unicorn in English Misericords', 153; Margaret B. Freeman, *The Unicorn Tapestries*. New York: Metropolitan Museum of Art 1976, 54; Parpola, 'The Harappan Unicorn', 131–3; Shepard, *The Lore of the Unicorn*, 234–8.

64 Liliane Châtelet-Lange, Renate Francisco, 'The Grotto of the Unicorn and the Garden of the Villa di Castello', *The Art Bulletin* 50:1 (March 1968), 52–5.

65 Contadini, *A World of Beasts*, 17–20, 21–2, 23–4, 52–3, fol. 211v–213r.

66 Aleksander Pluskowski, 'Narwhals or Unicorns: Exotic Animals as Material culture in medieval Europe', *European Journal of Archaeology* 7:3 (2004), 302; Cherry, *Mythical Beasts*, 56–60; Guido Schoenberger, 'A Goblet of Unicorn horn', *The Metropolitan Museum of Art Bulletin*, New Series 9:10 (1951), 284–8.

67 Carl Zimmer, 'The Mystery of the Sea Unicorn', *The Loom*, 18 March 2014, *National Geographic*. http://phenomena.nationalgeographic.com/2014/03/18/the-mystery-of-the-sea-unicorn/ (accessed 20 January 2016); Shepard, *The Lore of the Unicorn*, 97–9.

68 Benvenuto Cellini, *Autobiography*, translated by John Addington Symonds, Ch. LX, The Harvard Classics. New York: P.F. Collier & Son, 1909–14 www.bartleby.com/31/ (accessed 20 January 2016).

69 Shepard, *The Lore of the Unicorn*, 156–90.

70 Stephen Bamforth, 'On Gesner, Marvels and Unicorns', *Nottingham French Studies* 49:3 (2010), 125, 132–8; Andrea Marini, (medico), Discorco … contra la falsa opinione dell'alicorno. Venice 1566; Andrea Bacci, *L'Alicorno, discorso dell'eccellente medico et filosofo* Florence, 1573.

71 Gotfredsen, *The Unicorn*, 162–3; Thomae Bartholini. *De unicornu observationes novæ* / [Bartholin, Thomas,]. – Secunda editione / Auctores & emendatiores editæ à filio Casparo Bartholino. – Amstelædami: Apud JHenr. Wetstenium, 1678.

72 Bamforth, 'On Gesner, Marvels and Unicorns', 110–45; Gotfredsen, *The Unicorn*, 164–5; Lavers, *The Natural History of Unicorns*, 99–100.

73 Hans Sloane, 'An Account of Elephants Teeth and Bones Found under Ground', *Philosophical Transactions* (1683–1775), 35 (1727–8), 459–62.

74 Richard Fortey, 'In Retrospect: Leibniz's Protogaea', Review of *Protogaea* by Gottfried Wilhelm Leibniz. Translated by Claudine Cohen and Andre Wakefield. Chicago: University of Chicago Press, 2008. *Nature* (2008), 35; Roger Ariew, 'Leibniz on the Unicorn and Various other Curiosities', *Early Science and Medicine* 3:4 (1998) Protogaea chapter 35, 276.

75 F. J. Cole, 'Bibliographical Reflections of a Biologist', *Osiris* 8 (1948), 292–5; Ariew, 'Leibniz on the Unicorn', 278 n.34, 279.

76 Lavers, *The Natural History of Unicorns*, Chapter 6, 112–50; B. Laufer, 'Arabic and Chinese Trade in Walrus and Narwhal Ivory', *T'oung pao* 14 (1913), 315–70; R. Ettinghausen 'The Unicorn', *Freer Gallery of Art Occasional Papers* I (Washington, 1950), 1, 3; Catelan, *Histoire de la nature*, 11.

77 Rachel Dicker, US News 28 March 2016 (accessed 24 September 2017). https://www.usnews.com/news/articles/2016-03-28/newly-discovered-fossil-reveals-when-siberian-unicorns-last-roamed-the-earth?src=usn_.

78 Willy Ley, *The Lungfish, the Dodo, & the Unicorn: An Excursion Into Romantic Zoology*. New York: Viking Press, 1948; Newton, *Hidden Animals*, 185.

79 Lavers, *The Natural History of Unicorns*, 151–3.

80 Shepard, *The Lore of the Unicorn*, 219–24; Lavers, *The Natural History of Unicorns*, 13.

81 Lavers, *The Natural History of Unicorns*, chapters 1 and 2, 1–43.

82 Ibid., 155–8; Shepard, *The Lore of the Unicorn*, 211; Nikolai Przhevalskii, *Mongolia,* The Tangut Country and the Solitudes of Northern Tibet. 2 vols, translated by E. Delmar Morgan, London: Sampson Low, Marston, Searle & Rivington, 1876.

83 Lavers, *The Natural History of Unicorns*, 157–8, 168–9.

84 Ibid., 176–87.

85 Ibid., 196–216; Shepard, *The Lore of the Unicorn*, 226–8.

86 Marta Falconi, 'Unicorn deer' Rome, Associated Press. http://news.nationalgeographic.com/news/2008/06/080612-AP-unicorn-photo.html (accessed 9 August 2015).

87 William Brockbank, 'Sovereign Remedies: A Critical Depreciation of the 17th Century London Pharmacopoeia', *Medical History* 8:01 (1964), 1–14.

88 Aubrey Beardsley, *Under the Hill*. New York and London: John Lane 1904, 29, 36.

89 The term was first brought to my attention as part of the New York Club scene about 2008 when I enquired about some elaborately decorated headgear fashioned as unicorn horns.

90 Gian Carlo Menotti, 'The Unicorn, the Gorgon and the Manticore or The three Sundays of a poet: A madrigal fable for chorus, ten dancers and nine instruments' (1957).

91 Anne Morrow Lindbergh, *Bring Me a Unicorn: Diaries and Letters of Anne Morrow Lindbergh, 1922-1928*. Boston: G. K. Hall, 1973.

92 David Jones, *Order: An Occasional Catholic Review* 1–4 (May 1928–November 1929) issue 1, 1928, 29.

93 W. B. Yeats and Lady Gregory, *The Unicorn from the Stars, and Other Plays*. New York: Macmillan, 1908; Patricia Ann McFate, William E. Doherty, 'W. B. Yeats's '"Where There Is Nothing" Theme and Symbolism', *Irish University Review* 2:2 (Autumn 1972), 154–7.

94 James Thurber, 'The Unicorn in the Garden' from *Fables for Our Time* reprinted in *The Thurber Carnival*. New York: Harper and Brothers, 1945, 268–9.

95 Wolf Mankowitz, *A Kid for Two Farthings*. London: André Deutsch, 1953; *A Kid for Two Farthings*, 1955 dir. Carol Reed.

96 This mixture of parallel or alternate-world fantasies occurs in several 'unicorn' novels. For example, Margaret Lathrop, *The Colt from Moon Mountain* (1941) and Elizabeth Gouge, *The Little White Horse* (1946).

97 The Final Fantasy Art of Yoshitaka Amano. http://kotaku.com/5917619/the-beautiful-final-fantasy-art-of-yoshitaka-amano (accessed 23 April 2017).

98 Scott Bukataman, *Blade Runner*. London: British Film Institute, 1997, 80–3.

99 Michael Bracewell and Alun Rowlands, 'The Dark Monarch: Magic and Modernity in British Art', Tate St Ives, 10 October–10 January, curated by Martin Clark, artistic director of Tate St Ives, in Tate Etc. (Autumn issue 17, 2009). (accessed 13 February 2012).

100 Borges, *The Book of Imaginary Beings*, 148–9.

101 James C. Y. Wyatt, 'The Giraffe as the Mythical Qilin in Chinese Art: A Painting and a Rank Badge in the Metropolitan Museum', *Metropolitan Museum Journal* 43 (2008), 111–5; Julia K. Murray, 'Illustrations of the Life of Confucius: Their Evolution, Functions, and Significance in Late Ming China', *Artibus Asiae* 57:1/2 (1997), 78–82, 101, 102.

102 Shepard, *The Lore of the Unicorn*, 94–7; Borges, *The Book of Imaginary Beings*, 148–9; Wyatt, 'The Giraffe as the Mythical Qilin in Chinese Art', 111–5; Murray, 'Illustrations of the Life of Confucius', 73–134.

103 Fuyumi Ono, illustrator, Yamada Akihiro, *The Twelve Kingdoms*. Tokyo: Kodansha Ltd., 1992/2001, Translation and English Adaptation, Alexander O. Smith and Elye J. Alexander. Los Angeles: Tokyopop, 2006; *The Twelve Kingdoms* anime, directed Tsuneo Kobayashi, 2002–3.

104 Vicki Ellen Szabo, *Monstrous Fishes and the Mead-Dark Sea*: Whaling in the Medieval North. Leiden: Brill, 2008. Citing *The King's Mirror* Book XII, 187. https://archive.org/stream/kingsmirrorspecu00konuuoft/ kingsmirrorspecu00konuuoft_djvu.txt (accessed 1 December 2016).

105 Johan Fritzner, *Ordbog over det gamle norske sprog*. Kristiania: Feilberg & Landmark, 1867; I wish to express my thanks to Professor John Hines for this information from the online *Dictionary of Old Norse Prose*. http://onp. ku.dk/english/ (accessed 10 November 2012).

106 See discussion of sea serpent in Chapter 4.

107 Shepard, *The Lore of the Unicorn*, 259.

108 Pluskowski, 'Narwhals or Unicorns', 294.

109 Cherry, *Mythical Beasts*, 66–8.

110 Martin Frobisher quoted in *Purchas, His Pilgrimage*. London, 1613, 621; Pluskowski, 'Narwhals or Unicorns', 294–300; Cherry, *Mythical Beasts*, 58–60.

111 See p. 26.

112 Thomas Browne, *Pseudodoxia Epidemica* 1650 (ed. 2) III. xxiii. 137.

113 Gotfredsen, *The Unicorn*, 166, 69–81; Shepard, *The Lore of the Unicorn*, 262, 270–1.

114 Schoenberger, 'A Goblet of Unicorn horn', 284–8.

115 Van Duzer, *Sea Monsters*, 93.

116 The Angel warns Tobias, Florike Egmond and Peter Mason, eds, *The Whale Book: Whales and Other Marine Animals as Described by Adriaen Coenen in 1585*. London: Reaktion, 2003, 82–3; Adriaen Coenen *Visboek* (1577). https://www.kb.nl/en/themes/middle-ages/adriaen-coenens-visboek (accessed 7 August 2014).

117 Pierre Pomet, *Histoire Generale des Drogues*. Paris, 1694; Ambrose Paré, *Discours .... de la Licorne*, des venins et de la peste. Paris, 1582.

118 Pierre Martin de la Martiniére, *A New Voyage to the North*, 1700; William Henry Dewhurst, *The Natural History of the Order of Cetacea and the Oceanic Inhabitants of the Arctic Region*. London, 1834.

119 Jules Verne, *Vingt mille lieues sous les mers*, illustrations by Alphonse de Neuville and Eduard Riou, Paris: Hetzel, 1871. Illustrations by the French artist Alphonse Marie de Neuville for the version published by Pierre-Jules Hetzel in 1871; *Twenty Thousand Leagues Under the Sea.* London, 1870, chapters 1 & 2.

120 Gotfredsen, *The Unicorn*, 178–9; Jørn Rønnau (accessed 23 December 2011). http://www.visitaarhus.com/international/en-gb/menu/turist/om-aarhus/sevaerdigheder/naturomraader/skulpturtraeer/skulpturtraeer.htm.

121 'Enlisted "sea unicorns" reveal unexpected sea warming'. (*New Scientist* updated 16 December 2010); Jules Verne, *Vingt mille lieues sous les mers*, English Edition 1872.

122 Amy Turner, 'No hymns and, so far, no unicorns', *The Sunday Times* 01.08.10, p. 6. http://en.wikipedia.org/wiki/Invisible_Pink_Unicorn (accessed 7 August 2016).

123 This unicorn-like animal, called variously *karkodann* or *kardunn* or *cartazon*, appears in multiple sources.

124 Scott D. Westrem, *The Hereford Map: A Transcription and Translation of the Legends with Commentary.* Terrarvm orbis 1. Turnhout: Brepols, 2001, 110–11.

125 Benton, *Medieval Menagerie*, 71–3; Barber, *Bestiary*, 47.

126 'A true Relation of the dreadful combate between More of More-Hall and the Dragon of Wantley'. London, 1685; Jacqueline Simpson, *British Dragons.* Ware: Wordsworth Editions and The Folklore Society, 2001, 146–50.

127 Wilma George, 'The Yale', *Journal of the Warburg and Courtauld Institutes* 31 (1968), 423–5.

128 George, 'The Yale', 425, Westrem, *The Hereford Map*, 123.

129 George, 'The Yale', 426–8.

130 G. C. Druce, 'Notes on the History of the Heraldic Jale or Yale', *Archeological Journal* 68 (1911), 173–99.

131 Benton, *Medieval Menagerie*, 21–3; H. S, 'A Romanesque Archivolt', *The Metropolitan Museum of Art Bulletin* 18:1 (January 1923), 9–10.

132 Stephanie Young, 'manticore', in Jeffrey Andrew Weinstock, ed., *The Ashgate Encyclopedia of Literary and Cinematic Monsters.* Farnham: Ashgate, 2014, 398–400.

133 Barber, *Bestiary*, 63.

134 Westrem, *The Hereford Map*, 98–101.

135 Roger Sherman Loomis and Laura Hibbard Loomis, *Arthurian Legends in Medieval Art.* Oxford and New York: Oxford University Press, 1938, Plate 192.

136 Margaret Robinson, 'Some Fabulous Beasts', *Folklore* 76:4 (Winter, 1965), 273–87; Doris Jones-Baker, 'The Graffiti of Folk Motifs in Cotswold Churches', *Folklore* 92:2 (1981), 160–7. http://bestiary.ca/beasts/beast550.htm (accessed 6 July 2015).

137 Edward Topsell, *The History of Four-Footed Beasts*. London, 1607, and *A Description of the Nature of Four-Footed Beasts* with their figures engraved in brass by Joannes Jonstonus, London: M. Pitt, 1678.

138 Schick, *Heroic Worlds*, 129–30, 230–1.

139 E. R. Eddison, *The Worm Ouroboros*. London: Jonathan Cape, 1922, Chap. XII, 205–7.

140 'The Book of Beasts' by E. Nesbit, *The Book of Dragons*. London and New York: Harper & Bros, 1901, 1–19.

141 William J. Travis, 'Of Sirens and Onocentaurs: A Romanesque Apocalypse at Montceaux-l'Etoile', *Artibus et Historiae* 23:45 (2002), 33, 49. Brussels Physiologus, Bibliotheque Royale, MS lat. 10074, fol. 146v.

142 Cherry, *Mythical Beasts*, 141–3, 154–5; Benton, *Medieval Menagerie*, 22–31; Sidney Colvin, 'On Representations of Centaurs in Greek Vase-Painting', *The Journal of Hellenic Studies* 1 (1880), 107–67.

143 References summarized in Colvin, 'On Representations of Centaurs', 107–21.

144 Colvin, 'On Representations of Centaurs', 118–24, 152.

145 Susan Langdon, 'The Awkward Age: Art and Maturation in Early Greece', *Hesperia Supplements* 41, Constructions of Childhood in Ancient Greece and Italy (2007), 177–9.

146 A fourteenth-century copy of the *Vitae Patrum*, Pierpont Morgan Library MS M 626, fol. 2v depicts this scene; Walter Map, *De Nugis Curialium: Courtier's Trifles*, edited and translated by M. R. James revised by C. N. L. Brooks and R. A. B. Mynors. Oxford: Clarendon Press, 1983, Distinctio 2, c. 15.

147 Travis, 'Of Sirens and Onocentaurs', 39; Pierpont Morgan Library MS M 453, fol. 132r.

148 Pierpont Morgan Library MS M.32, fol. 26r.

149 http://bestiary.ca/beasts/beastgallery384.htm# (accessed 20 February 2013).

150 Pierpont Morgan Library MS M 1004, fol. 22r; Pierpont Morgan Library MS M 969, fol. 339r.

151 D. E. Strong, 'A Lady Centaur', *The British Museum Quarterly* 30:1/2 (Autumn 1965), 36–7.

152 Shepard, *The Lore of the Unicorn*, 273–6.

Chapter 2

1 John Nott, *Cook's & Confectioner's Dictionary* or the accomplished housewife's companion London printed for Charles Rivington, 1723.

2 Wood, 'Harpy', in Jeffrey Andrew Weinstock, ed., *The Ashgate Encyclopedia of Literary and Cinematic Monsters*. Farnham: Ashgate, 2014, 411–15.

3   Travis, 'Of Sirens and Onocentaurs', 33–9.

4   Guillaume le Clerc, *Bestiaire Divin*, translated by Hippeau, 1952, 114–17.

5   See centaur discussion, 45–47; Travis, 'Of Sirens and Onocentaurs', 39–45.

6   Elizabeth Rodini, 'Baroque Pearls: Renaissance Jewelry in the Alsdorf
       Collection', *Art Institute of Chicago Museum Studies* 25:2 (2000), 68–71,
       106; A. Luchs, *The Mermaids of Venice, Fantastic Sea Creatures in Venetian
       Renaissance Art*. London: Harvey Miller, 2010.

7   Madam White Snake, p. 147.

8   Clay, 'The Generation of Monsters in Hesiod', 107–15.

9   Bo Almqvist, 'The Mélusine Legend in the Context of Irish Folk Tradition',
       Béaloideas 67 (1999), 13–69; Juliette Wood, 'The Fairy Bride Legend in
       Wales', *Folklore* 103:1 (1992), 56–72

10 Bo Almqvist, 'Of Mermaids and Marriages: Seamus Heaney's "Maighdean
       Mara" and Nuala Ní Dhomhnaill's "anMhaighdean Mhara" in the Light of
       Folk Tradition', *Béaloideas* 58 (1990), 4–9, 17–18, 29–31; Juliette Wood,
       'The Mélusine Legend in Wales: Modern Period', in Jeanne-Marie Boivin
       and Prionsias MacCana, eds, *Mélusines continentales et Insulaires*. Paris:
       Honoré Champion, 1999, 297–314.

11 Almqvist, 'Of Mermaids and Marriages', 17–18, 29–31.

12 Wood, 'The Fairy Bride Legend in Wales', 56–72.

13 Jean d'Arras, *Mélusine: or the Noble History of Lusignan* (1393). Translated
       by Donald Maddox and Sara Sturm-Maddox. University Park, PA:
       Pennsylvania University Press, 2011.

14 Wood, 'The Mélusine Legend in Wales', 297–314.

15 'The Overflowing of Lough Neagh and the Story of Liban the Mermaid',
       in *Old Celtic Romances* from the Gaelic 1879, translated by P. W. Joyce;
       introduction Juliette Wood. Ware, Hertfordshire: Wordsworth Editions/The
       Folklore Society, 2000, 87–94.

16 Maureen Murphy, 'Siren or Victim? The Mermaid in Irish Legend and Poetry',
       in Donald E. Morse and Cilla Bertha, eds, *More Real Than Reality: The
       Fantastic in Irish Literature and the Arts*. New York: Greenwood Press, 1991,
       29–40.

17 Almqvist, 'Of Mermaids and Marriages', 41; Seamus Heaney, 'Maighdean
       Mara' in *Wintering Out*, London: Faber and Faber, 1972, 60–68; Nuala Ní
       Dhomhnaill, 'An Mhaighdean Mhara', in *Selected Poems: Rogha Dánta*,
       translated by Michael Hartnett. Dublin: Raven Arts Press, 1988, 81–3; Nuala
       Ní Dhomhnaill, *The Fifty Minute Mermaid*, translated by Paul Muldoon.
       Loughcrew and Ireland: Gallery Press, 2008.

18 David Atkinson, 'The Child Ballads from England and Wales in the James
       Madison Carpenter Collection', *Folk Music Journal* 7 (1998), 434–49; Steve
       Roud and Julia Bishop, *The New Penguin Book of English Folksongs*. London
       and New York: Penguin Classics, 2012, 885–7.

19 Herbert Wright, 'The Source of Matthew Arnold's Forsaken Merman',
       Modern Language Review 13 (1918), 90–4; Julia Cresswell, *Legendary
       Beasts of Britain*. Oxford: Shire Publications, 2013, 30–3.

20 Frédérick Laugrand and J. G. Oosten, *The Sea Woman: Sedna in Inuit Shamanism and Art in the Eastern Artic*. Fairbanks: University of Alaska Press, 2008, 35–8.

21 H. Rink and F. Boas, 'Eskimo Tales and Songs', *The Journal of American Folklore*, 2:5 (1889), 127–8; Knud Rasmussen, *Eskimo Folk-Tales*. Edited and translated by W. Worster. London: Gyldendal, 1921, 113–19, 155–6.

22 Laugrand and Oosten, *The Sea Woman*, 20–1, 34, n.2; Mundkur, 'Human Animality', 171.

23 Laugrand and Oosten, *The Sea Woman*, 111–22; Mundkur, 'Human Animality', 173.

24 Birgitte Sonne, 'The Acculturative Role of Sea Woman, Early Contact Relations between Inuit and Whites as Revealed in the Origin Myth of Sea Woman', *Man and Society* 13 (1990), 1–34; H. N. Wardle, 'The Sedna Cycle', *American Anthropologist* 2 (1900), 568–80.

25 Laugrand and Oosten, *The Sea Woman*, 58–71, 75–80.

26 Ibid., 91–111.

27 Ibid., 131–4.

28 'Serek-A the mermaid (Arua version)', trans. Betty Mindlin and Indigenous Storytellers, in *Barbecued Husbands and Other Stories From the Amazon*, translated by Donald Slatoff. New York: Verso, 2002, 249–52, 275.

29 H. W. Bates, *The Naturalist on the River Amazon*, 2 vols. London: Murray, 1863.

30 M. A. Cravalho, 'Shameless Creatures, an Ethnozoology of the Amazon River Dolphin', *Ethnology* 38:1 (1999), 47–58; W. Gravena et al., 'Amazon River Dolphin Love Fetishes: From Folklore to Molecular Forensics', *Marine Mammal Science* 24:4 (2008), 969–8.

31 Rowan Hooper, '"Pretty in Pink" meet the Amazon river dolphin', *New Scientist*, 17 December 2001, 25.

32 Martha Warren Beckwith, 'Hawaiian Shark Aumakua', *American Anthropologist*, New Series 19:4 (October–December 1917), 512–14.

33 Beckwith, 'Hawaiian Shark Aumakua', 508–10; Martha Beckwith, *Hawaiian Mythology* (1910). Honolulu: University of Hawaii Press, 1970, 256–68.

34 Lucia Sá, *Rain Forest Literatures: Amazonian Texts and Latin American Culture*. Minnesota: University of Minnesota Press, 2004, 35–68.

35 Phyllis Galembo, *Divine Inspiration from Benin to Bahia*. Albuquerque: University of New Mexico Press, 1993, 3–7, 111.

36 Marilyn Houlberg, 'Sirens and Snakes: Water Spirits in the Arts of Haitian Vodou', *African Arts*, Special Issue: Arts of Vodou, 29:2 (Spring, 1996), 30–5; Henry John Drewal, 'Mermaids, Mirrors, and Snake Charmers: Igbo Mami Wata Shrines', *African Arts* 21:2 (February 1988), 38–45.

37 Item: NLW WS.S 1604(2). http://education.gtj.org.uk/en/item1/26001 GTJ64526 (accessed 5 May 2014).

38 Adriaen Coenen, *Visboek* (1578) fol. 54–5. https://www.kb.nl/en/themes/middle-ages/adriaen-coenens-visboek (accessed 15 May 2014).

39 Van Duzer, *Sea Monsters*, 42.

40 Juliette Wood, 'Walter Map and the Context of *De Nugis Curialium*', *Transactions of the Honorable Society of Cymmrodorion* (1985), 91–103; Map, *De Nugis Curialium,* Walter Map and Colá Pesce, Distinction 4, section 39.

41 Alan Bruford, 'Trolls, Hillfolk, Finns and Picts: The Identity of the Good Neighbours in Orkney and Shetland', in Peter Narváez, ed., *The Good People: New Fairylore Essays*. New York and London: Garland Publishing, 1991, 116–41.

42 Richard Stoneman, *Alexander the Great: A Life in Legend*. New Haven and London: Yale University Press, 2008, 143–8.

43 Sophie Morrison, *Manx Fairy Tales*. London: D. Nutt, 1911, 70–4.

44 Arthur Waugh, 'The Folklore of the Merfolk', *Folklore* 71:2 (June 1960), 73–84.

45 Jennifer Westwood and Jacqueline Simpson, *The Lore of the Land: A Guide to England's Legends*. London: Penguin, 2005, 326–7.

46 J. D. Lewis-Williams, 'Ezeljagdspoort Revisited: New Light on an Enigmatic Rock-Painting', *The South African Archaeological Bulletin* 32:126 (December 1977), 165–9; Juliette Wood, 'The Mermaids of Karoo', *FLS News The Newsletter of the Folklore Society* no. 60, February 2001, 5.

47 Dublin, Trinity College Library, MS 58, fol. 213r.

48 http://bestiary.ca/beasts/beast283.htm

49 William Bottrell, *Traditions and Hearthside Stories of West Cornwall, Second Series*. Penzance: Beare and Son, 1873, reprint Whitefish, MT: Kessinger Publishing, 2009; Waugh, 'The Folklore of the Merfolk', 82–3.

50 R. J. Knecht, *Catherine de Medici*. London and New York: Longman, 1998; Roy Strong, *Art and Power: Renaissance Festivals, 1450–1650*. Woodbridge, UK: Boydell Press, 1984.

51 Frank E. Reynolds 'Ramayana, Rama Jataka, and Ramakien: A Comparative Study of Hindu and Buddhist Traditions', in Paula Richman, ed., *Many Ramayanas: The Diversity of a Narrative Tradition in South Asia*. Berkeley: University of California Press, 1991, 56–9. http://ark.cdlib.org/ark:/13030/ft3j49n8h7/ (accessed 17 March 2015).

52 Ritvo, *The Platypus and the Mermaid*, 6–7, 178–81; Steven C. Levi, 'P. T. Barnum and the Feejee Mermaid', *Western Folklore*, 36:2 (1977), 149–54; Feegee mermaid. http://www.showhistory.com/Feegee.Wolff.html (accessed 10 July 2016).

53 Personal communication from Dr Simpson, February 2010.

54 Kellerman's costumes, Powerhouse Museum, Sydney Australia. http://www.powerhousemuseum.com/collection/database/?irn= 9167&collection=Annette+Kellerman+Costume#ixzz0wESEAGhu (accessed 15 August 2016).

55 Maryan Pelland and Dan Pelland, *Weeki Wachee Springs*. Charleston and Chicago: Arcadia Publishing, 2006, 12; Lu Vickers and Sara Dionne, *Weeki Wachee, City of Mermaids: A History of One of Florida's Oldest Roadside*

Attractions. Gainesville: University Press of Florida, 2007. http://www.
weekiwachee.com/ (accessed 15 August 2014).

56 Lucy Fraser, *The Pleasures of Metamorphosis Japanese and English Fairy
Tale Transformation of 'The Little mermaid'*. Detroit Wayne State University
Press, 2017, 46–62, 67–9.

57 Thompson, *The Mystery and Lore of Monsters*, 106–15.

58 Van Duzer, *Sea Monsters*, 100, 102.

59 John Swan, *Speculum Mundi or A Glasse Representing the Face of the
World*. Cambridge, 1635; Thompson, *The Mystery and Lore of Monsters*,
106–15.

60 Michael Newton, 'Stronsay Beast', *Encyclopedia of Cryptozoology: A Global
Guide*. London: McFarland & Company, 2005, 442–3; Newton, *Hidden
Animals*, 79–80; Ritvo, *The Platypus and the Mermaid*, 6–7, 178–81.

61 James O'Donoghue, 'The Hunt for Predator X', *New Scientist* (31 October
2009), 32–5. www.newscientist.com/article/dn18047-real-sea-monsters-the-
hunt-for-predator-x/ (accessed 10 August 2015).

62 Ritvo, *The Platypus and the Mermaid*, 6–7, 178–81; see above p. 59.

63 www.chickenofthesea.com (accessed 15 January 2015).

64 http://www.metmuseum.org/collection/the-collection-online/search/210103
(accessed 29 June 2016).

65 Carl Pyrdum, 'The Other Starbucks Mermaid Cover-Up', 2010. http://www.
gotmedieval.com/2010/08/the-other-starbucks-mermaid-cover-up.html
(accessed 23 February 2013).

66 Israeli mermaid. http://www.livescience.com/5642-mermaid-sightings-
claimed-israel.html (accessed 15 March 2013).

67 Ritvo, *The Platypus and the Mermaid*, 182.

68 'Mermaids: The Body Found' (27 May 2012), 'Mermaids: The New Evidence'
(26 May 2013). http://www.dailymail.co.uk/news/article-2333515/Mermaid-
hoax-How-mockumentary-gave-Animal-Planet-biggest-audience-EVER.html
(accessed January 2015).

69 John K. Papadopoulos and Deborah Ruscillo, 'A Ketos in Early Athens: An
Archaeology of Whales and Sea Monsters in the Greek World', *American
Journal of Archaeology* 106:2 (April, 2002), 187–227.

70 Van Duzer, *Sea Monsters*, 50–2, 83.

71 Cornelia Caitlin Coulter, 'The Great Fish in Ancient and Medieval Story',
Transactions of the American Philological Association 57 (1926), 32–50.

72 Coulter, 'The Great Fish in Ancient and Medieval Story', 33–6.

73 Van Duzer, *Sea Monsters*, 49, 116; W. R. J. Barron and Glyn S. Burgess,
eds, *The Voyage of Saint Brendan: Representative Versions of the Legend
in English Translation*. Exeter: University of Exeter Press, 2002. Jasconius
appears in the Latin *Navigatio Brendani* in sections x, xvi, xxvii (pp. 35,
47, 62) and in Caxton's translation (1483), 331, 335, 341.

74 'The First Voyage of Sinbad the Sailor', in Andrew Lang, ed., *The Arabian
Nights Entertainment*. London: Longmans Green and Co, 1898, 126–7.

75 Coulter, 'The Great Fish in Ancient and Medieval Story', 36–7.

76 Van Duzer, *Sea Monsters*, 77–8.

77 Emma Lacey-Bordeaux and Dave Alsup, 'Seaplane almost Lands on Whale', CNN.com, 16 July 2014 (accessed 16 July 2014).

78 Jan Ziolkowski, 'Folklore and Learned Lore in Letaldus' Whale Poem', *Viator* 15 (1984), 111.

79 Ziolkowski, 'Folklore and Learned Lore', 107–11; William Hansen, *Ariadne's Thread: A Guide to International Tales Found in Classical Literature*. Ithaca: Cornell University Press, 2002, 261–4.

80 Charles Speroni, 'More on the Sea-Monsters', *Italica* 35:1 (March, 1958), 21–4; Allan Gilbert, 'The Sea Monster in Ariosto's Cinque Canti and Pinocchio', *Italica* 33:4 (December 1956), 260–3.

81 Edward Davis, 'A Whale of a Tale: Fundamentalist Fish Stories', *Perspectives on Science and Christian Faith* 43 (1991), 224–37.

82 Cockatrice, see pp. 119–124.

83 Walter Traill Dennison, 'Orkney folklore, Sea Myths 3', *The Scottish Antiquary* 5 (1891), 131–2.

84 Hermann Oesterley, ed., *Gesta Romanorum*. Berlin: Weiderman, 1872, cap 251 app 55, 655–7.

85 Nancy L. Canepa, trans., *Pentamerone Giambattista Basile's The Tale of Tales, or, Entertainment for Little Ones*. Detroit: Wayne State University Press, 2007, 427–32.

86 St Margaret of Antioch, See, p. 149.

87 Vikki Ellen Szabo: 'Bad to the Bone: The Unnatural History of Monstrous Medieval Whales', *The Heroic Age, A Journal of Early Medieval Northwestern Europe* 8 (June 2005), 1–18.

88 Van Duzer, *Sea Monsters*, 37–8, 81–6.

89 Anne Brydon, 'The Predicament of Nature: Keiko the Whale and the Cultural Politics of Whaling in Iceland', *Anthropological Quarterly* 79:2 (Spring, 2006), 225–60; Yixing Jiang, et al., 'Public Awareness, Education, and Marine Mammals in Captivity', *Tourism Review International* 11:3 (2007), 237–49.

90 *The Voyage of Saint Brendan*, edited by Barron and Burgess, *Navigatio*, section 16; Arthur Waugh, 'The Folklore of the Whale', *Folklore* 72:2 (June 1961), 361–71.

91 A. H. McLintock, *An Encyclopaedia of New Zealand*. Wellington, NZ: R. E. Owen, Government printer, 1966.

92 Edward Sapir, 'Indian Legends from Vancouver Island', *Journal of American Folklore* 72:284 (April–June 1959), 108–14.

93 E. Sapir, 'A Flood Legend of the Nootka Indians of Vancouver Island', *The Journal of American Folklore* 32:124 (April–June 1919), 351–5.

94 Margaret Lantis, 'The Alaskan Whale Cult and Its Affinities', *American Anthropologist* New Series, 40:3 (1938), 438–64; Michael Harkin, 'Whales, Chiefs, and Giants: An Exploration into Nuu-Chah-Nulth Political Thought', *Ethnology* 37:4 (Autumn, 1998), 317–32.

95 C. Lee Miller, 'The Younger Pliny's Dolphin Story ("Epistulae" IX 33): An Analysis', *The Classical World* 60:1 (September 1966), 6–8; H. C. Montgomery, 'The Fabulous Dolphin', *The Classical Journal* 61:7 (April 1966), 311–14; T. F. Higham, 'Nature Note: Dolphin-Riders. Ancient Stories Vindicated', *Greece & Rome*, Second Series, 7:1 (March, 1960), 82–6.

96 Deborah Howard, 'Venice as a Dolphin: Further Investigations into Jacopo de' Barbari's View', *Artibus et Historiae* 18:35 (1997), 101–11.

97 Gervase of Tilbury, *Otia Imperialia: Recreation for an Emperor*, edited and translated by S. E. Banks and J. W. Binns. Oxford: Clarendon Press, 2002, Bk 3, ch. 63.

98 Adriaen Coenen's *Visboek*, 1577 fol.189v. https://www.kb.nl/en/themes/middle-ages/adriaen-coenens-visboek (accessed 10 February 2014).

99 Caroline Williams, 'Behind the Smile: What Dolphins Really Think', *New Scientist*, 24 September 2014. https://www.newscientist.com/article/mg22329880-700-behind-the-smile-what-dolphins-really-think/ (accessed 10 January 2015); John Lilly, *Man and Dolphin: Adventures of a New Scientific Frontier* (1st edn). Garden City, NY: Doubleday, 1961; *The Mind of the Dolphin: A Nonhuman Intelligence* (1st edn). Garden City, NY: Doubleday, 1967.

100 Justin Gregg, *Are Dolphins Really Smart? The Mammal Behind the Myth*. Oxford: Oxford University Press, 2013; Clearwater Marine Aquarium. http://www.seewinter.com/ (accessed 11 July 2015).

101 David Tatham, 'Elihu Vedder's "Lair of the Sea Serpent"', *American Art Journal* 17:2 (1985), 33–47; 'Report of a Committee of the Linnaean Society of New England relative to a large Marine Animal supposed to be a Serpent, seen Near Cape Ann, Massachusetts in August 1817' (Boston, 1817), 1–22; Constantine S. Rafinesque, 'Dissertation on Water Snakes, Sea Snakes, and Sea Serpents', *American Monthly Magazine and Critical Review* 1:6 (October, 1817), 431–5.

102 Michael Brown Chandos, 'The Gloucester Sea Serpent, Knowledge, Power and the culture of Science in Antebellum America', *American Quarterly* 42:3 (September, 1990), 402–36; Eugene Batcheldor, *A Romance of the Sea Serpent or The Ichthyosaurus*. Cambridge: J. Bartlett, 1849; William Crafts, *The Sea Serpent; or, Gloucester Hoax: A Dramatic Jeu d'Esprit in Three Acts*. Charleston: Miller, 1819.

103 Henri de Blainville, 'Sur un nouveau genre de Serpent, Scoliophis, et le Serpent de mer vue en Amerique', *Journal de physique* 56 (1818), 299–301; A. C. Oudemans, *The Great Sea-Serpent: An Historical and Critical Treatise, with Reports of the 187 Appearances (including those in the appendix), the Suppositions and Suggestions of Scientific and non-Scientific Persons, and the Author's Conclusions*. London, 1892. However, a very balanced study by Rupert Thomas Gould, *The Case for the Sea Serpent*. New York: P. Allen, 1930, 54 questioned the so-called independent testimony.

104 'The New England Sea Serpent', Folklore in the News *Western Folklore* 7:1 (January 1948), 67.

105 Eric Pontoppidan, *Natural History of Norway*, translated by Andreas Berthelson. London, 1755.

106 A. E. Verrill, 'The Florida Sea-Monster', *The American Naturalist* 31:364 (April, 1897), 304–7.

107 Herman Melville, *Moby Dick*. New York: Harper Brothers, 1851, chapter 59, 'Squid'.

108 R. Ellis, *The Search for the Giant Squid* 1998; The Colossal Squid Exhibition. http://squid.tepapa.govt.nz/ (accessed 10 August 2015).

109 Sidney K. Pierce, Steven E. Masay, Nicholas E. Curtis, Gerald N. Smith, Carlos Olavarria and Timothy K. Maugel, 'Microscopic Biochemical and Molecular Characteristics of the Chilean Blob and a Comparison with the Remains of Other Sea Monsters: Nothing but Whales', *Biological Bulletin* 206:3 (2004), 125–33.

110 Jules Verne, *Vingt mille lieues sous les mers*, Illus. by Alphonse de Neuville and Eduard Riou. Paris: Hetzel, 1970, English Edition 1872.

111 T. S. Miller, 'From Bodily Fear to Cosmic Horror and Back Again: The Tentacle Monster from Primordial Chaos to Hello Cthulu', *Lovecraft Annual* 5 (2011), 121–54.

112 Marion Lawrence, 'Ships, Monsters and Jonah', *American Journal of Archaeology* 66:3 (July 1962), 289–96.

113 Van Duzer, *Sea Monsters*, 16–19.

114 J. F. Campbell, *Táin bó Froích. The Celtic Dragon Myth*. With the Geste of Fraoch and the dragon; translated with introduction by George Henderson. Edinburgh: J. Grant, 1911, 1–17.

115 N. J. A. Williams, 'Of Beast and Banner, the Origin of the Heraldic Enfield', *The Journal of the Royal Society of Antiquaries of Ireland* 119 (1989), 63–6.

116 Patrick Tohall, 'The Dobhar-Chu Tombstones of Glenade, Co Leitrim', *The Journal of the Royal Society of Antiquaries of Ireland* 78 (1948), 128–9.

117 'The King Who Couldn't Sleep', in Sean O'Sullivan, edited and translated, *Folktales of Ireland*. London: Routledge & K. Paul, 1969, 21–37.

118 John R. Swanton, *Tlingit Myths and Texts*, Smithsonian Institution Bureau of *American Ethnology Bulletin*. Washington, DC: Government Printing Office, 1909, 29–33.

119 Van Duzer, *Sea Monsters*, 31–2.

Chapter 3

1 John Pollard, *Seer Shrines and Sirens*. London: George Allen & Unwin, 1965, 137–45.

2 F. J. Tritsch, 'The Harpy Tomb at Xanthus', *The Journal of Hellenic Studies* 62, (1942), 39–50; J. Wood, 'Furies', in Jeffrey Andrew Weinstock, ed., *The Ashgate Encyclopedia of Literary and Cinematic Monsters*. Farnham: Ashgate, 2014, 243–5.

3 Bibliotèque nationale de France, Latin MS 6838B, fol. 25v.

4 Cresswell, *Legendary Beasts of Britain*, 15.

5   Wood, 'Harpy', in Weinstock, ed., *The Ashgate Encyclopedia of Literary and Cinematic Monsters*, 308–10.

6   George C. Druce, 'On the Legend of the Serra or Sawfish', *Proceedings of the Society of Antiquaries*, 2nd series 31(1919), 20–35; 'A Harpy Drawn from Life, An Amphibious Monster now Alive in Spain'. *The John Johnson Collection: An Archive of Printed Ephemera*. Oxford: Bodleian Library. http://johnjohnson.chadwyck.co.uk (accessed 9 August 2016).

7   *Hortus sanitatis,* printed Jacob Meydenbach. Mainz, 1497, 528; Ulisse Aldrovandi, *Monstrorum Historia*, 1642; John Jonston, *Historiae naturalis de quadrupedibus.* 1657.

8   Eva Baer, *Sphinxes and Harpies in Medieval Islamic Art: An Iconographical Study.* Jerusalem: Israel Oriental Society, 1965.

9   *Melchior Lorck: Drawings from the Evelyn Collection at Stonor Park, England, and from the Department of Prints and Drawings, the Royal Museum of Fine Arts, Copenhagen*, Erik Fischer, ed., Copenhagen: Statens Museum for Kunst, 1962.

10 Bodleian Library MS. Holkham misc. 48, p. 19. owned by Earls of Leicester. http://www.bodley.ox.ac.uk/dept/scwmss/wmss/medieval/mss/holkham/misc/048.a.htm (accessed 9 August 2016).

11 Lawrence Schick, *Heroic Worlds*, 106–7.

12 Harold Johnson, Steve Winter, Peter Adkison, Ed Stark, and Peter Archer, *30 Years of Adventure: A Celebration of Dungeons & Dragons*. Renton, WA: Wizards of the Coast, 2004.

13 Wood, 'Harpy', in Weinstock, ed., *The Ashgate Encyclopedia of Literary and Cinematic Monsters*, 308–10.

14 P. D. A. Harvey, *Mappa Mundi: The Hereford World Map*. London: Hereford Cathedral & the British Library, 1996; Griffins guard a gem-studded hill in the illustration for the Scythia section of a fifteenth-century *Livre des merveilles du monde*. Pierpont Morgan Library MS M.0461, fol. 22v.

15 Matias Michovius cited by Peter Armour, in Cherry, ed., *Mythical Beasts*, 98–100.

16 John Timbs, *Popular Errors Explained and Illustrated* (New edn). London: D. Bogue, 1856, 340–3.

17 Wood, 'Griffin', in Weinstock, ed., *The Ashgate Encyclopedia of Literary and Cinematic Monsters*, 305–10.

18 Adrienne Mayor and Michael Heaney, 'Griffins and Arimaspaeans', *Folklore* 104:1/2 (1993), 40–66.

19 Stoneman, *Alexander the Great*, 114–20.

20 Christa A. Tuczay, 'Motifs in "The Arabian Nights" and in Ancient and Medieval European Literature: A Comparison', *Folklore* 116:3 (2005), 272–91.

21 Bernard Goldman, 'The Development of the Lion-Griffin', *American Journal of Archaeology* 64:4 (October 1960), 319–32.

22 A fourteenth-century copy of Dante's *Divine Comedy* illustrates Christ as griffin (Pierpont Morgan Library MS M.676, fol. 83v, 85v, 87v).

23 Vauxhall Motors History (accessed 13 July 2015). http://www.theguardian.com/business/2009/sep/10/vauxhall-historym

24 Mercedes Lackey and Larry Dixon's fantasy books, *The Black Gryphon, The White Gryphon and The Silver Gryphon*, (dates 1994–96) featured a griffin called Skandranon who has the power of speech. Diana Wynne Jones's *The Dark Lord of Derkholm* (1998) and *The Year of the Griffin* (2000) concern a gentle wizard whose five griffin and two human children have many adventures.

25 Frank R. Stockton, *The Griffin and the Minor Canon*, illustrated by Maurice Sendak. New York: Holt, Reinhardt and Winston, 1964.

26 Henrietta McCall, 'Sphinxes', in Cherry, ed., *Mythical Beasts*, 104–6.

27 Pierpont Morgan Seal collection: Hero Grasping Two Male Sphinxes: Mesopotamia, (c. 1000–539 BCE.) Seal no. 757 & King Standing on Sphinxes Persia, (c. 550–330 BCE) Seal no. 824. http://www.themorgan.org/collection/ ancient-near-eastern-seals-and-tablets (accessed 9 August 2016).

28 Cherry, *Mythical Beasts*, 118.

29 Ibid., 118–19.

30 Ibid.,123.

31 Scott D. Westrem, *The Hereford Map*, 135.

32 *Athanasii Kircheri … Œdipus Ægyptiacus*, hoc est vniuersalis hieroglyphicæ veterum doctrinæ … instauratio. Rom. 1652-54, Col. 1655.

33 Cherry, *Mythical Beasts*, 126–31.

34 Alciato's emblems. http://www.emblems.arts.gla.ac.uk/alciato/index.php (accessed 10 February 2014).

35 *Land of Myths: The Art of Gustave Moreau*, edited by Ferenc Tóth, Marie-Cécile Forest, and Pierre Maréchaux. Budapest: Museum of Fine Arts, 2009.

36 Daniel Ogden, *Dragons, Serpents & Slayers in the Classical and Early Christian Worlds: A Sourcebook*. Oxford: Oxford University Press, 2013, 75–9.

37 Marilyn Low Schmitt, 'Bellerophon and the Chimaera in Archaic Greek Art', *American Journal of Archaeology* 70:4 (October 1966), 341–7.

38 Dominic Perring, '"Gnosticism" in Fourth-Century Britain: The Frampton Mosaics Reconsidered', *Britannia* 34 (2003), 97–127.

39 Christine de Pizan, British Library MS Harl. 4431, fol. 183, fol. 98v.

40 John M. Steadman, '"Perseus upon Pegasus" and Ovid Moralized', *The Review of English Studies* 9:36 (November 1958), 407–9.

41 A. Dawson, *Masterpieces of Wedgwood in the British Museum* (2nd edn). London: British Museum Press, 1995.

42 Michael Wilson, *Nature and Imagination: The Work of Odilon Redon*. New York: Dutton, 1978.

43 http://racing.channel4.com/news/newsid=1240535/index.html (accessed 9 August 2016).

44 Wood, 'Hippogriff', in Weinstock, ed., *The Ashgate Encyclopedia of Literary and Cinematic Monsters*, 328–30.

45 Tuczay, 'Motifs', 272–91.

46 John Harrington, *Orlando furioso in English*, printed by G. Miller for T. Parker, 1634.

47 Ludovico Ariosto, *Orlando furioso* (1516, revised 1521 and 1532), translated by William Stewart Rose. http://sacred-texts.com/neu/orl/index.htm; for a complete modern text *Ludovico Ariosto, Orlando furioso* (*The Frenzy of Orlando*) *A Romantic Epic*, translated with an introduction by Barbara Reynolds, 2 vols. Harmondsworth: Penguin, 1975–7.

48 Gustav Doré, *Doré's Illustrations for Ariosto's 'Orlando furioso'*. New York and London: Dover Constable, 1980.

49 Thomas Blount, *Glossographia; or, a Dictionary Interpreting the Hard Words of Whatsoever Language, Now Used in Our Refined English Tongue*. London, 1656.

50 Ambrose Bierce, *Devil's Dictionary* (1906) HIPPOGRIFF, n. 'An animal (now extinct) which was half horse and half griffin. The griffin was itself a compound creature, half lion and half eagle. The hippogriff was actually, therefore, a one-quarter eagle, which is two dollars and fifty cents in gold. The study of zoology is full of surprises.' https://www.gutenberg.org/files/972/972-h/972-h.htm (accessed 12 August 2014).

51 Paul Quinet, *Merlin l'enchanteur*, 2 vols. Paris: Levy, 1860.

52 Lord Dunsany, *The Book of Wonder: A Chronicle of Little Adventures at the Edge of the World*. London, 1912.

53 Nesbit, *The Book of Dragons*. Mineola, NY: Dover Publications, 2004, 1–19.

54 Schick, *Heroic Worlds*, 106–10.

55 Gerald K. Gresseth, 'The Myth of Alcyone', *Transactions and Proceedings of the American Philological Association* 95 (1964), 88–98.

56 Philemon Holland, trans., *Pliny History of the World* I. x. xxxii. (R.). https://archive.org/details/plinysnaturalhis00plinrich (accessed 9 August 2016).

57 Aberdeen Bestiary. https://www.abdn.ac.uk/bestiary/translat/54v.hti (accessed 9 March 2014).

58 Gresseth, 'The Myth of Alcyone', 91–93; Ovid *Metamorphoses* XI, 410–748; Hyginus *Fabulae* 65; Pseudo-Apollodorus I, 7.4; A. H. F. Griffin, 'The Ceyx Legend in Ovid, Metamorphoses, Book XI', *The Classical Quarterly* New Series, 31:1 (1981), 147–54.

59 Rudolph Wittkower, '"Roc": An Eastern Prodigy in a Dutch Engraving', *Journal of the Warburg Institute* 1:3 (January 1938), 255.

60 'The First Voyage of Sinbad the Sailor', 126–7.

61 Tuczay, 'Motifs', 280–1.

62 Ibid., 275.

63 Frau Mauro Map. http://www.bl.uk/magnificentmaps/map2.html (accessed 9 August 2016).

64 Wittkower, '"Roc"', 255–7.

65 Gary Gygax and Dave Arneson, *Dungeons & Dragons*. TSR Hobbies, 1974.

66 Nili Wazana, 'The Anzu and Ziz: Great Mythical Birds in Ancient Near Eastern Biblical and Rabbinic Traditions', *Journal of the Ancient Near Eastern Society* 31: 111–35.

67 Prudence Oliver Harper, 'The Simurv', *The Metropolitan Museum of Art Bulletin*, New Series, 20:3 (November 1961), 95–101.

68 The Cambridge Shanama Project. http://persian.pem.cam.ac.uk/projects/shahnama-project (accessed 10 June 2016).

69 *The Conference of the Birds* by Farid al-Din Attar, edited and translated by Afkham Darbandi and Dick Davis. Harmondsworth: Penguin Classics, 1984.

70 A blue phoenix sits amid flames atop a hill in a miniature which illustrates the land of Arabia in *Livre de merveilles du monde*, c. 1460. Pierpont Morgan Library MS M.461, fol.10r.

71 Westrem, *The Hereford Map*, 123.

72 Aberdeen Bestiary, 'phoenix'. https://www.abdn.ac.uk/bestiary/translat/55v.hti (accessed 9 August 2016).

73 W. R. S. Ralston, *Russian Fairy Tales: A Choice Collection of Muscovite Folk-lore*. New York: Arno Press, 1977, 217–19.

74 Alan Priest, 'Phoenix in Fact and Fancy', *The Metropolitan Museum of Art Bulletin*, New Series, 1:2 (October 1942), 97–101.

75 Adrienne Mayor, *The First Fossil Hunters: Palaeontology in Greek and Roman Times*. Princeton, NJ: Princeton University Press, 2000; new edn, 2011.

76 R. McN. Alexander, 'The Evolution of the Basilisk', *Greece & Rome* Second Series, 10:2 (1963), 170–81; Laurence A. Breiner, 'The Career of the Cockatrice', *Isis* 70:1 (1979), 30–47.

77 Wood, 'Cockatrice'—, in Weinstock, ed., *The Ashgate Encyclopedia of Literary and Cinematic Monsters*, 99–101.

78 *De materia medica*. Pierpont Morgan Library MS M.652, fol. 326r. This tenth-century Greek paraphrase of the *Theriaca* and other classical medical treatises has a drawing of a scarlet, cockerel-headed serpent marked *basiliskos*.

79 Loomis and Loomis, *Arthurian Legends in Medieval Art*, Plates 152–3.

80 Cockatrice, basilisk, regulus. http://bestiary.ca/beasts/beastgallery265.htm# (accessed 9 August 2016).

81 Mike Dash, 'On the trail of the Warsaw Basilisk', *Smithsonian.com*, 23 July 2012, 3. http://www.smithsonianmag.com/history/on-the-trail-of-the-warsaw-basilisk-5691840/?no-ist (accessed 10 March 2016).

82 Breiner, 'The Career of the Cockatrice', 30–47.

83 Dash, 'On the trail of the Warsaw Basilisk', 1–11.

84 The Flying Serpent, etc. Reproduced in facsimile … with introduction by R. M. Christy. Saffron Walden 1885; Sarah Perry, *The Essex Serpent*. London: The Serpent's Tail, 2016.

85 Dash, 'On the trail of the Warsaw Basilisk', 5–9.

86 Oesterley, ed., *Gesta Romanorum*, ch. 139 (131), 493–494.

87 The coat of arms of Moscow shows St George slaying a dragon-like creature which is identified as a heraldic basilisk.

88 Breiner, 'The Career of the Cockatrice', 30–47.

89   Edward Topsell, *History of Serpents* (1608) published in 1658 as *The History of Four-Footed Beasts and Serpents*, Cockatrice, 667.

90   Jacqueline Simpson, *British Dragons*. Ware: Wordsworth & The Folklore Society, 1980, rpr 2001, 46–7.

91   http://gatherer.wizards.com/Pages/Search/Default.aspx?name=+%5bBasilisk (Accessed 15 February 2012).

92   *Alien* (1979 Ridley Scott), *Aliens* (1986 James Cameron), *Alien 3* (1992 David Fincher), *Alien Resurrection* (1997 Jean-Pierre Jeunet).

93   http://bestiary.ca/beasts/beast274.htm (accessed 10 January 2016).

94   http://www.newadvent.org/fathers/3003.htm (accessed 10 January 2016).

95   Jacqueline Simpson, 'Fifty British Dragon Tales: An Analysis', *Folklore* 89:1 (1978), 79–93; Peregrine Horden, 'Disease, Dragons and Saints: The Management of Epidemics in the Dark Ages', in Terence Ranger and Paul Slack, eds, *Epidemics and Ideas: Essays on the Historical Perception of Pestilence*. Cambridge: Cambridge University Press, 1992, 45–76.

96   Owen Wynne Jones (Glasynys), *Cymru Fu*. Wrecsam: Hughes & Son, 1862, 424–433.

97   Glasynys, *Cymru Fu*, 431.

98   Ibid., 424, 425, 430; T. Gwyn Jones, *Welsh Folklore and Folk-custom*. Cambridge: Brewer, 1979, 83.

99   Marie Trevelyan, *Folk Lore and Folk Stories of Wales*. London: E. Stock, 1909, 167; Elias Owen, *Welsh Folk-lore: A Collection of the Folk Tales and Legends of North Wales*. Oswestry: Woodall, Minshall, 1896, 349–50.

100   J. Dacres Devlin, *Helps to Hereford History*, Civil and Legendary …: The Mordiford dragon; and other subjects. London: J.R. Smith, 1848, 22–3, 48–51.

101   Trevelyan, *Folk Lore and Folk Stories of Wales*, 168–70.

102   Glasynys, *Cymru Fu*, 432.

103   http://www.pandorapedia.com, (accessed 14 February 2012); Michael G. Richard, (16 February 2010). 'Y'Know the Flying Dragons in Avatar? Tiny Real-Life Version Discovered in Indonesia'. http://www.treehugger.com/files/2010/02/tiny-dragon-indonesia-like-avatar.php (Retrieved 17 February 2010).

104   See above, PP. 96–97.

Chapter 4

1   Ezekiel 32:2–4. https://www.biblegateway.com/ (accessed 5 January 2014).

2   Theodore J. Lewis. 'CT 13.33-34 and Ezekiel 32: Lion-Dragon Myths', *Journal of the American Oriental Society* 116:1 (January–March 1996), 28–47.

3   Priscilla Bawcutt, *The Poems of William Dunbar*, 2 vols. Glasgow: Association for Scottish Literary Studies, 1998.

4 Loomis and Loomis, *Arthurian Legends in Medieval Art*, plate 343.

5 Horus. http://www.louvre.fr/en/oeuvre-notices/horus-horseback (accessed 15 January 2016).

6 Richard E. Johnson, *Saint Michael the Archangel in Medieval English Legend*. Woodbridge: Boydell Press, 2005, 140–68. For example, the Introit for the Feast of Archangel Michael in a thirteenth-century manuscript is illustrated with the Archangel transfixing the jaws of a dragon with his spear, Pierpont Morgan Library MS M.855, fol. 72v.

7 French Book of Hours, (fifteenth century), Pierpont Morgan Library MS M.348, fol. 231r.

8 Book of Hours, (fifteenth century), Pierpont Morgan Library MS M.7, fol. 83v.

9 Johnson, *Saint Michael the Archangel*, 69–70.

10 Lewis, 'CT 13.33-34 and Ezekiel 32: Lion-Dragon Myths', 41–7; Ogden, *Dragons, Serpents & Slayers in the Classical and Early Christian Worlds: A Sourcebook*. Oxford: Oxford University Press, 2015, 39–44; S. H. Hooke, *Middle Eastern Mythology: From the Assyrians to the Hebrews* (1963). London: Penguin, 1991, 41–6.

11 A cylinder seal c. 1049–609 BCE depicts a god riding a bull-headed dragon, Pierpont Morgan Library cylinder seal no. 689.

12 Hansen, *Ariadne's Thread*, 119–31.

13 Ogden, *Dragons, Serpents & Slayers*, 75–81. http://www.theoi.com/Heros/ Bellerophontes.html (accessed 10 May 2016).

14 Margaret Schlauch, 'Geoffrey of Monmouth and Early Polish Historiography: A Supplement', *Speculum* 44:2 (1969), 261; Albina I. Kruszewska and Marion M. Coleman, 'The Wanda Theme in Polish Literature and Life', *American Slavic and East European Review* 6:1/2 (May, 1947), 19–35; W. S. Lach-Szyrma, 'Folk-Lore Traditions of Historical Events', *The Folk-Lore Record* 3:2 (1880), 157–68.

15 See above, pp. 80–1.

16 Simpson, *British Dragons*, 70–1.

17 Basil Hall Chamberlain, *Ko-ji-ki … or, Records of Ancient Matters*, vol. I. Yokohama, London and Lane: Crawford & Co. Trübner, 1883, 71–2; William George Aston, *Nihongi: Chronicles of Japan from the Earliest Earliest Times to A.D.697*. 1896, 2 vols, vol. I, 52–9.

18 *The Prose Edda of Snorri Sturluson*, 'Gylfaginning', translated by Arthur Gilchrist Brodeur (1916) ch. xxxiv, 42, xlviii–xlvix, 68–70, li, 78–80. http:// www.sacred-texts.com/neu/pre/pre04.htm (accessed 10 May 2017); Ursula Dronke, ed. and trans., *Völuspá, The Poetic Edda*, 2 vols. Oxford: Oxford University Press, 1969–97, vol. II, 22.

19 Preben Meulengracht Sørensen, 'Þorr's fishing Expedition' (Hymoslviða), translated by Kirsten Williams, in Paul Acker and Carolyne Larrington, eds, *The Poetic Edda, Essays on Old Norse Mythology*. New York & London: Routledge, 2002, 119–38.

20 Sørensen, 'Þorr's fishing Expedition', 128–32.

21 Life of St George (accessed 10 July 2016). http://sourcebooks.fordham.edu/basis/goldenlegend/GoldenLegend-Volume3.asp#George

22 Simpson, *British Dragons*, 54–5.

23 Richard Johnson, *The Famous History of the Seven Champions of Christendom* (1596).

24 Samantha Riches, *St George: A Saint for All*. London: Reaktion Books, 2015, 29–34, 84–99.

25 Thomas H. H. Caine, ed., *King Albert's Book: A Tribute to the Belgian King and his People*. London: Daily Telegraph & Hodder and Stoughton, 1914.

26 Riches, St George by Dutch artist, Oswald Wenckebach, 37.

27 Zurab Tsereteli, 'Good Defeats Evil', St George defeating a dragon composed of broken pieces of Soviet and American ballistic missiles. *New York Times*, 30 September 1990. http://www.nytimes.com/1990/09/30/nyregion/world-summit-for-children-how-st-george-ended-up-at-the-un.html (accessed 13 January 2016).

28 St Sylvester (accessed 5 June 2016). http://sourcebooks.fordham.edu/basis/goldenlegend/GoldenLegend-Volume2.asp#Silvester.

29 Jacques Le Goff, *Time Work and Culture in the Middle Ages*, translated by Arthur Goldhammer. Chicago: University of Chicago Press, 1980, 160–9.

30 Christine Rauer, *Beowulf and the Dragon Parallels and Analogues*. Cambridge: D.S. Brewer, 2000, 174–93; Simpson, 'Fifty British Dragon Tales', 79–93.

31 G. H. Doble, *The Saints of Cornwall*. Part 5. Truro: Dean and Chapter, 1970, 80–103.

32 'The Martyrdom of Censurinus', *Acta Sanctorum* September, II, pp. 521–4. http://www.ostia-antica.org/~atexts/actasanc.htm#aass11 (accessed 10 January 2016).

33 Mary Lovett Cameron, 'The Dragon of La Trinità: An Italian Folk-Tale', *Folklore* 21:3 (September 1910), 349–50.

34 St Philip http://sourcebooks.fordham.edu/basis/goldenlegend/GoldenLegend-Volume3.asp#Philip%20the%20Apostle (accessed 5 June 2016).

35 Ogden, *Dragons, Serpents & Slayers*, 207–20.

36 Ibid., 242–3.

37 Donald R. Rawe, *Padstow's Obby Oss and May Day Festivities: A Study in Folklore & Tradition*. Padstow: Lodenek Press, 1999, 13.

38 Hilda R. Ellis Davidson, 'The Hill of the Dragon: Anglo-Saxon Burial Mounds in Literature and Archaeology', *Folklore* 61:4 (December 1950), 169–85.

39 J. R. R. Tolkien, 'Beowulf: The Monsters and the Critics', *Proceedings of the British Academy* 22 (1936), 245–95.

40 Rauer, *Beowulf and the Dragons*, 9–51, 89–124.

41 Annelise Talbot, 'Sigemund the Dragon-Slayer', *Folklore* 94:2 (1983), 153–62.

42 Rauer, *Beowulf and the Dragons*, 41–2; Paul Acker, 'Dragons in the Eddas and in Early Nordic Art', in Acker and Larrington, eds, *Revisiting the Poetic*

Edda, 57–68; Edgar Haimerl, 'Siguðr, A Medieval Hero: A Manuscript-Based Interpretation of the "Young Siguðr Poems"', in *Revisiting the Poetic Edda*, 32–52.

43 Ogden, *Beowulf and the Dragons*, 266.

44 A. T. Hatto, *The Nibelungenlied*. Harmondsworth: Penguin Classics, 1965, 121–2.

45 Pierpont Morgan Library MS M.815, fol.14r; Janet Backhouse, 'A Further Illuminated Devotional Book for the Use of Lady Margaret Beaufort', in Bernard J. Muir, ed., *Reading Texts and Images: Essays on Medieval and Renaissance Art and Patronage in Honour of Margaret M. Manion*. 221–35 227 n. 30, Exeter: University of Exeter Press, 2002.

46 Loomis and Loomis, *Arthurian Legends in Medieval Art*, plate 236.

47 *The Mabinogion,* translated by Sioned Davies. Oxford: Oxford University Press, 2007; 'Lludd and Llefelys', 111–15.

48 Carl Lofmark, *A History of the Red Dragon*, edited by G. A. Wells. Llanrwst: Gwasg Carreg Gwalch, 1995; Linda Malcor, 'Merlin and the Pendragon King Arthur's Draconarius', *Arthuriana* 10:1 (2000), 3–13.

49 Margaret Deanesly, 'Roman Traditionist Influence among the Anglo-Saxons', *The English Historical Review* 58 (1943), 131,135–8; J. C. N. Coulston, 'The "*draco*" standard', *Journal of Roman Military Equipment Studies* 2 (1991), 101–14.

50 Hermann Oesterley, ed., *Gesta Romanorum*, 145 (137), 503–4.

51 Reidar Th. Christiansen, *The Migratory Legends: A Proposed List of Types with a Systematic Catalogue of Norwegian Variants*. Helsinki: Suomalainen Tiedeakatemia, 1958, ML7060 Disputed Site for a Church/ Putting spirit to rest.

52 *The Mabinogion,* translated by Davies, *Iarlles y Ffynnwn*, 'Lady of the Well', 116–38.

53 Loomis and Loomis, *Arthurian Legends in Medieval Art*, plate 3.

54 *The Mabinogion*, trans., Davies, 116–38.

55 See Campbell, *Táin bó Froích*.

56 Simpson lists other localized versions in *British Dragons*, 137–55.

57 Loomis and Loomis, *Arthurian Legends in Medieval Art*, plate 53 (Chertsey tile, c. 1270), plates 66–7 (Runkelstein Murals c. 1400), plate 76 (Wienhausen embroidery c. 1310), plate 86 six panels in a German embroidery (Victoria and Albert Museum, c. 1370), plate 83 (Erfurt Cathedral cloth c. 1370).

58 Westwood and Simpson, *The Lore of the Land*, 286–7.

59 Map, *De Nugis Curialium*, Division II, section vi.

60 Simpson, *British Dragons*, 39,141–2.

61 Alex Scobie, 'An Ancient Greek Drakos – Tale in Apuleius' Metamorphoses VIII, 19–21', *The Journal of American Folklore* 90 (July–September 1977), 339–43.

62 Simpson, *British Dragons*, 61, 70, 99, chapter 3, pp. 123–24.

63 Cockatrice, pp. 119–24.

64 Simpson, *British Dragons*, 143–5.

65 Westwood and Simpson, *The Lore of the Land*, 651.

66 Simpson, *British Dragons*, 130; A True Relation of the Dreadful Combat between More of More-Hall, and the Dragon of Wantley (Broadside ballad 1685).

67 Owen Wister, *The Dragon of Wantley; His Rise, His Voracity and His Downfall. A Romance* …. Philadelphia: J. B. Lippincott Co., 1892.

68 *The Tall Tales of Davy Crockett: The Second Nashville Series of Crockett Almanacs, 1839-1841*. Knoxville: University of Tennessee Press, 1987.

69 Rauer, *Beowulf and the Dragons*, 168–73.

70 Robert Chambers, *The Book of Days: A Miscellany of Popular Antiquities*. Edinburgh and London: W & R Chambers, 1864, 541. Simpson, *British Dragons*, 38, 51; Jennifer Westwood and Sophia Kingshill, *The Lore of Scotland: A Guide to Scottish Legends*, London: Random House, 2009, 334.

71 Van Duzer, *Sea Monsters*, 52–3.

72 Ibid., 42–3.

73 *Historia Monachorum in Aegypto*, Pierpont Morgan Library MS M.626, fol. 43v; MS M.625, fol. 53r.

74 R. Macdonald Robinson, *Selected Highland Folktales*. Edinburgh: Oliver and Boyd, 1961, 140–3.

75 Ogden, *Dragons, Serpents & Slayers*, 125–33.

76 Riches, *St George: A Saint for All*, 103–7.

77 Hansen, *Ariadne's Thread*, 128–30.

78 Ogden, *Dragons, Serpents & Slayers*, 97–108.

79 D. J. A. Ross, 'Olympias and the Serpent: The Interpretation of a Baalbek Mosaic and the Date of the Illustrated Pseudo-Callisthenes', *Journal of the Warburg and Courtauld Institutes* 26:1/2 (1963), 1–21.

80 Nectanebus father of Alexander; Fights with serpents and dragons, chap. liv, lxi, lxii. Appendix 1 from the *Prose Alexander*, Nigel Bryant, trans., *The Medieval Romance of Alexander: The Deeds and Conquests of Alexander the Great*. Cambridge: Cambridge University Press, 2013, 299–301.

81 Whelan Lai, 'From Folklore to the Literate theatre: Unpacking Madam White Snake', *Asian Folklore Studies* 51:1 (1992), 51–66.

82 Kinga Ilona Márkus-Takeshita, 'From Iranian Myth to Folk Narrative: The Legend of the Dragon-Slayer and the Spinning Maiden in the Persian Book of the Kings', *Asian Folklore Studies* 60:2 (2001), 203–14; Dick Davis, *Shahnameh: The Persian Book of Kings*. New York: Penguin Books, 2004, 544–53.

83 Brent D. Shaw, 'The Passion of Perpetua', *Past & Present* 139 (May 1993), 26–30, 43–44.

84 St Margaret. http://sourcebooks.fordham.edu/basis/goldenlegend/goldenlegend-volume4.asp#Margare (accessed 1 June 2016).

85   'Tarasque', *Folklore Society Miscellany*, Jacqueline Simpson. http://folklore-society.com/miscellany/tarasque (accessed 14 September 2017).

86   Charles Fillingham Coxwell, *Siberian and Other Folktales*. London: C.W. Daniel, 1925, 300–1. This collection reworks a number of traditions from various central Asian cultures.

87   Francis James Child, ed., *English and Scottish Ballads*, 4 vols. Boston, MA: Little & Brown, 1857–9.

88   Joseph Jacobs, ed., *English Fairy Tales*. London: D. Nutt, 1890, 190–6; Simpson *British Dragons*, 58–60.

89   Brooklyn Museum Costume Collection at The Metropolitan Museum of Art, Gift of the Brooklyn Museum, 2009; Gift of Anna May Wong, 1956, Accession Number: 2009.300.1507.

90   *Western Mail* cartoonist Joseph Morewood Staniforth; Hywel Teifi Edwards, *The National Pageant of Wales*. Llandysul: Gomer, 2009, 107.

91   Barber, *Bestiary*, 181–2.

92   J. Roosval, 'St. George of Stockholm', *The Burlington Magazine for Connoisseurs* 40:228 (1922), 111–13.

93   Carmen C. Bambach, ed., *Leonardo da Vinci: Master Draftsman (exhibition)*. New York: Metropolitan Museum of Art, 2003. 'Study of Cats and Dragon', 632.

94   http://www.britishmuseum.org/research/collection_online/collection_object_details.aspx?objectId=86159&partId= (accessed 20 June 1016).

95   Parade saddle. http://www.metmuseum.org/art/collection/search/21991 (accessed 10 March 2014).

96   Diane Barre, 'Sir Samuel Hellier (1736-84) and His Garden Buildings: Part of the Midland's Garden Circuit in the 1760s-1780s', *Garden History* 36:2 (Winter 2008), 317.

97   C. S. Lewis, *The Allegory of Love: A Study in Medieval Tradition*. Oxford: The Clarendon Press, 1936, *The Pilgrim's Regress: An Allegorical Apology for Christianity, Reason and Romanticism*. London: Shed & Ward, 1935.

98   Arnie Fenner and Cathy Fenner, eds, *Icon, Frank Frazetta: A Retrospective by the Grand Master of Fantastic Art*. Grass Valley, CA: Underwood Books, 1999; Schick, *Heroic Worlds*, 18–32.

99   David Buckingham, 'Studying Computer Games', in Diane Carr, et al., eds, *Computer Games: Text, Narrative and Play*. Cambridge: Polity, 2007, 1–14, 6–8.

100   Schick, *Heroic Worlds*, 89–92, 128–9, 130–3; DragonQuest, Simulations Publication TSR 1980 (board RPG); Dragon Quest (console RPG) Enix, 1986.

101   *Dragonlance*, Laura and Tracey Hickman, and Margaret Weis (TSR Inc.) 1984–2011. http://www.trhickman.com/my-works/novels/dragonlance/ (accessed 17 February 2015).

102   Peter Meredith and John Marshall, 'The Wheeled Dragon in the Luttrell Psalter', *Medieval English Theatre* 2 (1980), 70–3.

103   Philip Butterworth, 'Late Medieval Performing Dragons', *Yearbook of English Studies* vol. 43, *Early English Drama* (2013), 322–29.

104 Riches, *St George: A Saint for All*, 51–7.

105 Mrs Gutch, 'Saint Martha and the Dragon', *Folklore* 63:4 (December 1952), 193–203.

106 F. J. Daniels, 'Snake and Dragon lore of Japan', *Folklore* 71 (1960), 158–60.

107 'The Welsh Dragon Leads the Pageant in Wales's Festival', *Times Archive, The Times*, Wednesday 4 February 2009, 4.

108 Butterworth, quoting John Bates, 336–7.

109 John Babington, *Pyrotechnia or a Discourse of Artificial Fireworks*, London, Thomas Harper, 1635. http://lhldigital.lindahall.org/cdm/ref/collection/eng_tech/id/4897 (accessed 10 June 2016).

110 Butterworth, 'Late Medieval Performing Dragons', 339–42.

111 Ibid., 318–21.

112 Brenda S. A. Yeoh and Peggy Teo, 'From Tiger Balm Gardens to Dragon World: Philanthropy and Profit in the Making of Singapore's First Cultural Theme Park', Geografiska Annaler. Series B. *Human Geography* 78:1 (1996), 27–42.

113 Barry Atkins, *More Than a Game: The Computer Game as Fictional Form*. Manchester and New York: Manchester University Press, 2003, 1–26.

114 Alfred Reginald Radcliffe-Brown, 'The Rainbow-Serpent Myth of Australia', *Journal of the Royal Anthropological Institute* 56 (1926), 19–25; Mundkur, 'Human animality', 162–78.

115 Boa, see pp. 122–3.

116 Herbert J. Spinden, 'Myths of the Nez Percé Indians', *The Journal of American Folklore* 21 (January–March 1908), 13–15.

117 J. E. L. 'Ch'en Jung's Picture of Nine Dragons', *Boston Museum of Fine Arts Bulletin* 15:92 (December 1917), 67–73.

118 Sheila R. Canby, in Cherry, ed., *Mythical Beasts*, 14–33; Q. Zhao, 'Dragons: The Symbol of China', *Oriental Art* 37:2 (1991), 72–80.

119 F. J. Daniels, 'Snake and Dragon lore of Japan', 157.

120 Yei Theodora Osaki, trans., *The Japanese Fairy Book*. New York: Dutton and Company, 1903; 'The Story of Prince Yamato Take', 224–44. https://archive.org/stream/japanesefairyboo00oza#page/n19/mode/2up (accessed 10 June 2016).

121 Ibid., 'My Lord Bag of Rice', 1–12.

122 F. J. Daniels, 'Snake and Dragon lore of Japan', 160–4.

123 Ryūnosuke Akutagawa, 'Dragon: The Old Potter's Tale', *Rashōmon and 17 Other Stories*, translated by Jay Rubin. New York City: Penguin Group, 2006, xi–xl, 3–9.

124 Gregory of Tours, *History of the Franks,* translated by Ernest Brehaut (extended selections), Records of Civilization 2, New York: Columbia University Press, 1916. http://legacy.fordham.edu/halsall/basis/gregory-hist.asp#book10 (accessed 10 January 2016).

125 George Monger, 'Dragons and Big Cats', *Folklore* 103:2 (1992), 203–6.

126   Simpson, *British Dragons*, 54–5.

127   Topsell, *The History of Four-Footed Beasts and Serpents*, 701–15.

128   Devlin, *Helps to Hereford history* (1848).

129   Mayor and Heaney. 'Griffins and Arimaspaeans', 40–66; Adrienne Mayor, *The First Fossil Hunters: Dinosaurs, Mammoths, and Myth in Greek and Roman Times* (2nd edn). Princeton, NJ: Chichester Princeton University Press, 2011.

130   Deborah Ruscillo, 'The First Fossil Hunters: Palaeontology in Greek and Roman Times by Adrienne Mayor Review', *American Journal of Archeology* 107:2 (2003), 293–5; Gerard Naddaf, 'The Bones of Giants' *The First Fossil Hunters: Palaeontology in Greek and Roman Times* by A. Mayor' Review, *The Classical Review* New Series 53:1 (April 2003), 195–7.

131   Paul Acker, 'Dragons in the Eddas', 2013, 53–4, 57–68; David S. Reese, 'Men, Saints, or Dragons?' *Folklore* 87:1 (1976), 89–95.

132   J. G. M. Thewissen, S. T. Hussain and M. Arif, 'Fossil Evidence for the Origin of Aquatic Locomotion in Archaeocete Whales', *Science* 263 (1994), 210–12.

133   Simpson, *British Dragons*, 18–22, 124–6.

134   Carl Sagan, *The Dragons of Eden: Speculations on the Evolution of Human Intelligence*. New York: Random House, 1977.

135   Peter Dickenson, *The Flight of Dragons*. UK: Pierrot Publishing and the New English Library, 1979.

136   Dugald Steer, *Dragonology: The Complete Book of Dragons*. UK: Templar Publishing, US: Candlewick Press, 2003.

137   'The Last Dragon'. http://www.imdb.com/title/tt0433367/ (accessed 10 December 2015).

138   William Douglas Burden, *Dragon Lizards of Komodo*. New York and London: G. P. Putnam Sons, 1927, 112.

139   Deborah Cadbury, *The Dinosaur Hunters*. London: Fourth Estate, 2000, 150–1, 159, 162.

140   http://www.telegraph.co.uk/news/science/dinosaurs/12111363/Dragons-really-did-roam-Wales-Dracoraptor-dinosaur-unveiled.htm (accessed 15 February 2014); Jonathan Amos, Welsh dinosaur named 'dragon thief', *BBC News*, 20 January 2016 (accessed 30 January 2016); Ian Sample, 'Zhenyuanlong suni: Biggest Ever Winged Dinosaur is Found in China', *The Guardian*, 16 July 2016 (accessed 30 January 2016).

141   Deepika Gupta, Bruce Bleakley and Rajinder K. Gupta, 'Dragon's Blood: Botany, Chemistry and Therapeutic uses', *Journal of Ethnopharmacology* 115 (2008), 362–3. http://www.smgrowers.com/info/dragonsblood_tree_botanyetc.pdf (accessed 1 June 2016).

142   Ding Wenlei, 'Discovery: the Dragon Bone Collectors', *Beijing Review* no 15, 10 April 2008. http://www.bjreview.com.cn/science/txt/2008-04/04/content_108818.htm# (accessed 10 June 2016).

143   E. Lovett, 'Folk medicine in London', *Folklore* 24:1 (1913), 120–1.

144　George C. Druce, 'The Elephant in Medieval Legend and Art', *Journal of the Royal Archaeological Institute* 76 (1919), 30.

145　Kim M. Phillips, *Before Orientalism: Asian Peoples and Cultures in European Travel Writing, 1245-1510*. Philadelphia: University of Pennsylvania Press, 2014, 98–9.

146　Burn and Carr, 'Defining Game Genres', in Carr, et al., eds, *Computer Games*, 14–15.

Primary sources

This section includes references to web resources, museum collections, manuscripts and pamphlets. In order to provide the reader with access to easily accessible translations, the primary sources indicated in brackets in the text refer, where possible, to standard editions and translations available on the internet. Where this has not been possible, I have included details of primary sources in the Selected Bibliography.

Aberdeen Bestiary
https://www.abdn.ac.uk/bestiary/translat/54v.hti

Acta Sanctorum September, II, pp. 521–4
http://www.ostia-antica.org/~atexts/actasanc.htm#aass11

Aelian, *On the Nature of Animals*. 3 volumes. Translated by A. F. Scholfield. Loeb Classical Library London: Heinemann, 1958–9
https://archive.org/details/L446AelianCharacteristicsOfAnimalsI15
https://archive.org/details/L448AelianCharacteristicsOfAnimalsII611
https://archive.org/details/L449AelianCharacteristicsOfAnimalsIII1217

Andrea Alciato (1492–1550), *Emblemata*
http://www.emblems.arts.gla.ac.uk/alciato/index.php

Al-Kazwini, *The Wonders of the World* (British Library Or.2784)
http://www.bl.uk/reshelp/findhelplang/arabic/arabicsection/arabicmanuscripts/large15917.html

Batholomew Anglicus, *De Proprietatibus Rerum*–
John Trevisa's translation of *Bartholomaeus Anglicus De proprietatibus rerum*: a critical text Editors, M. C. Seymour and others Oxford, Clarendon Press, 1975–

Mediaeval Lore from Bartholomew Anglicus, edited Robert Steele, London: Alexander Moring, The King's Classics 1893/1905
http://www.gutenberg.org/ebooks/6493

Apollonius of Rhodes, *The Argonautica*. Translated by R. C. Seaton http://www.theoi.com/Text/ApolloniusRhodius1.html

Ludovico Ariosto, *Orlando furioso* (1516, revised 1521 and 1532), translated William Stewart Rose (1823–31)
http://sacred-texts.com/neu/orl/index.htm

Aristotle,
History of Animals Book 2, ch 1 trans D'Arcy Wentworth Thompson
http://classics.mit.edu/Aristotle/history_anim.html
On the Parts of Animals Book 3 ch. 2 trans. William Ogle.
http://classics.mit.edu/Aristotle/parts_animals.html

Avatar
http://www.pandorapedia.com

Babington, John, *Pyrotechnia, or a Discourse of Artificial Fireworks*, London,
Thomas Harper, 1635
http://lhldigital.lindahall.org/cdm/ref/collection/eng_tech/id/4897

Beowulf (translation Lawrence Gummere)
http://literatureproject.com/beowulf/beowulf_32.htm

Bierce, Ambrose, *Devil's Dictionary* (1906)
https://www.gutenberg.org/files/972/972-h/972-h.htm (accessed 12 August 2015).

Bestiary
http://bestiary.ca/beasts/beast265.htm

Browne, Thomas, *Pseudodoxia Epidemica* 1650
http://penelope.uchicago.edu/pseudodoxia/pseudodoxia.shtml

Chapman, George, 'The Revenge of Bussy d'Ambois' [A facsimile of the edition of
1613]. Menston: Scolar Press, 1968

Geoffrey Chaucer, *The Canterbury Tales*
http://sourcebooks.fordham.edu/source/CT-prolog-para.html

Benvenuto Cellini, *Autobiography*, translated by John Addington Symonds. Vol.
XXXI.
The Harvard Classics. New York: P.F. Collier & Son, 1909–14
www.bartleby.com/31/.

Chicken of the Sea website
www.chickenofthesea.com

Child Ballads
The English and Scottish Popular Ballads Collected and Edited by Francis James
Child
4 vols. Boston: Houghton Mifflin, 1882–1898
http://www.sacred-texts.com/neu/eng/child/ch035.htm

Cicero, *De Natura Deorum*, translated by H. Rackham, (1933), The Loeb Classical
Library.   http://penelope.uchicago.edu/Thayer/E/Roman/Texts/Cicero/de_Natura_
Deorum/2A*.html

Clearwater Marine Aquarium
http://www.seewinter.com/explore-cma/exhibits-and-animals/meet-the-animals/
current-residents/dolphins

Adriaen Coenen's *Visboek* 1577
https://www.kb.nl/en/themes/middle-ages/adriaen-coenens-visboek

The Colossal Squid Exhibition, Museum of New Zealand
http://squid.tepapa.govt.nz/

Cosmas Indicoplaestes *The Christian Topography of Cosmas Indicopleustes*.
Edited by J.W. McCrindle, Hakluyt Society, 1897.
http://www.tertullian.org/fathers/cosmas_11_book11.htm

St Crescentiis
(http://www.newadvent.org/fathers/3003.htm

Ctesias, *La Perse, L'Inde* trans. R Henry Brussels 1947
Ctesias 390 BCE *Indica* quoted by Photius
http://www.livius.org/ct-cz/ctesias/photius_indica.html

Dante Alighieri's *Divine Comedy*,
http://classics.mit.edu/Virgil/aeneid.html

Dante's Divine Comedy owned by Earls of Leicester
Bodleian Library MS. Holkham misc. 48
http://www.bodley.ox.ac.uk/dept/scwmss/wmss/medieval/mss/holkham/
misc/048.a.htm

'The Dark Monarch: Magic and Modernity in British Art', Michael Bracewell and
Alun Rowlands ,Tate St Ives, 10 October – 10 January, curated by Martin Clark,
artistic director of Tate St Ives, in *Tate Etc*. Autumn issue 17 (2009).
http://www.tate.org.uk/whats-on/tate-st-ives/exhibition/dark-monarch

Dash, Mike. 'On the Trail of the Warsaw Basilisk' Smithsonian.com July 23, 2012
1-11   http://www.smithsonianmag.com/history/on-the-trail-of-the-warsaw-basilisk-
5691840/?no-ist

Diodorus of Sicily, *Library of Hist*ory trans. C. F. Oldfather
http://penelope.uchicago.edu/Thayer/E/Roman/Texts/Diodorus_Siculus/4D .html

Dictionary of Old Norse Prose.
http://onp.ku.dk/english/

'Dragons Really did Roam Wales'
http://www.telegraph.co.uk/news/science/dinosaurs/12111363/Dragons-really-did-
roam-Wales-Dracoraptor-dinosaur-unveiled.htm

Dragonlance
http://www.trhickman.com/my-works/novels/dragonlance/

The Essex Serpent
A Discourse relating a strange and monstrous Serpent (or Dragon) lately discovered, and yet living, to the great Annoyance and divers Slaughters both of Men and Cattell, by his strong and violent Person. In Sussex, two miles from Horsham, in a Woode called St Leanard. (1614) https://archive.org/stream/truewonderfulldi00arrauoft/truewonderfulldi00arrauoft_djvu.txt

Falconi, Marta *'Unicorn deer'* Rome, Associated Press
http://news.nationalgeographic.com/news/2008/06/080612-AP-unicorn-photo.html

Feegee mermaid
http://www.showhistory.com/Feegee.Wolff.html

Fra Mauro World Map (1450).
Source: Piero Falchetta 'Fra Mauro's World Map'. http://cartographic-images.net/Cartographic_Images/249_Fra_Mauros_Mappamundi.html

Geoffrey of Monmouth, *Historia Regum Brittainiae*
http://www.yorku.ca/inpar/geoffrey_thompson.pdf

Conrad Gesner, *Historiae animalium.* Zurich 1551-1558, 1587
Book 1 De qadrupedibus viviparis, 1551; Book 2. De qadrupedibus oviparis, 1554
Book 3. Qui est de avium natura, 1555; Book 4. Qui est de piscium et aquatilium animantium natura, 1558; Book 5. De serpentium natura, 1587 (posthumous)
https://ceb.nlm.nih.gov/proj/ttp/flash/gesner/gesner.html

John Gower, *Confessio Amantis* edited by G.C. Macaulay
http://gowertranslation.pbworks.com/w/page/53690519/Confessio%20Amantis

Grand National Advertisement 2015
http://racing.channel4.com/news/newsid=1240535/index.html

The Thomas L. Gravell Watermark Archive. 1996-Mosser, Daniel W., Ernest W. Sullivan II, with Len Hatfield and David H. Radcliffe. www.gravell.org.

Gregory of Tours, *History of the Franks*, trans. Ernest Brehaut (extended selections), Records of Civilization 2, New York: Columbia University Press, 1916
http://legacy.fordham.edu/halsall/basis/gregory-hist.asp#book10

'A Harpy Drawn from Life, An Amphibious Monster now Alive in Spain'.
The John Johnson Collection: An Archive of Printed Ephemera. Bodleian Library, Oxford. http://johnjohnson.chadwyck.co.uk

Harvard Art Museum
http://www.harvardartmuseums.org/collection

Herodotus, *The Histories* trans A.D. Godley
http://www.perseus.tufts.edu/hopper/text?doc=Perseus:text:1999.01.0126

Hesiod, *Theogony* trans Hugh G. Evelyn-White http://www.perseus.tufts.edu/hopper/text?doc=Perseus%3Atext%3A1999.01.0130%3Acard%3D304

Hesiod, *The Catalogue of Women* trans Hugh G. Evelyn-White http://www.theoi.com/Text/HesiodCatalogues.htm

Hildegard von Bingen's *Physica* (1098–1179) trans. Priscilla Throop Rochester: Healing Arts Press, 1998

Historia Brittonum
https://sourcebooks.fordham.edu/basis/nennius-full.asp

Philemon Holland trans. *The Historie of the World*. Commonly called, The Natural Histories of C. Plinius Secundus. 1601
http://penelope.uchicago.edu/Holland/index.html

Homer, *The Iliad*, trans. Richmond Lattimore
http://digital.library.northwestern.edu/homer/

Homer, *The Odyssey* trans Samuel Butler
http://classics.mit.edu/Homer/odyssey.html

Hortus sanitatis (1491)
Cambridge Digital Library
http://cudl.lib.cam.ac.uk/view/PR-INC-00003-A-00001-00008-00037/1

Horus on horseback
http://www.louvre.fr/en/oeuvre-notices/horus-horseback

Hyginus *Fabulae*, trans. Mary Grant
http://www.theoi.com/Text/HyginusFabulae2.html

Isidore. *The Etymologies of Isidore of Seville*, trans. Stephen A Barney, et al. Cambridge University Press: Cambridge, 2006 http://sfponline.org/Uploads/2002/st%20isidore%20in%20english.pdf

Israeli mermaid
http://www.livescience.com/5642-mermaid-sightings-claimed-israel.html

Jacobus de Voragine, *The Golden Legend*; Caxton Edition 1483,
reprint edited by F. S. Ellis, Temple Classics, 1900
Saint Paul the Hermit (vol. 2)
http://en.wikisource.org/wiki/The_Golden_Legend (accessed 5 January 2014).

St Jerome, *Life of St Paul the Hermit*
Vitae Patrum (1628 edition)
http://www.vitae-patrum.org.uk/page5.html

Johnson, Richard (1596), *The Famous History of the Seven Champions of Christendom*. St George of England, St Denis of France, St James of Spain, St Anthony of Italy,

St Andrew of Scotland, St Patrick of Ireland and St David of Wales. Shewing their honourable battels by sea and land: their tilts, justs, turnaments, for ladies: their combats with gyants, monsters and dragons: their adventures in foreign nations: their enchantments in the Holy Land: their knighthoods, prowess and chivalry in Europe, Africa and Asia with their victories against the enemies of Christ. Also the true manner and places of their deaths, being seven tragedies: and how they came to be called the seven saints of Christendom.
http://quod.lib.umich.edu/e/eebo/A46926.0001.001/1:10..23?rgn=div3;view=fulltext

The King's Mirror (Speculum regale-Konungs skuggsjá) translated from the old Norwegian by Laurence Marcellus Larson
https://archive.org/stream/kingsmirrorspecu00konuuoft/kingsmirrorspecu00konuuoft_djvu.txt

Kitāb Na't al-Ḥayawān (Book of the Characteristics of Animals), (British Library Or.2784)
http://www.bl.uk/reshelp/findhelplang/arabic/arabicsection/arabicmanuscripts/large15917.html

Annette Kellerman Costume Collection, Powerhouse Museum, Sydney Australia
http://www.powerhousemuseum.com/collection/database/?irn=9167&collection=Annette+Kellerman+Costume#ixzz0wESEAGhu

The Last Dragon
http://www.imdb.com/title/tt0433367/

Brunetto Latini, Li Livres dou Trésor
http://www.florin.ms/tresor1.html

Legenda Aurea (Golden Legend)
http://sourcebooks.fordham.edu/basis/goldenlegend/

Lucian, Dialogue of the Sea Gods
http://lucianofsamosata.info/DialoguesOfTheSeaGods.html

Lucian, True history, Verae Historiae, translated by H. W. Fowler and F. G. Oxford
https://lucianofsamosata.info/TheTrueHistory.html

Megasthenes, Indica (1846), E. A. Schwanbeck, ed., Sumptibus Pleimesii, bibliopolae (Oxford University).
http://books.google.co.uk/books?id=J1MOAAAAQAAJ&redir_esc=y

'Mermaids: The Body Found' (27 May 2012), 'Mermaids: The New Evidence' (26 May 2013) http://www.dailymail.co.uk/news/article-2333515/Mermaid-hoax-How-mockumentary-gave-Animal-Planet-biggest-audience-EVER.html.

'Mermaids' Fight to Save Florida Roadside Attraction.
Kimberly Ayers and Boyd Matson in Weeki Wachee Springs, Florida National Geographic on Assignment, 22 March 2004.

http://news.nationalgeographic.com/news/2004/03/0322_040322_TVmermaid.html

Middle English Marian Lyrics. Karen Stone (editor) Kalamazoo, Michigan: Medieval Institute Publications, 1997.
http://d.lib.rochester.edu/teams/text/saupe-middle-english-marian-lyrics-poems-in-celebration-of-mary (accessed 5 May 2016).

John Milton, *Paradise Lost*
http://literature.org/authors/milton-john/paradise-lost/

The Narwhal Tusk Research Project
http://eloka-arctic.org/communities/narwhal/interviews.html

The New York Metropolitan Museum of Art
http://www.metmuseum.org/collection/the-collection-online/search/210103

O'Donoghue, James, 'The Hunt for Predator X'. *New Scientist* (31 October 2009): 32–5. www.newscientist.com/article/dn18047-real-sea-monsters-the-hunt-for-predator-x/

Ovid, *Metamorphoses* translated by Antony S. Kline
http://ovid.lib.virginia.edu/trans/Ovhome.htm#askline

Pausanias, *Description of Greece*
http://www.perseus.tufts.edu/hopper/text?doc=Perseus%3Atext%3A1999.01.0160

The Pendine mermaid
'Most strange and true report of a monsterous fish, that appeared in the forme of a woman, from her waste upwards: seene in the sea by diuers men of good reputation ...'.
National Library of Wales Item: NLW WS.S 1604(2)
http://education.gtj.org.uk/en/item1/26001 GTJ64526

The Periplus of the Erythraean Sea: Travel and Trade in the Indian Ocean by a Merchant of the First Century, edited by William H. Schoff,
New York: Longmans, Green, and Co., 1912.
https://depts.washington.edu/silkroad/texts/periplus/periplus.html

Philostratus, *Life of Apollonius of Tyana* trans. Conybeare
http://www.livius.org/sources/content/philostratus-life-of-apollonius/
Physiologus, translated by M. J. Curley, Austin Texas: University of Texas, 1979

The Pierpont Morgan Library and Museum, New York
http://www.themorgan.org/collection/medieval-and-renaissance-manuscripts

Plato, *The Republic* trans Benjamin Jowett
http://classics.mit.edu/Plato/republic.html

Pliny the Elder, *Natural History*. trans. John Bostock
http://www.perseus.tufts.edu/cgi-bin//ptext?lookup=Plin.+Nat.+8.31.

Plutarch, *Parallel Lives* trans. Bernadette Perrin
http://penelope.uchicago.edu/Thayer/E/Roman/Texts/Plutarch/Lives/home.html

Pseudo-Apollodorus trans. James Frazer
http://www.theoi.com/Text/Apollodorus1.html

Rabelais, François. *The Lives, Heroic Deeds and Sayings of Gargantua and his son Pantagruel* (c. 1532), translated into English by Sir Thomas Urquhart of Cromarty and Peter Antony Motteux
https://ebooks.adelaide.edu.au/r/rabelais/francois/r11g/book4.59.html

Richard, Michael G. (16 February 2010). 'Y'Know the Flying Dragons in Avatar? Tiny Real-Life Version Discovered in Indonesia'. *Treehugger.com*. http://www.treehugger.com/files/2010/02/tiny-dragon-indonesia-like-avatar.php

Jørn Rønnau
http://www.visitaarhus.com/international/en-gb/menu/turist/om-aarhus/sevaerdigheder/naturomraader/skulpturtraeer/skulpturtraeer.htm

Steve Roud, *Folk Song Index* 'The Lion and the Unicorn' no. 20170
http://library.efdss.org;

Shahnameh, *The Epic of Kings* by Ferdowsi. Translated by Helen Zimmern
http://classics.mit.edu/Ferdowsi/kings.html

The Cambridge Shanama Project
http://persian.pem.cam.ac.uk/projects/shahnama-project

'Search for the unicorn'. Metropolitan Museum of Art Exhibition, 2013
http://www.metmuseum.org/exhibitions/listings/2013/search-for-the-unicorn

'Enlisted "sea unicorns" reveal unexpected sea warming'. https://www.newscientist.com/article/dn19658-arctic-narwhals-reveal-climate-model-errors/

Solinus, The excellent and pleasant worke of Iulius Solinus Polyhistor Contayning the noble actions of humaine creatures, the secretes and prouidence of nature, the description of countries, the maners of the people: with many meruailous things and strange antiquities, seruing for the benefitt and recreation of all sorts of persons. Translated out of Latin into English, by Arthur Golding. Gent.
http://quod.lib.umich.edu/cgi/t/text/text-idx?c=eebo;idno=A12581

Edmund Spenser, *The Faerie Queene*
http://www.online-literature.com/edmund-spenser/faerie-queene/

Strabo, *Geography*.
http://penelope.uchicago.edu/Thayer/E/Roman/Texts/Strabo/15A3 .html

Suda On Line: Byzantine Lexicography
http://www.stoa.org/sol/

The Plays of William Shakespeare
http://www.shakespeare-online.com/plays/

The Starbucks mermaid
http://www.starbucks.com/blog/so-who-is-the-siren (accessed 10 July 15).

'The Other Starbucks Mermaid Cover Up' Carl Pyrdum
http://www.gotmedieval.com/2010/08/the-other-starbucks-mermaid-cover-up.html
(accessed 10 July 2015).

Theoi Greek Myths
http://www.theoi.com/Thaumasios/Basiliskoi.html

Edward Topsell, *The History of Four-Footed Beasts* (London 1607)
http://eebo.chadwyck.com/search/full_rec?ACTION=ByID&SOURCE=pgimages.
cfg&ID=V23166

Edward Topsell, *The History of Four-Footed Beasts and Serpents* (London 1658)
https://archive.org/details/historyoffourfoo00tops

Edward Topsell, *The History of Four-Footed Beasts* London 1607, and *A description of the nature of four-footed beast with their figures engraved in brass* by Joannes Jonstonus London: M. Pitt 1678; Edward Topsell's The History of Four-Footed Beasts and Serpents 1658
https://archive.org/stream/historyoffourfoo00tops#page/714/mode/2up

The Travels of Sir John Mandeville
http://www.romanization.com/books/mandeville/

Tsereteli, Zurab, 'Good Defeats Evil', St George defeating a dragon composed of broken pieces of Soviet and American ballistic missiles. *New York Times* 1990, 30 September
http://www.nytimes.com/1990/09/30/nyregion/world-summit-for-children-how-st-george-ended-up-at-the-un.html (accessed 13 January 2016).

Virgil, *Aeneid* trans. John Dryden
http://classics.mit.edu/Virgil/aeneid.html

Virgil, *Eclogues*. trans. H R. Fairclough
http://www.theoi.com/Text/VirgilAeneid1.html

Vauxhall Motors History
http://www.theguardian.com/business/2009/sep/10/vauxhall-history

Warhammer
http://warhammeronline.wikia.com/wiki/

Weechee Wachee mermaids, Florida
http://www.weekiwachee.com/

Wenlei, Ding, 'Discovery: the Dragon Bone Collectors', *Beijing Review* no 15, 10 April 2008
http://www.bjreview.com.cn/science/txt/2008-04/04/content_108818.htm#

Williams, Caroline, 'Behind the smile: what dolphins really think'. *New Scientist* 24 September 2014 https://www.newscientist.com/article/mg22329880-700-behind-the-smile-what-dolphins-really-think/

Zimmer, Carl. 'The Mystery of the Sea Unicorn'. *The Loom*, 18 March 2014, National Geographic. http://phenomena.nationalgeographic.com/2014/03/18/the-mystery-of-the-sea-unicorn

Selected bibliography and references

Acker, Paul. 'Dragons in the Eddas and in Early Nordic Art'. In *Revisiting the Poetic Edda: Essays on Old Norse Heroic Legend*, edited by Paul Acker and Carolyne Larrington, 53–75. New York: Routledge, 2013.

Acker, Paul, and Carolyne Larrington, eds. *The Poetic Edda, Essays on Old Norse Mythology*. New York and London: Routledge, 2002.

Acker, Paul, and Carolyne Larrington, eds. *Revisiting the Poetic Edda: Essays on Old Norse Heroic Legend*. New York: Routledge, 2013.

Aharoni, Israel. 'On Some Animals Mentioned in the Bible'. *Osiris* 5 (1938): 461–78.

Akutagawa, Ryūnosuke. *Rashōmon and 17 Other Stories*, Translated by Jay Rubin. New York City: Penguin Group, 2006.

Aldrovandi, Ulisse. *Monstrorum Historia*. Bologna, 1642.

Aldrovandi, Ulyssis. *Serpentum, et draconum historiæ libri duo*, 1640, https://archive.org/details/UlyssisAldrovanlAldr.

Alexander, R. McN. 'The Evolution of the Basilisk'. *Greece & Rome*, Second Series 10: 2 (1963): 170–81.

Almqvist, Bo. 'The Mélusine Legend in the Context of Irish Folk Tradition'. *Béaloideas* 67 (1999): 13–69.

Almqvist, Bo. 'Of Mermaids and Marriages: Seamus Heaney's "Maighdean Mara" and Nuala Ní Dhomhnaill's "An Mhaighdean Mhara" in the Light of Folk Tradition'. *Béaloideas* 58 (1990): 1–74.

Amos, Jonathan. 'Welsh dinosaur named "dragon thief"'. *BBC News*, 20 January 2016, http://www.bbc.co.uk/news/science-environment-35364711.

Ariew, Roger. 'Leibniz on the Unicorn and Various other Curiosities'. *Early Science and Medicine* 3: 4 (1998): 267–88.

Ariosto, Ludovico. *Orlando furioso* (The frenzy of Orlando: A romantic epic, translated with an introduction by Barbara Reynolds. 2 vols. Penguin classics, Harmondsworth Penguin 1975–7.

Armour, Peter. 'Griffins'. In *Mythical Beasts*, edited by John Cherry, 98–100. San Francisco and London: Pomegranate & British Museum Press, 1995.

Aston, William George, trans. *Nihongi: Chronicles of Japan from the Earliest Times to A.D.697*. 2 vols. London: Kegan Paul, 1896.

Atkins, Barry. *More Than a Game the Computer Game as Fictional Form*. Manchester and New York: Manchester University Press, 2003.

Atkinson, David. 'The Child Ballads from England and Wales in the James Madison Carpenter Collection'. *Folk Music Journal* 7: 4 (1998): 434–49.

Attar, Farid al-Din. *The Conference of the Birds*, edited and translated by Afkham Darbandi and Dick Davis. Harmondsworth: Penguin Classics, 1984.

Bacci, Andrea. *L'Alicorno*, ... nel quale si tratto della natura dell'alicorno & delle sue virtù eccellentissime.... Florence: Giorgio Marescotti, 1573.

Backhouse, Janet. 'A Further Illuminated Devotional Book for the Use of Lady Margaret Beaufort'. In *Reading Texts and Images: Essays on Medieval and Renaissance Art and Patronage in Honour of Margaret M. Manion*, edited by Bernard J. Muir, 221–35, 227 n. 30. Exeter: University of Exeter Press, 2002.

Baer, Eva. *Sphinxes and Harpies in Medieval Islamic Art: An Iconographical Study*. Jerusalem: Israel Oriental Society, 1965.

Bambach, Carmen C. ed. *Leonardo da Vinci: Master Draftsman* (exhibition). New York: Metropolitan Museum of Art, 2003.

Bamforth, Stephen. 'On Gesner, Marvels and Unicorns'. *Nottingham French Studies* 49: 3 (Autumn 2010): 110–45.

Barber, Richard. *Bestiary*. Woodbridge: The Boydell Press, 1999.

Barre, Diane. 'Sir Samuel Hellier (1736-84) and His Garden Buildings: Part of the Midland's Garden Circuit in the 1760s-1780s'. *Garden History* 36: 2 (Winter 2008): 310–27.

Barron, W. R. J., S. Glyn and S. Burgess, eds. *The Voyage of Saint Brendan: Representative Versions of the Legend in English Translation*. Exeter: University of Exeter Press, 2002.

Bartholin, Caspar. *De unicorn ejusque affinibus et succedaneis opusculum*; Thomas Bartholin De Unicornu observations novae (1645).

Bartholini, Thomae. *De unicornu observationes novæ*, Secunda editione, Auctores & emendatiores editæ à filio Casparo Bartholino.-- Amstelædami : Apud JHenr. Wetstenium, 1678.

Bartlett, J. *A Romance of the Sea-Serpent, or the Ichthyosaurus*. Also a collection of the ancient and modern authorities, with letters from distinguished merchants and men of science. Cambridge, MA, 1849.

Bartlett, Robert. *The Natural and the Supernatural in the Middle Ages*. Cambridge: Cambridge University Press, 2008.

Batcheldor, Eugene. *A Romance of the Sea Serpent or the Ichthyosaurus*. Cambridge: J. Bartlett, 1849.

Bates, Henry Walter. *The Naturalist on the River Amazon*. 2 vols. London: Murray, 1863.

Bawcutt, Priscilla. *The Poems of William Dunbar*. 2 vols. Glasgow: Association for Scottish Literary Studies, 1998.

Beardsley, Aubrey. *Under the Hill*. New York and London: John Lane, 1904.

Beckwith, Martha Warren. *Hawaiian Mythology* (1910). Honolulu: University of Hawaii Press, 1970.

Beckwith, Martha Warren. 'Hawaiian Shark Aumakua'. *American Anthropologist*, New Series 19: 4 (October–December 1917): 503–17.

Benton, Janetta Rebold. *Medieval Menagerie: Animals in the Art of the Middle Ages*. New York: Abbeville Press, 1992.

Bildhauer, Bettina, and Robert Mills, eds. *The Monstrous Middle Ages*. Cardiff: University of Wales Press, 2003.

Blainville, Henri de. 'Sur un nouveau genre de Serpent, Scoliophis, et le Serpent de mer vue en Amerique en 1817'. *Journal de physique* 56 (1818): 299–301.

Blount, Thomas. *Glossographia; or, a Dictionary Interpreting the Hard Words of Whatsoever Language, Now Used in Our Refined English Tongue*. London: Tho. Newcomb, 1656.

Boivin, Jean Marie, and Proinsias MacCana. *Mélusines continentales et insulaires*. Paris: Champion, 1999.

Borges, Jorge Luis with Margarita Guerrero. *The Book of Imaginary Beings*. Translated by Norman Thomas di Giovanni. London: Vintage, 2002.

Bottrell, William. *Traditions and Hearthside Stories of West Cornwall, Second Series*. Penzance: Beare and Son, 1873 reprint Whitefish, MT: Kessinger Publishing, 2009.

Breiner, Laurence A., 'The Career of the Cockatrice'. *Isis* 70: 1 (1979): 30–47.

Brockbank, William. 'Sovereign Remedies: A Critical Depreciation of the 17th Century London Pharmacopoeia'. *Medical History* 8: 01 (1964): 1–14.

Brodbeck, Simon Pearse. *The Mahabharata Patriline: Gender, Culture and the Royal Hereditary*. Farnham: Ashgate, 2009.

Brodbeck, Simon Pearse. 'Putrika Interpretation of the Mahabharata'. In *Samskrtavimarsah*, New Series World Sanskrit Conference. Special Rahtriya Sanskrit, 142–59. New Delhi: Santhan Deemed University, 2012.

Brodeur, Arthur Gilchrist, trans. *The Prose Edda of Snorri Sturlson*, 'Gylfaginning', (1916), http://www.sacred-texts.com/neu/pre/pre04.htm.

Bromwich, Rachel, ed. and trans. *Trioedd ynys Prydein: The Welsh Triads*, 4th edn. Cardiff: University of Wales Press, 2014.

Brown, Chandos Michael. 'The Gloucester Sea Serpent, Knowledge, Power and the Culture of Science in Antebellum America'. *American Quarterly* 42: 3 (September 1990): 402–36.

Bruford, Alan. 'Trolls, Hillfolk, Finns and Picts: The Identity of the Good Neighbours in Orkney and Shetland'. In *The Good People: New Fairylore Essays*, edited by Peter Narváez, 116–41. New York and London: Garland Publishing, 1991.

Bryant, Nigel, trans. *The Medieval Romance of Alexander: The Deeds and Conquests of Alexander the Great*. Cambridge: Cambridge University Press, 2013.

Brydon, Anne. 'The Predicament of Nature: Keiko the Whale and the Cultural Politics of Whaling in Iceland'. *Anthropological Quarterly* 79: 2 (Spring 2006): 225–60.

Buckingham, David. 'Studying Computer Games'. In *Computer Games: Text, Narrative and Play*, edited by Diane Carr, et al., 1–14. Cambridge: Polity, 2007.

Bukataman, Scott. *Blade Runner*. London: British Film Institute, 1997.

Burden, William Douglas. *Dragon Lizards of Komodo*. New York and London: G. P. Putnam Sons, 1927.

Burn, Andrew, and Diane Carr. 'Defining Game Genres'. In *Computer Games: Text, Narrative and Play*, edited by Diane Carr, et al., 14–29. Cambridge: Polity, 2007.

Butterworth, Philip. 'Late Medieval Performing Dragons'. *The Yearbook of English Studies*. vol. 43, *Early English Drama* (2013): 318–42.

Cadbury, Deborah. *The Dinosaur Hunters*. London: Fourth Estate, 2000.

Caine, Thomas H. H., ed. *King Albert's Book: A Tribute to the Belgian King and his People*. London: Daily Telegraph & Hodder and Stoughton, 1914.

Cameron, Mary Lovett. 'The Dragon of La Trinità: An Italian Folk-Tale'. *Folklore* 21: 3 (September 1910): 349–50.

Campbell, J. F., *Táin bó Fráich. The Celtic Dragon Myth*. With the Geste of Fraoch and the dragon; translated with introduction by George Henderson. Edinburgh: J. Grant, 1911.

Canby, Sheila R., 'Dragons'. In *Mythical Beasts*, edited by John Cherry, 14–33. San Francisco and London: Pomegranate & British Museum Press, 1995.

Canepa, Nancy L., trans. *Pentamerone; Giambattista Basile's The Tale of Tales, or, Entertainment for Little Ones*. Detroit: Wayne State University Press, 2007.

Carroll, Lewis. *Through the Looking-Glass, and What Alice Found There*. London: Macmillan, 1871.

Carr, Diane, David Buckingham, Andrew Burn, and Gareth Schott. *Computer Games: Text, Narrative and Play*. Cambridge: Polity, 2007.

Catelan, Lauren (Maistre apoticquaire de Montpelier). *Histoire de la nature, chasse, vertus, proprietes, et usage de la Lycorne*. Montpellier, 1624.

Cavallo, Adolfo Salvatore. *The Unicorn Tapestries at the Metropolitan Museum of Art*. New York: Harry Abrams, 1998.

Chamberlain, Basil Hall, trans. *Ko-ji-ki or, Records of Ancient Matters*. Yokohama London: Lane, Crawford & Co., Trübner, 1883.

Chambers, Robert. *The Book of Days: A Miscellany of Popular Antiquities*. Edinburgh and London: W & R Chambers, 1864.

Châtelet-Lange, Liliane, and Francisco Renate. 'The Grotto of the Unicorn and the Garden of the Villa di Castello'. *The Art Bulletin* 50: 1 (March 1968): 51–8.

Cherry, John, ed. *Mythical Beasts*. San Francisco and London: Pomegranate & British Museum Press, 1995.

Christiansen, Reidar Th., *The Migratory Legends: A Proposed List of Types with a Systematic Catalogue of Norwegian Variants*. Helsinki: Suomalainen Tiedeakatemia, 1958.

Clark, Willene B., and Meradith T. McMunn, eds. *Beasts and Birds of the Middle Ages: The Bestiary and its Legacy*. Philadelphia: University of Pennsylvania Press, 1989.

Clay, Jenny Strauss. 'The Generation of Monsters in Hesiod'. *Classical Philology* 88: 2 (April 1993): 105–16.

Cohen, Jeffrey Jerome. *Monster Theory: Reading Culture*. Minneapolis, MI: University of Minnesota Press, 1996.

Cole, F. J. 'Bibliographical Reflections of a Biologist'. *Osiris* 8 (1948): 289–315.

Colvin, Sidney. 'On Representations of Centaurs in Greek Vase-Painting'. *The Journal of Hellenic Studies* 1 (1880): 107–67.

Comes, Natalis. *De Venatione*. Venice: Apud Aldi filios, 1551.

Contadini, Anna. *A World of Beasts: A Thirteenth-Century Illustrated Arabic Book on Animals (the Kitāb Na't al-Ḥayawān) in the Ibn Bakhtīshū' Tradition*. Leiden: Brill, 2011.

Coulston, J. C. N. 'The "*draco*" Standard'. *Journal of Roman Military Equipment Studies* 2 (1991): 101–14.

Coulter, Cornelia Catlin. 'The "Great Fish" in Ancient and Medieval Story'. *Transactions and Proceedings of the American Philological Association* 57 (1926): 32–50.

Coxwell, Charles Fillingham. *Siberian and Other Folktales*. London: C. W. Daniel, 1925.

Crafts, William. *The Sea Serpent; or, Gloucester Hoax: A Dramatic Jeu d'Esprit in Three Acts*. Charleston: Miller, 1819.

Cravalho, M. A., 'Shameless Creatures, an Ethnozoology of the Amazon River Dolphin'. *Ethnology* 38: 1 (1999): 47–58.

Cresswell, Julia. *Legendary Beasts of Britain*. Oxford: Shire Publications, 2013.

Crockett, Davy. *The Tall Tales of Davy Crockett: The Second Nashville Series of Crockett Almanacs, 1839-1841*. Knoxville: University of Tennessee Press, 1987.

Csapo, Eric. *Theories of Mythology*. Oxford: Oxford University Press, 2005.

Curley, Michael J. *Physiologus: A Medieval Book of Nature Lore*. Chicago: University of Chicago Press, 2009.

Daniels, F. J. 'Snake and Dragon Lore of Japan'. *Folklore* 71: 3 (1960): 145–64.

Darbandi, Afkham, and Dick Davis, ed. and trans. *The Conference of the Birds by Farid al-Din Attar*. Harmondsworth: Penguin Classics, 1984.

d'Arras, Jean. *Melusine; or, the Noble History of Lusignan*. Translated by Donald Maddox and Sara Sturm-Maddox. University Park, PA: Pennsylvania University Press, 2011.

Davidson, Hilda R. Ellis, ed. *Boundaries & Thresholds: Papers from a Colloquium of the Katharine Briggs Club*. Woodchester and Stroud: Thimble Press, 1993.

Davidson, Hilda R. Ellis. 'The Hill of the Dragon: Anglo-Saxon Burial Mounds in Literature and Archaeology'. *Folklore* 61: 4 (1950): 169–85.

Davies, Sioned, trans. *The Mabinogion*. Oxford: Oxford University Press, 2007.

Davis, Dick. *Shahnameh: The Persian Book of Kings*. New York: Penguin Books, 2004.

Davis, Edward. 'A Whale of a Tale: Fundamentalist Fish Stories'. *Perspectives on Science and Christian Faith* 43 (1991): 224–37.

Dawson, A. *Masterpieces of Wedgwood in the British Museum.*, 2nd edn. London: The British Museum Press, 1995.

Deanesly, Margaret. 'Roman Traditionist Influence among the Anglo-Saxons'. *The English Historical Review* 58: 230 (1943): 120–46.

DeLoughrey, Elizabeth M., and George B. Handley, eds. *Postcolonial Ecologies: Literatures of the Environment*. Oxford: Oxford University Press, 2011.

Dendle, Peter. 'Cryptozoology in the Medieval and Modern Worlds'. *Folklore* 117: 2 (August 2006): 190–206.

Dennison, Walter Traill. 'Orkney folklore, Sea Myths 3'. *The Scottish Antiquary* 5 (1891): 130–3.

Devlin, J. Dacres. *Helps to Hereford history*, civil and legendary, in an account of the ancient Cordwainers' Company of the city: The Mordiford dragon; and other subjects. London: J. R. Smith, 1848.

Dewhurst, William Henry. *The Natural History of the Order of Cetacea and the Oceanic Inhabitants of the Arctic Region*. London: the Author, 1834.

Dickenson, Peter. *The Flight of Dragons*. London: Pierrot Publishing and the New English Library, 1979.

Dicker, Rachel. 'Unicorns Were Real, and a New Fossil Shows When They Lived'. *US News*, 28 March, 2016, https://www.usnews.com/news/articles/2016-03-28/newly-discovered-fossil-reveals-when-siberian-unicorns-last-roamed-the-earth?src=usn_.

Doble, G. H. *The Saints of Cornwall*: part 5. Truro: Dean and Chapter, 1970.

Doré, Gustave. *Doré's illustrations for Ariosto's 'Orlando furioso'*. New York and London: Dover Constable, 1980.

Douglas, Mary. *Purity and Danger: Analysis of the Concepts of Pollution and Taboo*. London and New York: Ark Paperbacks, 1966.

Downey, Dara, Ian Kinane and Parker Elizabeth, eds. *Landscapes of Liminality: Between Space and Place*. London and New York: Rowman & Littlefield International, 2016.

Drewal, Henry John. 'Mermaids, Mirrors, and Snake Charmers: Igbo Mami Wata Shrines'. *African Arts* 21: 2 (February 1988): 38–45+96.

Dronke, Ursula, ed. and trans. *Vǫluspá, The Poetic Edda*. 2 vols. Oxford: Oxford University Press, 1969–97.

Druce, G. C. 'The Elephant in Medieval Legend and Art'. *Journal of the Royal Archaeological Institute* 76 (1919): 1–73.

Druce, G. C. 'Notes on the History of the Heraldic Jale or Yale'. *Archaeological Journal* 68 (1911): 173–99.

Druce, G. C. 'On the Legend of the Serra or Sawfish'. *Proceedings of the Society of Antiquaries*, 2nd series, 31 (1919): 20–35.

Dundes, Alan, ed. *Readings in the Theory of Myth*. Berkeley: University of California Press, 1984.

Dundes, Alan. 'Structuralism and Folklore'. *Studia Fennica* 20 (1976): 149–94.

Eddison, E. R., *The Worm Ouroboros*. London: Jonathan Cape, 1922.

Edwards, Hywel Teifi. *The National Pageant of Wales*. Llandysul: Gomer, 2009.

Egmond, Florike, and Peter Mason, eds. *The Whale Book: Whales and Other Marine Animals as Described by Adriaen Coenen in 1585*. London: Reaktion, 2003.

Ellis, Richard. *The Search for the Giant Squid*. New York: Lyons Press, 1998.

Elsner, John. 'Hagiographic Geography: Travel and Allegory in the Life of Apollonius of Tyana'. *The Journal of Hellenic Studies* 117 (1997): 22–37.

Erlande-Brandenburg, Alain. *La dame a la licorne* (new revised edn). Paris: Réunion des musées nationaux, 1993.

The Essex Serpent: The Flying Serpent, etc. Reproduced in facsimile .. with introduction by R. M. Christy. Saffron Walden, 1885

Ettinghausen, R., *The Unicorn* (Studies in Muslim Iconography). Freer Gallery of Art Occasional papers 1, 3 (Washington, 1950).

Evans, Oliver. 'Selections from the Bestiary of Leonardo Da Vinci'. *The Journal of American Folklore* 64 (1951): 393–6.

Fenner, Arnie, and Cathy Fenner, eds. *Icon, Frank Frazetta A Retrospective by the Grand Master of Fantastic Art*. Grass Valley, CA: Underwood Books, 1999.

Fine, Gary Alan. *Shared Fantasy: Role-Playing Games as Social Worlds*. Chicago and London: University of Chicago Press, 1983.

Forklaring over nogle Ord og Udtryk i det gamle norske Sprog / Af Johan Fritzner. Særskilt aftrykt af Vidensk, Selsk. Forhandlinger for 1871, Kristiania.

Fortey, Richard. 'In Retrospect: Leibniz's *Protogaea*', Review of *Protogaea* by Gottfried Wilhelm Leibniz. Translated by Claudine Cohen and Andre Wakefield. Chicago: University of Chicago Press, 2008, *Nature* 455 (2008): 35.

Fournival, Richard. *Le Bestiare d'amour*. Edited by C. Hippeau. Paris: Hippeau, 1860.

Fournival, Richard de. *Master Richard's Bestiary of Love*. Translated by Jeanette Beer. Berkeley: University of California Press, 1986.

Freeman, Margaret B. *The Unicorn Tapestries*. New York: Metropolitan Museum of Art, 1976 (1974).

Fritzner, Johan. *Ordbog over det gamle norske sprog*. Kristiania: Feilberg & Landmark, 1867.

Galembo, Phyllis. *Divine Inspiration from Benin to Bahia*. Albuquerque: University of New Mexico Press, 1993.

Gennrich, Friedrich, ed. *Le Romans de la dame à la lycorne et du beau chevalier au lyon*. Dresden: Gedruckt für die Gesellschaft für romanische literature, 1908.

George, Wilma. 'The Yale'. *Journal of the Warburg and Courtauld Institutes* 31 (1968): 423–8.

Gervase of Tilbury. *Otia Imperialia: Recreation for an Emperor,* edited and translated by S. E. Banks and J. W. Binns. Oxford: Clarendon Press, 2002.

Gilbert, Allan. 'The Sea Monster in Ariosto's Cinque Canti and Pinocchio'. *Italica* 33: 4 (December 1956): 260–3.

Godbey, A. H., 'The Unicorn in the Old Testament'. *The American Journal of Semitic Languages and Literatures* 56 (1939), 256–96.

Goldman, Bernard. 'The Development of the Lion-Griffin'. *American Journal of Archaeology* 64: 4 (October 1960): 319–28.

Gotfredsen, Lise. *The Unicorn.* Translated by Anne Brown. London: Harvill, 1999.

Gould, Rupert Thomas. *The Case for the Sea Serpent.* London: P. Allan, 1930.

Gravena, W., T. Hrbek, V. M. F. da Silva and I. P. Farias. 'Amazon River Dolphin Love Fetishes: From Folklore to Molecular Forensics'. *Marine Mammal Science* 24 (2008): 969–78.

Gregg, Justin. *Are Dolphins Really Smart? The Mammal Behind the Myth.* Oxford: Oxford University Press, 2013.

Gresseth, Gerald K. 'The Myth of Alcyone'. *Transactions and Proceedings of the American Philological Association.* 95 (1964): 88–98.

Griffin, A. H. F. 'The Ceyx Legend in Ovid, Metamorphoses, Book XI'. *The Classical Quarterly,* New Series, 31: 1 (1981): 147–54.

Grossinger, Christa. 'The Unicorn in English Misericords'. In *Medieval Art: Recent Perspectives, A Memorial Tribute to C.R. Dodwell,* edited by Gale R. Owen-Crocker and Timothy Graham, 142–58. Manchester and New York: Manchester University Press, 1998.

Guillaume le Clerc. *Le bestiaire divin de Guillaume, clerc de Normandie,* trouvère du XIIIe. Siècle, publié d'après les manuscrits de la Bibliothèque nationale ...par M. C. Hippeau. Caen: Chez A. Hardel, Imprimeur-Libraire, 1852 Geneva: Slatkine Reprints, 1970.

Gupta, Deepika, and Rajinder K. Bruce Bleakley. Gupta, 'Dragon's blood: Botany, Chemistry and Therapeutic Uses'. *Journal of Ethnopharmacology* 115 (2008) : 361–80.

Mrs Gutch. 'Saint Martha and the Dragon'. *Folklore* 63:4 (December 1952): 193–203.

Gygax, Gary. *Monster Manual: An Alphabetical Compendium of all of the Monsters* found in Advanced Dungeons & Dragons, Renton WA, Wizards of the coast, 1st edn, 1979.

Gygax, Gary, and Dave Arneson. *Dungeons & Dragons.* Fantasy Adventure Game Basic Rulebook. Lake Geneva: WT TSR Hobbies Inc, 1974–81.

Haimerl, Edgar. 'Siguðr, A Medieval Hero A Manuscript-Based Interpretation of the "Young Siguðr Poems"'. In *Revisiting the Poetic Edda: Essays on Old Norse Heroic Legend,* edited by Paul Acker and Carolyne Larrington, 32–52. New York: Routledge, 2013.

Hansen, William. *Ariadne's Thread: A Guide to International Tales Found in Classical Literature.* Ithaca: Cornell University Press, 2002.

Harkin, Michael. 'Whales, Chiefs, and Giants: An Exploration into Nuu-Chah-Nulth Political Thought'. *Ethnology* 37: 4 (Autumn 1998): 317–32.

Harper, Prudence Oliver. 'The Simurv'. *The Metropolitan Museum of Art Bulletin,* New Series, 20: 3 (November 1961): 95–101.

Harrington, John. *Orlando Furioso in English* printed by G. Miller for T. Parker, 1634

Harvey, P. D. A. *Mappa Mundi: The Hereford World Map.* London: Hereford Cathedral & the British Library, 1996.

Hatto, A. T. *The Nibelungenlied.* Harmondsworth: Penguin Classics, 1965.

Hayward, Philip. *Making a Splash Mermaids (and Mer-men) in 20th and 21st Century Audiovisual Media.* Bloomington: Indiana University Press, 2017.

Heaney, Seamus. 'Maighdean Mara'. In *Wintering Out,* 60–68. London: Faber and Faber, 1972.

Heuvelmans, Bernard. *In the Wake of the Sea-Serpents.* Translated by Richard Garnett. London: Hart-Davis, 1968.

Higham, T. F. 'Dolphin-Riders; Ancient Stories Vindicated'. *Greece & Rome, Second Series* 7: 1 (March 1960): 82–6.

Honko, Lauri. 'The Problem of Defining Myth'. In *Sacred Narrative Readings in the Theory of Myth,* edited by Alan Dundes, 41–52. Berkeley, Los Angeles and London: University of California Press, 1984.

Hooke, S. H. *Middle Eastern Mythology from the Assyrians to the Hebrews* (1963). Harmondsworth: Penguin, 1991.

Hooper, Rowan. 'Pretty in Pink' Meet the Amazon River Dolphin'. *New Scientist,* 17 December 2001, 25.

Horden, Peregrine. 'Disease, Dragons and Saints: The Management of Epidemics in the Dark Ages'. In *Epidemics and Ideas: Essays on the Historical Perception of Pestilence,* edited by Terence Ranger and Paul Slack, 45–76. Cambridge: Cambridge University Press, 1992.

(H)Ortus Sanitatis With Woodcuts. Strasbourg: Reinhard Beck, 1517.

Hortus deliciarum (Garden of delights) by Herrad of Landsberg, edited and translated by Aristide D. Caratzas. New Rochelle, NY: Caratzas Brothers, 1977.

Houlberg, Marilyn. 'Sirens and Snakes: Water Spirits in the Arts of Haitian Vodou'. *African Arts* Special Issue: Arts of Vodou 29: 2 (Spring 1996): 30–35+101.

Howard, Deborah. 'Venice as a Dolphin: Further Investigations into Jacopo de' Barbari's View'. *Artibus et Historiae* 18: 35 (1997): 101–11.

Ingold, Tim, ed. *What Is an Animal?* One World Archaeology, New edn. New York and London: Routledge, 1994.

Jacobs, Joseph, ed. *English Fairy Tales.* London: D. Nutt, 1890.

J. E. L., 'Ch'en Jung's Picture of Nine Dragons'. *Boston Museum of Fine Arts Bulletin* 15: 92 (December 1917): 67–73.

Jiang, Yixing, Michael Lück and E. C. M. Parsons. 'Public Awareness, Education, and Marine Mammals in Captivity'. *Tourism Review International* 11: 3 (2007): 237–49.

Johnson, Harold, Steve Winter, Peter Adkison, Ed Stark and Peter Archer. *30 Years of Adventure: A Celebration of Dungeons & Dragons.* Renton WA: Wizards of the Coast, 2004.

Johnson, Richard E. *Saint Michael the Archangel in Medieval English Legend.* Woodbridge: Boydell Press, 2005.

Jones, David. *Order: An Occasional Catholic Review.* London, 1928, vol. 1 (1–4: May 1928–November 1929).

Jones, T. Gwyn. *Welsh Folklore and Folk-Custom.* Cambridge: Brewer, 1979.

Jones, Owen Wynne (Glasynys). *Cymru Fu.* Wrecsam: Hughes & Son, 1862.

Jones-Baker, Doris. 'The Graffiti of Folk Motifs in Cotswold Churches'. *Folklore* 92: 2 (1981): 160–7.

Jonston, John. *Historiae naturalis de quadrupedibus*. Amsterdam: Johann Jacob Schipper, 1657.

Joyce, P. W., trans. *Old Celtic romances* from the Gaelic (1879). Introduction Juliette Wood. Ware and Hertfordshire: Wordsworth Editions/ The Folklore Society, 2000

Kay, Sarah. '"The English Bestiary," the Continental Physiologus, and the Intersections between Them'. *Medium Ævum* 85: 1 (2016): 118–42.

Kingshill, Sophia. *Mermaids*. Little Toller Monograph. Toller Fratrum, Dorset: Little Toller Books 2015.

Kircher, Athanasius. *Athanasii Kircheri .. Œdipus Ægyptiacus*, hoc est vniuersalis hieroglyphicæ veterum doctrinæ .. instauratio. Rome 1652-54, colophon 1655.

Knecht, R. J. *Catherine de' Medici*. London and New York: Longman, 1998.

The Knight of the Parrot (Le chevalier du papegau). Translated by Thomas E. Vesce. New York: Garland, 1986.

Kruszewska, Albina I., and Marion M. Coleman. 'The Wanda Theme in Polish Literature and Life'. *American Slavic and East European Review* 6: 1/2 (May 1947): 19–35.

Lacey-Bordeaux, Emma, and Dave Alsup. 'Seaplane almost Lands on Whale'. *CNN.com* 16 July 2014.

Lach-Szyrma, W. S. 'Folk-Lore Traditions of Historical Events'. *The Folk-Lore Record* 3: 2 (1880): 157–68.

Lai, Whelan. 'From Folklore to the Literate Theatre: Unpacking Madam White Snake'. *Asian Folklore Studies* 51: 1 (1992): 51–66.

Lang, Andrew. *The Arabian Nights Entertainment*. London: Longmans Green and Co, 1898.

Langdon, Susan. 'The Awkward Age: Art and Maturation in Early Greece'. *Hesperia Supplements*, vol. 41, *Constructions of Childhood in Ancient Greece and Italy* (2007): 173–91.

Lantis, Margaret. 'The Alaskan Whale Cult and Its Affinities'. *American Anthropologist*, New Series, 40: 3 (1938): 438–64.

Laufer, B. 'Arabic and Chinese Trade in Walrus and Narwhal Ivory'. *T'oung pao* 14 (1913): 315–70.

Laugrand, Frédéric, and Jarich Oosten. *The Sea Woman: Sedna in Inuit Shamanism and Art in the Eastern Arctic*. Fairbanks: University of Alaska Press, 2008.

Lavers, Chris. *The Natural History of Unicorns*. London: Granta, 2009.

Lawrence, Marion. 'Ships, Monsters and Jonah'. *American Journal of Archaeology* 66: 3 (July 1962): 289–96.

Le Goff, Jacques. *Time, Work & Culture in the Middle Ages*. Translated by Arthur Goldhammer. Chicago: University of Chicago Press, 1980.

Levi, Steven C. 'P. T. Barnum and the Feejee Mermaid'. *Western Folklore* 36: 2 (April 1977): 149–54.

Lewis, Theodore J. 'CT 13.33-34 and Ezekiel 32: Lion-Dragon Myths'. *Journal of the American Oriental Society* 116: 1 (January–March 1996): 28–47.

Lewis, C. S. *The Allegory of Love: A Study in Medieval Tradition*. Oxford: The Clarendon Press, 1936.

Lewis, C. S. *The Pilgrim's Regress: An Allegorical Apology for Christianity, Reason and Romanticism*. London: Shed & Ward, 1935.

Lewis-Williams, J. D. 'Ezeljagdspoort Revisited: New Light on an Enigmatic Rock-Painting'. *The South African Archaeological Bulletin* 32: 126 (December 1977): 165–9.

Ley, Willy. *The Lungfish, the Dodo, & the Unicorn: An Excursion into Romantic Zoology*. New York: Viking Press, 1948.

Lilly, John. *Man and Dolphin: Adventures of a New Scientific Frontier*, 1st edn. Garden City, NY: Doubleday, 1961.

Lilly, John. *The Mind of the Dolphin: A Nonhuman Intelligence*, 1st edn. Garden City, NY: Doubleday, 1967.

Lindbergh, Anne Morrow. *Bring Me a Unicorn: Diaries and Letters of Anne Morrow Lindbergh, 1922-1928*. Boston: G. K. Hall, 1973.

Lofmark, Carl. *A History of the Red Dragon*. Llanrwst: Gwasg Carreg Gwalch, 1995.

Loo, Oliver. *The Original 1812 Grimm Fairy Tales: A New Translation of the 1812 First Edition Kinder- und Hausmärchen / Children's and Household Tales, Collected Through the Brothers Grimm*. Vol. I, Self-published. 2014.

Loomis, Roger Sherman, and Laura Hibbard Loomis. *Arthurian Legends in Medieval Art* Modern Language Association of America 9, Oxford and New York: Oxford University Press, 1938.

Lovett, E. 'Folk medicine in London'. *Folklore* 24: 1 (1913): 120–1.

Luchs, Alison. *The Mermaids of Venice, Fantastic Sea Creatures in Venetian Renaissance Art*. London: Harvey Miller, 2010.

Malcor, Linda. 'Merlin and the Pendragon, King Arthur's Draconarius'. *Arthuriana* 10: 1 (2000): 3–13.

Mankowitz, Wolf. *A Kid for Two Farthings*. London: André Deutsch, 1953.

Map, Walter. *De Nugis Curialium: Courtier's Trifles*, edited and translated by M. R. James, revised by C. N. L. Brooks and R. A. B. Mynors. Oxford: Clarendon Press, 1983.

Marini, Andrea (medico). *Discorco ... contra la fasa opinione dell'alicorno*. Venice, 1566.

Márkus-Takeshita, Kinga Ilona. 'From Iranian Myth to Folk Narrative: The Legend of the Dragon-Slayer and the Spinning Maiden in the Persian Book of the Kings'. *Asian Folklore Studies* 60: 2 (2001): 203–14.

Martiniére, Pierre Martin de la. *A New Voyage to the North*. 1700, English translation 1706.

Mayor, Adrienne. *The First Fossil Hunters: Dinosaurs, Mammoths, and Myth in Greek and Roman Times*, 2nd edn. Princeton, NJ: Chichester Princeton University Press, 2011.

Mayor, Adrienne, and Michael Heaney. 'Griffins and Arimaspaeans'. *Folklore* 104: 1/2 (1993): 40–66.

McCall, Henrietta. 'Sphinxes'. In *Mythical Beasts*, edited by John Cherry. 104–37. San Francisco and London: Pomegranate & British Museum Press, 1995.

McFate, Patricia Ann, and William E. Doherty. 'W. B. Yeats's "Where There Is Nothing". Theme and Symbolism'. *Irish University Review* 2: 2 (Autumn 1972): 149–63.

Melchior Lorck: Drawings from the Evelyn Collection at Stonor Park, England, and from the Department of Prints and Drawings, the Royal Museum of Fine Arts, Copenhagen, edited by Erik Fischer. Copenhagen: Statens museum for kunst, 1962.

Meredith, Peter, and John Marshall. 'The Wheeled Dragon in the Luttrell Psalter'. *Medieval English Theater* 2 (1980): 70–3.

Miller, C. Lee. 'The Younger Pliny's Dolphin Story ("Epistulae" IX 33): An Analysis'. *The Classical World* 60: 1 (September 1966): 6–8.

Miller, T. S. 'From Bodily Fear to Cosmic Horror and Back Again: The Tentacle Monster from Primordial Chaos to Hello Cthulu'. *Lovecraft Annual* 5 (2011): 121–54.

Mindlin, Betty. *Barbecued Husbands and Other Stories from the Amazon* trans. by Betty Mindlin, Donald Slatoff and indigenous storytellers. New York: Verso, 2002.

Monger, George. 'Dragons and Big Cats'. *Folklore* 103: 2 (1992): 203–6.

Montgomery, H. C. 'The Fabulous Dolphin'. *The Classical Journal* 61: 7 (April 1966): 311–14.

Morrison, Sophia. *Manx Fairy Tales*. London: D. Nutt, 1911.

Morse, Donald E., and Bertha Cilla, eds. *More Real Than Reality: The Fantastic in Irish Literature and the Arts*. New York: Greenwood Press, 1991.

Muir, Bernard J., ed. *Reading Texts and Images: Essays on Medieval and Renaissance Art and Patronage in Honour of Margaret M. Manion*. Exeter: University of Exeter Press, 2002.

Muldoon, Paul, trans. *The Fifty Minute Mermaid Poems in Irish by Nuala Ní Dhomhnaill*. Loughcrew, Oldcastle, County Meath: Gallery Press, 2007.

Mundkur, Balaji. 'Human Animality, the Mental Imagery of Fear and Religiosity'. In *What Is an Animal?* edited by Tim Ingold, 141–80. London and New York: Routledge, 1994.

Murphy, Maureen. 'Siren or Victim? The Mermaid in Irish Legend and Poetry'. In *More Real Than Reality: The Fantastic in Irish Literature and the Arts*, edited by Donald E. Morse and Bertha Cilla, 29–40. New York: Greenwood Press, 1991.

Murray, Julia K. 'Illustrations of the Life of Confucius: Their Evolution, Functions, and Significance in Late Ming China'. *Artibus Asiae* 57: 1/2 (1997): 73–134.

Murray, Janet H. *Hamlet on the Holodeck: The Future of Narrative in Cyberspace*. New York and London: Free Press, 1997, update 2017.

Naddaf, Gerard. 'The Bones of Giants, *The First fossil hunters Palaeontology in Greek and Roman Times* by A. Mayor' Review. *The Classical Review*, New Series, 53: 1 (April 2003): 195–7.

Narváez, Peter, ed. *The Good People: New Fairylore Essays*. New York and London: Garland Publishing, 1991.

Nesbit, Edith. *The Book of Dragons*. London and New York: Harper & Bros, 1901; Mineola and New York: Dover publications, 2004.

Newton, Michael. *Hidden Animals: A Field Guide to Batsquatch, Chupacabra and Other Elusive Creatures*. Greenwood: ABC-CLIO, 2009.

Newton, Michael. 'Stronsay Beast'. *Encyclopedia of Cryptozoology: A Global Guide*. London: McFarland & Company, 2005.

Ní Dhomhnaill, Nuala. 'An Mhaighdean Mhara'. In *Selected Poems: Rogha Dánta*. Translated by Michael Hartnett, 81–3. Dublin: Raven Arts Press, 1988.

Ní Dhomhnaill, Nuala. *The Fifty Minute Mermaid*. Translated by Paul Muldoon. Loughcrew. Ireland: Gallery Press, 2008.

Nott, John. *Cook's and Confectioner's Dictionary*. London: Printed for C. Rivington, at the Bible and Crown, 1723.

Oesterley, Hermann, ed. *Gesta romanorum*. Berlin: Weiderman, 1872.

Ogden, Daniel. *Dragons, Serpents & Slayers in the Classical and Early Christian Worlds: A Sourcebook*. Oxford: Oxford University Press, 2015.

Ono, Fuyumi, illustrator, Yamada Akihiro, *The Twelve Kingdoms*. Tokyo: Kodansha Ltd, 1992/2001; Translation and English Adaptation, Alexander O. Smith and Elye J. Alexander. Los Angeles: Tokyopop, 2006.

Opie, Iona, and Peter Opie. *Oxford Dictionary of Nursery Rhymes*. Oxford: Oxford University Press, 1951.

Osada, Toshiki, and Hirishi Endo. *Linguistics, Archaeology and the Human Past*, edited by Indus project Occasional paper 12. Kyoto, Japan: Research Institute for Humanity and Nature, 2011.

Osaki, Yei Theodora, trans. *The Japanese Fairy Book*. New York: Dutton and Company, 1903, https://archive.org/stream/japanesefairyboo00oza#page/n19/mode/2up.

O'Sullivan, Sean, ed. and trans. *Folktales of Ireland*. London: Routledge & K. Paul, 1969.

Oudemans, A. C. *The Great Sea-Serpent: An Historical and Critical Treatise*, with Reports of the 187 Appearances (including those in the appendix), the Suppositions and Suggestions of Scientific and non-Scientific Persons, and the Author's Conclusions. Leiden and London: E. J. Brill, 1892.

Owen, Elias. *Welsh Folk-Lore: A Collection of the Folk-Tales and Legends of North Wales*. Oswestry: Woodall, Minshall, 1896.

Owen-Crocker, Gale R., and Graham, Timothy, eds. *A Memorial Tribute to C.R. Dodwell*. Manchester and New York: Manchester University Press, 1998.

Palsson, Gisli. 'The Idea of Fish: Land and Sea in Icelandic World-View'. In *What Is an Animal?* edited by Roy Willis, 119–29. London: Routledge, 1994.

Papadopoulos, John K., and Deborah Ruscillo. 'A Ketos in Early Athens: An Archaeology of Whales and Sea Monsters in the Greek World'. *American Journal of Archaeology* 106: 2 (April 2002): 187–227.

Paré, Ambrose. *Discours....de la Licorne, des venins et de la peste*. Paris: Gabriel Buon, 1582.

Parpola, Asko. 'The Harappan Unicorn in Eurasian and South Asian Perspectives'. In *Linguistics, Archaeology and the Human Past*, edited by Toshiki Osada and Hirishi Endo, Indus project Occasional paper 12, 125–88. Kyoto: Research Institute for Humanity and Nature, 2011.

Partridge, Christopher. *The Re-enchantment of the West: Alternative Spiritualities, Sacralization, Popular Culture and Occulture*, Vol. 1. Edinburgh: T &T Clark, 2005.

Pelland, Maryan, and Dan Pelland. *Weeki Wachee Springs*. Charleston and Chicago: Arcadia Publishing, 2006.

Perring, Dominic. '"Gnosticism" in Fourth-Century Britain: The Frampton Mosaics Reconsidered'. *Britannia* 34 (2003): 97–127.

Perry, Sarah. *The Essex Serpent*. London: The Serpent's Tail, 2016.

Phillips, Kim M. *Before Orientalism: Asian Peoples and Cultures in European Travel Writing, 1245-1510*. Philadelphia: University of Pennsylvania Press, 2014.

Pierce, Sidney K., Steven E. Masay, Nicholas E. Curtis, Gerald N. Smith, Carlos Olavarria and Timothy K. Maugel. 'Microscopic Biochemical and Molecular Characteristics of the Chilean Blob and a Comparison with the Remains of Other Sea Monsters: Nothing but Whales'. *Biological Bulletin* 206: 3 (2004): 125–33.

Platt, Peter G., *Wonders, Marvels, and Monsters in Early Modern Culture*. Newark: University of Delaware Press; London: Associated University Presses, 1999.

Pluskowski, Aleksander. 'Narwhals or Unicorns Exotic Animals as Material Culture in Medieval Europe'. *European Journal of Archaeology* 7: 3 (2004): 291–313.

Pollard, John. *Seer Shrines and Sirens*. London: George Allen & Unwin, 1965.

Pomet, Pierre. *Histoire Generale des Drogues*. Paris, 1694.

Pontoppidan, Eric. *Natural History of Norway*. Translated by Andreas Berthelson. London: Printed for A. Linde, 1755.

Priest, Alan. 'Phoenix in Fact and Fancy'. *The Metropolitan Museum of Art Bulletin*, New Series, 1: 2 (October 1942): 97–101.

Przhevalskii, Nikolai. *Mongolia, The Tangut Country and the Solitudes of Northern Tibet*. 2 vols. Translated by E. Delmar Morgan with introduction and notes by Colonel Henry Yule. London: Sampson Low, Marston, Searle & Rivington, 1876.

Purchas, Samuel. *His Pilgrimage*. London, 1613

Radcliffe-Brown, Alfred Reginald. 'The Rainbow-Serpent Myth of Australia'. *Journal of the Royal Anthropological Institute* 56 (1926): 19–25.

Rafinesque, Constantine S. 'Dissertation on Water Snakes, Sea Snakes, and Sea Serpents'. *American Monthly Magazine and Critical Review* 1: 6 (October 1817): 431–35.

Ralston, W. R. S. *Russian Fairy Tales: A Choice Collection of Muscovite Folk-lore* (1873). New York: Arno Press, 1977.

Ranger, Terence, and Paul Slack, eds. *Epidemics and Ideas: Essays on the Historical Perception of Pestilence*. Cambridge: Cambridge University Press, 1992.

Rasmussen, Knud. *Eskimo Folk-Tales*, edited and translated by W. Worster. London: Gyldendal, 1921.

Rauer, Christine. *Beowulf and the Dragon Parallels and Analogues*. Cambridge: D. S. Brewer, 2000.

Rawe, Donald R. *Padstow's Obby Oss and May Day Festivities: A Study in Folklore & Tradition*. Padstow: Lodenek Press, 1999.

Reese, David S. 'Men, Saints, or Dragons?' *Folklore* 87: 1 (1976): 89–95.

Reynolds, Frank E., 'Ramayana, Rama Jataka, and Ramkien: A comparative Study of Hindu and Buddhist Traditions'. In *Many Ramayanas: The Diversity of a Narrative Tradition in South Asia*, edited by Paula Richman, 51–9. Berkeley: University of California Press, 1991.

Riches, Samantha. *St George: A Saint for All*. London: Reaktion Books, 2015.

Rink H., and F. Boas. 'Eskimo Tales and Songs'. *The Journal of American Folklore* 2: 5 (1889): 123–31.

Richman, Paula, ed. *Many Ramayanas: The Diversity of a Narrative Tradition in South Asia*. Berkeley: University of California Press, 1991.

Ritvo, Harriet. *The Platypus and the Mermaid and Other Figments of Classifying Imagination*. Cambridge, MA: Harvard University Press, 1997.

Robinson, Margaret. 'Some Fabulous Beasts'. *Folklore* 76: 4 (Winter 1965): 273–87.

Robinson, R. Macdonald. *Selected Highland Folktales*. Edinburgh: Oliver and Boyd, 1961.

Rodini, Elizabeth. 'Baroque Pearls: Renaissance Jewelry in the Alsdorf Collection'. *Art Institute of Chicago Museum Studies* 25: 2 (2000): 68–71, +106.

'Le Roman de la dame à la lycorne et du beau chevalier au lyon: Text Image Rubril' *French Studies* January 1997, vol II.

Roosval, J. 'St. George of Stockholm'. *The Burlington Magazine for Connoisseurs* 40: 228 (1922): 111–13.

Ross, D. J. A. 'Olympias and the Serpent: The Interpretation of a Baalbek Mosaic and the Date of the Illustrated Pseudo-Callisthenes'. *Journal of the Warburg and Courtauld Institutes* 26: 1/2 (1963): 1–21.

Ross, Alexander. *Arcana Microcosmi or, The Hidden Secrets of Mans Body Disclosed…*With a Refutation of Doctor Browns Vulgar Errors, and the Ancient Opinions Vindicated. London, printed by Thomas Newcomb, 1651.

Roud, Steve, and Julia Bishop, eds. *The New Penguin Book of English Folk Songs*. London and New York: Penguin Classics, 2012.

Rowling, J. K. *Fantastic Beasts & Where to Find Them* by Newt Scamander. London: Bloomsbury, 2009.

Ruderman, David. *Kabbalah, Magic and Science The Cultural Universe of a Sixteenth Century Jewish Physician*. Cambridge, MA: Harvard University Press, 1988.

Ruderman, David. 'Unicorns, Great Beasts and the Marvellous Nature of Things in Nature in the Thought of Abraham Ben Hananiah Yagel'. In *Jewish Thought in the 17th Century*, edited by Bernard Septimus and Isaac Twersky, 343–64. Cambridge, MA: Harvard University Press, 1987.

Ruscillo, Deborah. 'The First Fossil Hunters: Paleontology in Greek and Roman Times by Adrienne Mayor Review'. *American Journal of Archeology* 107: 2 (2003): 293–5.

Sagan, Carl. *Dragons of Eden: Speculations on the Evolution of Human Intelligence*, 1st edn. New York: Random House, 1977.

Sample, Ian. 'Zhenyuanlong suni: Biggest Ever Winged Dinosaur is Found in China'. *The Guardian*, 16 July 2016, https://www.theguardian.com/science/2015/jul/16.

H. S. 'A Romanesque Archivolt'. *The Metropolitan Museum of Art Bulletin* 18: 1 (January 1923): 9–10.

Sá, Lucia. *Rain Forest Literatures: Amazonian Texts and Latin American Culture*. Minneapolis: University of Minnesota Press, 2004.

Sapir, Edward. 'A Flood Legend of the Nootka Indians of Vancouver Island'. *The Journal of American Folklore* 32: 124 (April–June 1919): 351–5.

Sapir, Edward. 'Indian Legends from Vancouver Island'. *The Journal of American Folklore* 72: 284 (April–June 1959): 106–14.

Schick, Lawrence. *Heroic Worlds: A History and Guide to Role-Playing Games*. Buffalo, NY: Prometheus Books, 1991.

Schlauch, Margaret. 'Geoffrey of Monmouth and Early Polish Historiography: A Supplement'. *Speculum* 44: 2 (1969): 258–63.

Schmitt, Marilyn Low. 'Bellerophon and the Chimaera in Archaic Greek Art'. *American Journal of Archaeology* 70: 4 (October 1966): 341–7.

Schoenberger, Guido. 'A Goblet of Unicorn Horn'. *The Metropolitan Museum of Art Bulletin*, New Series, 9: 10 (1951): 284–8.

Scobie, Alex. 'An Ancient Greek Drakos-Tale in Apuleius' Metamorphoses VIII, 19-21'. *The Journal of American Folklore* 90: 357 (July–September 1977): 339–43.

Seaver, Kirsten A. 'Desirable Teeth: The Medieval Trade in Arctic and African Ivory'. *Journal of Global History* 4 (2009): 271–92.

Segal, Robert A. *Myth: A Very Short Introduction*. Oxford: Oxford University Press, 2015.

Segal, Robert A. *Theorizing About Myth*. Amherst: University of Massachusetts, 1999.

Septimus, Bernard, and Isaac Twersky, eds. *Jewish Thought in the 17th Century*. Cambridge, MA: Harvard University Press, 1987.

Shaw, Brent D. 'The Passion of Perpetua'. *Past & Present* No. 139 (May 1993): 3–45.

Shepard, Odell. *The Lore of the Unicorn: Myths and Legends*. London: Allen & Unwin, 1930.

Simpson, Jacqueline. *British Dragons*. Ware: Wordsworth and The Folklore Society, 1980 reprint, 2001.

Simpson, Jacqueline. 'Fifty British Dragon Tales: An Analysis'. *Folklore* 89: 1 (1978): 79–93.

Simpson, Jacqueline. 'Tarasque'. *Folklore Society Miscellany*, http://folklore-society.com/miscellany/tarasque (accessed 14 September 2017).

Slatoff, Donald, trans. *Barbecued Husbands and Other Stories From the Amazon*. New York: Verso, 2002.

Slifkin, Natan. *Sacred Monsters: Mysterious and Mythical Creatures of Scripture, Talmud and Midrash*. Israel: Zoo Torah, 2007.

Sloane, Hans. 'An Account of Elephants' Teeth and Bones Found under Ground'. *Philosophical Transactions* (1683–1775) 35 (1727–8): 459–62.

Sonne, Birgitte. 'The Acculturative Role of Sea Woman, Early Contact Relations between Inuit and Whites as Revealed in the Origin Myth of Sea Woman'. *Man and Society* 13 (1990): 1–34.

Sørensen, Preben Meulengracht. 'Þorr's fishing Expedition' [Hymoslviða], trans. Kirsten Williams. In *The Poetic Edda, Essays on Old Norse Mythology*, edited by Paul Acker and Carolyne Larrington, 119–38. New York and London: Routledge, 2002.

Speroni, Charles. 'More on the Sea-Monsters'. *Italica* 35: 1 (March 1958): 21–4.

Spinden, Herbert J. 'Myths of the Nez Percé Indians'. *The Journal of American Folklore* 21 (January–March 1908): 13–23.

Steadman, John M. 'Perseus upon Pegasus and *Ovid Moralized*'. *The Review of English Studies* 9: 36 (November 1958): 407–10.

Steer, Dugald. *Dragonology: The Complete Book of Dragons*. London; Somerville: Templar Publishing; Candlewick Press, 2003.

Stockton, Frank R. *The Griffin and the Minor Canon* illustrated by Maurice Sendak. New York: Holt, Reinhardt and Winston, 1964.

Stoneman, Richard. *Alexander the Great: A Life in Legend*. New Haven: Yale University Press, 2008.

Strong, D. E. 'A Lady Centaur'. *The British Museum Quarterly* 30: 1/2 (Autumn 1965): 36–40.

Strong, D. E. *Art and Power: Renaissance Festivals, 1450–1650*. Woodbridge, UK: Boydell Press, 1984.

Swan, John. *Speculum Mundi or A Glasse Representing the Face of the World*. Cambridge: Printed by the printers to the University of Cambridge, 1635.

Swanton, John R. *Tlingit Myths and Texts*. Smithsonian Institution Bureau of American Ethnology Bulletin. Washington DC: Government Printing Office, 1909.

Szabo, Vikki Ellen. 'Bad to the Bone: The Unnatural History of Monstrous Medieval Whales'. *The Heroic Age, A Journal of Early Medieval Northwestern Europe* 8 (June 2005): 1–18, http://www.heroicage.org/issues/8/szabo.html.

Szabo, Vikki Ellen. *Monstrous Fishes and the Mead-Dark Sea Whaling in the Medieval North Atlantic*. Leiden: Brill, 2008.

Talbot, Annelise. 'Sigemund the Dragon-Slayer'. *Folklore* 94: 2 (1983): 153–62.

Tatham, David. 'Elihu Vedder's "Lair of the Sea Serpent"'. *American Art Journal* 17: 2 (1985): 33–47.

Thewissen, J. G. M., S. T. Hussain and M. Arif. 'Fossil Evidence for the Origin of Aquatic Locomotion in Archaeocete Whales'. *Science* 263: 5144 (1994): 210–12.

Thomas E. Vesce, trans. *The Knight of the Parrot* (Le chevalier du papegau). New York: Garland, 1986.

Thompson, C. J. S., *The Mystery and Lore of Monsters*. With accounts of some giants, dwarfs and prodigies, etc. London: Williams & Norgate, 1930.

Thurber, James. 'The Unicorn in the Garden'. In *Fables for Our Time*, 268–69, reprinted in *The Thurber Carnival* New York: Harper and Brothers, 1945.

Timbs, John. *Popular Errors Explained and Illustrated,* New edn. London: D. Bogue, 1856.

Times Archive. 'The Welsh dragon leads the pageant in Wales's festival', *The Times* Wednesday 4 February (2009): 4.

Tohall, Patrick. 'The Dobhar-Chu Tombstones of Glenade, Co Leitrim'. *The Journal of the Royal Society of Antiquaries of Ireland* 78 (1948): 127–9.

Tolkien, J. R. R. 'Beowulf: The Monsters and the Critics'. *Proceedings of the British Academy* 22 (1936): 245–95.

Tóth, Ferenc, and Marie-Cécile Forest, Pierre Maréchaux, eds. *Land of Myths: The Art of Gustave Moreau.* Budapest: Budapest Museum of Fine Arts, 2009.

Travis, William J. 'Of Sirens and Onocentaurs: A Romanesque Apocalypse at Montceaux-l'Etoile'. *Artibus et Historiae* 23: 45 (2002): 29–62.

Trevelyan, Marie. *Folk-Lore and Folk-Stories of Wales*. London: E. Stock, 1909.

Tritsch, F. J. 'The Harpy Tomb at Xanthus'. *The Journal of Hellenic Studies* 62 (1942): 39–50.

Tuczay, Christa A. 'Motifs in "The Arabian Nights" and in Ancient and Medieval European Literature, A Comparison'. *Folklore* 116: 3 (December 2005): 272–91.

Urreta, Father Luis de. *Historia Ecclesiastica Politica*, Natural, y Moral, de los Grandes y Remotes Reynos de la Etiopia, Monarchia del Emperador, llamado Preste Juan de las India, Valencia, 1610.

van Buitenen, J. A. B., ed. and trans. *The Mahabharata*. Chicago: University of Chicago Press, 1975.

van Duzer, Chet. *Sea Monsters on Medieval and Renaissance Maps*. London: The British Library, 2014.

Verne, Jules. *Vingt mille lieues sous les mers*, Illustration by Alphonse de Neuville and Eduard Riou. Paris: Hetzel, 1871 (English Edition 1872).

Verrill, A. E. 'The Florida Sea-Monster'. *The American Naturalist* 31: 364 (April 1897): 304–7.

Vickers, Lu and Sara Dionne. *Weeki Wachee, City of Mermaids: A History of One of Florida's Oldest Roadside Attractions*. Gainesville: University Press of Florida, 2007.

Wardle, H. N. 'The Sedna Cycle'. *American Anthropologist* 2 (1900): 568–80.

Waugh, Arthur. 'The Folklore of the Merfolk'. *Folklore* 71: 2 (June 1960): 73–84.

Waugh, Arthur. 'The Folklore of the Whale'. *Folklore* 72: 2 (June 1961): 361–71.

Wazana, Nili. 'The Anzu and Ziz: Great Mythical Birds in ancient near Eastern Biblical and Rabbinic Traditions'. *Journal of the Ancient Near Eastern Society* 31: 111–35.

Weinstock, Jeffrey Andrew, ed. *The Ashgate Encyclopedia of Literary and Cinematic Monsters*. Farnham: Ashgate, 2014.

Westrem, Scott D. *The Hereford Map*: A transcription and translation of the legends with commentary. Terrarvm orbis 1. Turnhout: Brepols, 2001.

Westwood, Jennifer, and Jacqueline Simpson. *The Lore of the Land: A Guide to England's Legends*. London: Penguin, 2005.

Westwood, Jennifer, and Sophia Kingshill. *The Lore of Scotland: A Guide to Scottish Legends*. London: Random House, 2009.

White, T. H. *The Book of Beasts Being a Translation of a Latin Bestiary of the 12th century*. London: Cape, 1954.

Williams, Kirsten, trans. Preben Meulengracht Sørensen. 'Þorr's fishing Expedition' [Hymoslviða] 119–38. In *The Poetic Edda*, edited by Paul Acker and Carolyne Larrington, *The Poetic Edda, Essays on Old Norse Mythology*. New York and London: Routledge, 2002.

Williams, N. J. A. 'Of Beast and Banner, the Origin of the Heraldic Enfield'. *The Journal of the Royal Society of Antiquaries of Ireland* 119 (1989): 62–78.

Willis, Roy, ed. *Signifying Animals: Human Meaning in the Natural World*. London: Routledge, 1994.

Wilson, Michael. *Nature and Imagination: The Work of Odilon Redon*. New York: Dutton, 1978.

Wister, Owen. *The Dragon of Wantley; His Rise, His Voracity and His Downfall. A Romance*. Philadelphia: J. B. Lippincott Co., 1892.

Wittkower, Rudolph. '"Roc": An Eastern Prodigy in a Dutch Engraving'. *Journal of the Warburg Institute* 1: 3 (January 1938): 255–7.

Wood, Juliette. 'Another Island Close at Hand: The Irish Imramma and the Travelogue'. In *Boundaries & Thresholds: Papers from a Colloquium of the Katharine Briggs Club*, edited by Hilda Ellis Davidson, 54. Stroud: Thimble Press for the Katherine Briggs Club, 1993.

Wood, Juliette. 'The Fairy Bride Legend in Wales'. *Folklore* 103: 1 (1992): 56–72.

Wood, Juliette. 'The Mélusine Legend in Wales: Modern Period'. In *Mélusines continentales et Insulaires*, edited by Jeanne-Marie Boivin, Prionsias MacCana, 297–314. Paris: Honoré Champion, 1999.

Wood, Juliette. 'The Mermaids of Karoo'. *FLS News* The newsletter of the Folklore Society no 60 Feb 2001, 5

Wood, Juliette. 'Walter Map and the Context of De Nugis Curialium'. *Transactions of the Honorable Society of Cymmrodorion* (1985): 91–103.

Wood, Juliette. 'Cockatrice', 99-101, 'Furies', 243-245, 'Harpy', 308-310, 'Hippogriff' 328-330, 'Mermaid and Merman' 411–415. In *The Ashgate Encyclopedia of Literary and Cinematic Monsters*, edited by Jeffrey Andrew Weinstock. Farnham: Ashgate, 2014.

Wright, Herbert. 'The Source of Matthew Arnold's Forsaken Merman'. *Modern Language Review* 13 (1918): 90–4.

Wyatt, James C. Y. 'The Giraffe as the Mythical Qilin in Chinese Art: A Painting and a Rank Badge in the Metropolitan Museum'. *Metropolitan Museum Journal* 43 (2008): 111–15.

Yeats, W. B., and Lady Gregory. *The Unicorn from the Stars, and Other Plays*. New York: Macmillan, 1908.

Yeoh, Brenda S. A., and Peggy Teo. 'From Tiger Balm Gardens to Dragon World: Philanthropy and Profit in the Making of Singapore's First Cultural Theme Park'. *Human Geography* 78: 1 (1996): 27–42.

Zhao, Q. 'Dragon: The Symbol of China'. *Oriental Art* 37: 2 (1991): 72–80.

Ziolkowski, Jan. 'Folklore and Learned Lore in Letaldus' Whale Poem'. *Viator* 15 (1984): 107–17.

Index